*Brief Treatment in
Clinical Social Work
Practice*

Brief Treatment in Clinical Social Work Practice

MARIA D. CORWIN
Bryn Mawr College

BROOKS/COLE

™

THOMSON LEARNING

Australia • Canada • Mexico • Singapore • Spain • United Kingdom • United States

BROOKS/COLE

™

THOMSON LEARNING

Executive Acquisitions Editor: *Lisa Gebo*
Assistant Editors: *Shelley Gesicki,*
 JoAnne von Zastrow
Marketing Team: *Caroline Concilla,*
 Megan Hanson, Margaret Parks
Editorial Assistant: *Sheila Walsh*
Production Project Manager: *Laurel Jackson*
Production Service: *G & S Typesetters, Inc.*
Manuscript Editor: *Carolyn Russ*

Permissions Editor: *Sue Ewing*
Cover Design: *Denise Davidson*
Cover Photo: *Photodisc*
Interior Illustration: *Glenda Hassinger/*
 G & S Typesetters, Inc.
Print Buyer: *Vena Dyer*
Typesetting: *G & S Typesetters, Inc.*
Printer: *Webcom, Ltd.*

For more information about this or any other Brooks/Cole product, contact:
BROOKS/COLE
511 Forest Lodge Road
Pacific Grove, CA 93950 USA
www.brookscole.com
1-800-423-0563 (Thomson Learning Academic Resource Center)

Printed in Canada

10 9 8 7 6 5 4 3 2 1

Library of Congress Cataloging-in-Publication Data
Corwin, Maria DeOca, [date]
  Brief treatment in clinical social work practice / Maria DeOca Corwin.
    p. cm.
  Includes bibliographical references and index.
  ISBN 0-534-36768-2 (pbk.)
  1. Psychiatric social work. 2. Brief psychotherapy. 3. Managed care plans
(Medical care) I. Title.
HV689.C66 2002
362.2′0425—dc21   2001025175

This book is printed on acid-free recycled paper.

Contents

Chapter 3

Levels of Intervention: The Engagement and Assessment Process   27

Chapter 4

Levels of Intervention: Case Conceptualization and Treatment Plan   55

Chapter 5

The Intervention Phase   75

Chapter 6

Brief Treatment with Children and Families: Family Service Agencies   110

Chapter 7

Working Briefly with Complex Clinical Problems: Community Mental Health Care   146

Chapter 8

Brief Social Work Practice in Health Care   181

Preface

This book was written to help the many practicing social workers who recognize that they will need to apply concepts of brief treatment in their work but are unsure how to start. It will also help new students training in and intending to practice modern social work.

Concerns about Brief Treatment

At workshops and training programs on brief treatment that I have conducted at social service and mental health agencies over the last 15 years, certain reactions to and concerns about time-limited work have surfaced repeatedly. For a significant number of participants, there is a general resistance or reluctance to doing brief treatment. This resistance appears to be partly related to a general unhappiness with the loss of professional autonomy under managed mental health care, with its imposition of time limits and restrictions on methods of treatment. These individuals assume that brief treatment is a by-product of the cost-containment strategies of insurance and managed care companies rather than a discipline with a history and rationale of its own. Some clinicians, particularly those trained in long-term exploratory therapies, also feel that brief treatment is inherently inferior to and less satisfying than longer-term work. However, in my experience, much of the resistance to brief treatment seems to stem from clinicians' lack of confidence that they can effect solutions to clients' problems or meet clients' needs in a limited period of time. Even clinicians and students who have accepted—perhaps reluctantly—the reality of managed care continue to find time-limited work daunting, particularly with clients who have multiple and complex problems.

Special Tasks in Brief Treatment

Some of the more difficult tasks of brief treatment include engaging clients in a working relationship, conducting a full assessment, and developing a working treatment plan within the first few sessions. Some clinicians are concerned that they will not have enough time to explore clients' needs and problems to understand them adequately—that is, to learn the underlying causes of problems—and that this will result in an unsatisfactory outcome. There is an even greater concern that there will not be enough time to establish rapport and gain a client's trust, particularly when the client's participation is involuntary or reluctantly offered. Even when they complete an assessment to their satisfaction, many of these clinicians report feeling overwhelmed by the number of problems that their clients typically present with. They are also confused about how to keep the treatment focused so that it does not drift into the scattershot approach that often results in response to the multiple stresses and crises in clients' lives. Although most of these clinicians express a strong interest in learning more effective assessment and intervention strategies, they remain highly skeptical that it is possible to provide sufficient help in a limited amount of time.

Why This Book Is Needed

The impetus for writing this book came from a desire to address clinicians' concerns, objections, and doubts about brief treatment and thereby help them to gain a sense of competency and confidence in conducting brief treatment and to increase their motivation to work creatively within managed care constraints. This book also will prepare clinicians and students to meet the changed job performance expectations of the new behavioral health care environment. Increasingly, workers will be expected to have the specialty skills needed to work within a managed care context and to meet changing standards of care. Given current cost containment pressures, it is unlikely that there will be a return to the long-term, fee-for-service, self-monitoring mental health care delivery system of the past. It is more likely that there will continue to be restrictions on the length and type of care and increasing demands for accountability. Clinicians must be prepared to justify in their treatment plans that they are providing clients with the appropriate level of care, selecting the best practice methods, and incorporating means of measuring progress. Therefore, all social workers will have to be knowledgeable about and proficient in focused, problem-solving treatment methods and in management of outcomes. In turn, graduate and continuing-education programs will have to include content on brief treatment in their training and provide opportunities for hands-on experience and supervision in focused treatment.

Social work education and continuing-education programs have been relatively slow in responding to the changes in training required by the paradigm

shifts in behavioral health care. This may be due to the scarcity of general social work texts on brief treatment. This book addresses the need for a foundation text. In addition, it provides more specialized clinical social work knowledge through an examination of the treatment needs of people in diverse social
service and mental health settings. Thus, the beginning chapters of the book
provide a context and rationale for doing brief treatment and then describe the
fundamental principles and techniques. Subsequent chapters look at practice
needs and methods in family and children's service agencies, community mental health plans, health care settings, and health maintenance and employee
assistance programs.

Goals of the Book

Given the educational needs, the central aim of this book is to help students
and clinical workers gain a sense of competency and confidence in doing time-
limited work. The specific goals are to give workers (1) a way of conceptualizing their services that will help them to see how their existing skills and theoretical frameworks can be adapted to time-limited work and enable them to
discover the power and possibilities of strategic, focused interventions; (2) a
conceptual framework for assessing clients' problems and needs, prioritizing
problems, and selecting the appropriate level of care, with the aim of increasing
clinicians' competence and confidence in assessment and treatment planning;
(3) the basic brief treatment intervention strategies and techniques that are part
of the repertoire of new behavioral health care skills; and (4) the means for
adapting the basic brief treatment techniques to diverse clinical settings and
with diverse clinical populations. The behavioral health care skills that this book
focuses on are (1) performing rapid, comprehensive biopsychosocial evaluations and risk assessments; (2) developing precise, strategic treatment plans
based on existing best-practices guidelines; (3) using problem-solving treatment
techniques that can rapidly reduce clients' symptoms and improve functioning;
(4) understanding interdisciplinary and interagency teamwork and using community resources for enhancing clinical treatment; and (5) measuring and managing treatment outcomes.

Case Illustrations and Exercises

The case illustrations in each chapter provide students with concrete examples
of how to do time-limited assessments and interventions. Each chapter contains a case study in which excerpts from treatment sessions are presented, giving readers a more detailed description of brief treatment strategies and techniques. At the end of the chapters on assessment, treatment, and practice in
various settings, there are assessment or assessment-intervention exercises
that give the reader an opportunity to conceptualize a clinical problem from a

brief treatment perspective and to apply the principles and techniques to actual case material.

The bibliography provides the reader with an introduction to the principal concepts and practices that form the foundation of the discipline of brief treatment.

Acknowledgments

I would like to thank the following reviewers for their valuable comments and suggestions: Dennis Cogswell, Radford University; Diane Davis, Eastern Washington University; Cynthia G. S. Franklin, University of Texas at Austin; and Jane Peller, Northeastern Illinois University.

Maria D. Corwin

Brief Treatment in Clinical Social Work Practice: Context and Rationale

Introduction

The recent upsurge of interest in brief treatment is not the first. Interest in brief, focused treatments has increased when there was a need to respond quickly to large numbers of people in need of services, for example, during and after World War II, when many people were suffering from war-related stress reactions. The establishment of community mental health centers in the 1960s and the emergence of health maintenance organizations (HMOs)[1] in the 1970s as important providers of health and mental health services also spurred interest in the development of time-limited practice models in order to help more of the large populations these organizations had contracted to serve. In addition, there have been several social work practice models (e.g., the functional school model, the task-centered model, and the crisis intervention model) that have placed time limits on services, based on theory and empirical evidence on how people change and most effectively use services. Currently, the emergence of managed care in the behavioral health care system has created renewed interest in time-limited, focused treatment methods and has spurred professional schools to train students in the principles and techniques of brief treatment.

Students entering the field of clinical social work are entering a work environment that has undergone dramatic changes in organization and service delivery methods. A drive to contain costs in the health care system began in the 1980s, resulting in a decreasing number of insurance programs that allowed members to see clinicians of their choice on a fee-for-service basis or permitted the clinician to determine the methods and length of treatment. In the new system there are restrictions on both the choice of health care providers and on the length and type of treatment. In addition, most health care and social service providers are no longer self-monitoring but are instead accountable to an outside

---

[1] Acronyms introduced in this chapter: HMO, health maintenance organization; EAP, employee assistance program; MCO, managed care organization; PPO, preferred provider organization; EPO, exclusive provider organization.

managed care organization for the quality and cost efficiency of the services they provide.

Today enrollment in health maintenance organizations stands at 79.3 million members, with an additional 89.1 million enrollees in preferred provider organizations (PPOs) and 13 million in exclusive provider organizations (EPOs), making the total national managed care enrollment 181.4 million (Medical Source, 1999). Health maintenance organizations usually limit the number of treatment sessions a member may have per year (as in staff and group model HMOs). Individual-provider-association HMOs require that clinicians joining their panels of providers be knowledgeable and skilled in brief treatment (Hoyt, 1995). Clearly, students preparing themselves for entering the field and practitioners adapting to this new behavioral health care environment will need to understand how managed care evolved, what its future direction will most likely be, and what the implications of these changes will be for social work. Students and workers will also have to be knowledgeable about the effect of managed care policies and procedures on standards of care and service delivery and about the brief, problem-focused therapies that are the preferred practice methods.

Organization and Service Delivery Changes

The health care revolution, specifically the emergence of managed care, has brought major changes over the past decade in the organization, financing, and delivery of mental health services and, more recently, social services. It is a revolution that is not complete. Significant changes are still appearing and will continue to appear as we enter what some have termed the third stage of the health care revolution (Seaburn, Lorenz, Gunn, Gawinski, & Mauksch, 1996) or the second wave of managed care (Cummings & Sayama, 1995). The first stage of the health care revolution, occurring in the middle of the 20th century, was characterized by major advances in medical technology; tremendous growth in health delivery systems, including ones related to mental health and substance abuse; and by "privatization of health care expenditures," with the suppliers of the services (e.g., mental health professionals) controlling the cost of the services. Health care professionals had no incentive to contain escalating costs. In the 1980s, mental health and chemical dependency services came under particular scrutiny because they had become the health care cost leaders. While only 5% of health insurance beneficiaries used mental health and chemical dependency benefits, payments for these benefits accounted for 25% of total health care costs (Goodman, Brown, & Dietz, 1992). In response to ever-increasing health care costs, employers turned to managed care companies to bring costs under control, ushering in the period of cost containment, the second stage of the revolution. In the emerging third stage, it appears that there will be a dual emphasis on cost containment and on quality and adequacy of care in order for HMOs and other managed care organizations to stay competitive. In a market reaching the saturation point in terms of numbers of managed care companies and the point of diminishing returns in cost savings gained from restrictions on services, other ways will have to be found to contain costs (Cummings & Sayama, 1995).

The second stage of the revolution (the first phase of managed care) introduced the concept of accountability to an outside reviewer to mental health and social services programs; that is, employers or insurance providers designated a managed care organization to monitor costs and ensure quality of services (Strom-Gottfried, 1997). Managed mental health care organizations seek to control costs by matching clients' needs to appropriate treatment resources, which are then monitored to ensure that those who receive services truly need them, that the treatment itself is likely to be effective (Corcoran & Vandiver, 1996), and that the outcome is positive in terms of quality and value. This has meant the gradual ending of such features of the mental health–chemical dependency delivery system as free choice of care and care provider, elective admissions, long-term hospitalization, and open-ended treatment. In their place have come regulation of the utilization of services through external review, case management, triage protocols, restriction of services to authorized providers, brief hospital stays, and highly focused interventions (Garnick, Hendricks, Dulski, Thorpe, & Horgan, 1994).

Under managed care, the preferred mode of service delivery has become outpatient treatment, which is far less costly than inpatient. Programs that once were primarily inpatient, such as substance abuse treatment, are now primarily outpatient. Inpatient treatment is used mainly for "assessment and stabilization purposes, with length of stay based on clinical need, as opposed to being 'programmatically driven'" (Winegar, 1993, p. 175). The goal is the rapid return of the patient to the community. Consequently there has been a greater emphasis on community-based intermediate programs such as in-home crisis intervention, intensive case management, and wraparound programs[2] as methods of preventing more costly hospital or residential treatment stays. Two other methods by which managed care has sought to control costs and quality are the use of standardized treatment protocols for determining level of care, length of treatment, suitability of care, and quality and consistency of care delivery, and the use of case management techniques to coordinate services and prevent duplication (Paulson, 1996).

Two primary forms of managed mental health care systems have emerged. One form is based on the capitated, self-contained organization model, such as HMOs, EAPs, and community mental health organizations. In this model,

---

[2] The term *wraparound services* refers to an intensive level of care in which an individual who is at risk of placement out of the community receives a variety of services at home or in the community, thus enabling the individual to remain in and function in his or her usual family and community settings.

funding is provided on a prospective, per capita basis per year, and the organizations provide most of the mental health services themselves or serve as external reviewers when services are contracted out. The other type of managed care system consists of associations of preferred providers and independent practitioners, which are independent fee-for-service organizations that agree to accept reduced fees and the utilization review management's requirements for service delivery (Corcoran & Vandiver, 1996).

As private insurers turned to managed care organizations to bring down costs and manage expenditures, the sector initially affected was private, for-profit health and mental health services. Public agencies, faced with the loss of support for government programs and the constant threat of decreases in federal and state funding of public programs such as Medicare, Medicaid, and child welfare, are likewise turning to for-profit managed care companies to manage public programs (Paulson, 1996). Not-for-profit social service agencies, too, are increasingly affected as more and more of their funding sources, both private and public, are turning to managed care companies. In addition, many not-for-profit social service agencies are being bought by managed care companies to be run for profit, and contracts for providing services to publicly funded clients such as the chronically or mentally ill, who were mainly served by social service agencies in the past, are now being awarded to for-profit managed care companies. As Paulson (1996) notes, the merging of the public and private sectors is likely to continue and will have a great impact on social work.

The merging of the public and private sectors will not necessarily mean a loss of jobs for social workers. As the for-profit companies start providing services for vulnerable populations once served by social service agencies, other venues for social work services may open up. An example of this is the movement of HMOs into the public school system. School-based health centers and health plans that are the result of partnerships between schools and managed care organizations will offer a broad range of prevention and early intervention health care services. Preventive mental health services, psychotherapy, and social services are included along with primary care services in the comprehensive health-plus-mental-health packages that are being developed by these partnerships (School Health Policy Initiative, 1996).

There is no question that, with downsizings and mergers taking place almost daily in the health field and in publicly funded health and mental health services, and with the acquisition by managed care companies of social service agencies and social work departments in hospitals, social work jobs will be lost. It remains to be seen whether the trend toward devolution of health care services into the community from large medical centers and the trend toward integration of primary care and mental health services, of which the above HMO–school partnership is one example, will offset the loss of jobs due to downsizings and mergers. Certainly, in the push toward community-based health and mental health services, there should be a significant role for social workers because of the preference by managed care companies for using mental health professionals other than psychologists and psychiatrists to provide mental health services (Cummings & Sayama, 1995). This is a cost containment decision, but social work may also be favored in community-based practice because of the expertise and experience of social workers in working within a host setting, on interdisciplinary teams, and collaboratively with community agencies and leaders (Dhooper, 1997).

Community-based practice and the integration of mental health services are a part of the third stage of the health care revolution that will be driven by consumer demand for affordable coverage and quality and adequacy of services. The expectation is that the market will be dominated by network–individual-provider associations, which are now the fastest growing segment of managed care organizations, because employers prefer the network model. Employers prefer having a choice of treatment sites (as opposed to the centralized group and staff HMO models), and they perceive the network model as offering more choices of services and better quality of care (McCall-Perez, 1994). In addition, the community consortium model of managed care is expected to become a dominant market force as health care providers and nonemployer insurance buyers such as unions seek to provide low-cost services and better quality of care without the high overhead of the current profit-driven managed care companies. These "practitioner equity" or "community accountable health-care network" models will accelerate the drive toward quality and toward capitated, comprehensive, community-based health care (Cummings & Sayama, 1995, p. 38).

The savings that could be realized from downsizing and from restricting or controlling services through utilization review have largely been made. Further savings will have to come from other cost containment measures such as coordination of services through case management, development of precise practice guidelines, integration of health and mental health services, and an emphasis on preventive and early intervention methods, especially medical cost offset efforts (Strom-Gottfried, 1997). Examples of precise practice guidelines are triage protocols for determining appropriate level of care and "critical path models" for selecting the service plans that have proven to be the most effective for particular health–mental health problems and psychosocial profiles. Capitated, comprehensive, community-based health and mental health programs will be the vehicle for delivering cost-efficient, quality health services.

Implications of Managed Care for Practice

To succeed in the new behavioral health care environment, social workers will need to understand the population-based approach to mental health services and the integrated health–mental health "wellness" model of health care that inform program development and service delivery today. To succeed in this health care environment, workers will need to be proficient in prevention, early intervention, and relapse prevention skills. A population-based orientation to practice means that the worker conceptualizes his or her practice as being a commitment to serving a population and not just the individual client or family. Furthermore, the worker thinks in terms of how best to serve the population of clients with a particular problem—for example, individuals with a chronic health problem such as diabetes, with chronic mental illness, or with stress reactions related to a community event such as the loss of a place of employment. Thus, rather than focusing exclusively on the individual with a presenting problem, the focus would be on serving the population through interventions such as health education, developmental life cycle, crisis management, bereavement, or relapse prevention groups (Sabin, 1991).

Workers in integrated health–mental health, community-based programs will need greater flexibility in role performance. Social workers will have to conceive of themselves as working for a community within a network of services and not just within an organization. This will mean having the skills and comfort level to work in a variety of venues within the network (Paulson, 1996). They will need to learn how to function effectively on an interdisciplinary team, particularly in collaborative work with health care providers, and how to work with a variety of community leaders to develop preventive and early intervention strategies. Knowledge of community resources and skills in utilizing formal and informal social support networks will also be valuable in the new managed care environment, as coordination of services and a greater emphasis on client and community strengths and resources will be utilized as cost containment measures (Seaburn et al., 1996).

Other skills will be needed by social workers in the step-down or intermediate care programs formed by managed care as a means for preventing hospitalization, rehospitalization, or placement of children and adolescents outside the home. These skills are in crisis management, intensive adult and child case management, wraparound services, outpatient rehabilitation and relapse prevention, individual and family psychoeducation, family life education, and health maintenance (Strom-Gottfried, 1997).

There will undoubtedly be an even greater emphasis on the biopsychosocial approach to practice as advances in brain psychiatry lead to a better understanding of the neurobiological origins of severe and persistent mental disorders and as more targeted medications are developed (Paulson, 1996). Workers will need to keep current not only on psychotropic medications but also on clinical research literature in order to know when to refer a client for medication and how to assess the interaction between the client's biological illness and psychosocial stresses.

Brief Therapy and Managed Care

Central to the managed mental health care approach to cost containment and quality assurance has been the substitution of brief therapy for open-ended treatment. Managed care sought to control "therapeutic drift," the prolongation of services for as long as the patient was willing to attend, by holding practitioners accountable for the efficiency and effectiveness of their therapeutic interventions (Cummings & Sayama, 1995). Under the managed care philosophy of health care, practitioners are required to work to return the patient as rapidly as possible to a normal level of functioning. Treatment is viewed as something to be used parsimoniously, with the least invasive procedures, on an as-needed, intermittent basis throughout the life cycle. This means that practitioners have to be able to set realistic, achievable treatment goals and be able to document that the selected treatment approach will be (or was) helpful in achieving such goals. If the treatment is not working, the practitioner must be ready and able to use other methods and then be ready to terminate therapy when goals have been achieved. Brief therapy approaches have been seen as most compatible with these managed care goals and philosophy of health care and, therefore, have become the preferred practice mode (Winegar, 1992).

Social workers, then, will need to be knowledgeable about focused, intermittent, across-the-life-cycle, solution-oriented treatment strategies. Single-session work will continue to be an important mode of service delivery in health care because providing early intervention psychosocial services to medical patients experiencing emotional distress has been found to reduce utilization of medical services (Cummings & Sayama, 1995). Moreover, the ability to write precise treatment plans that have clear linkages between defined, targeted problems, goals, objectives, and intervention strategies and that are congruent with approved practice methods—that is, with practice guidelines—will be a primary skill for social workers in the future (Jongsma & Peterson, 1995). Knowledge of practice guidelines, treatment protocols, and critical path models will also be essential, as will staying abreast of the empirically based practice literature, in order to know which treatment approaches have good outcomes for particular problems and populations (Garnick et al., 1994). A high level of competence in assessment and diagnosis will be fundamental for carrying out all of the above functions in a managed care environment.

Finally, workers will need to develop critical thinking and creative problem-solving skills in order to develop effective treatment methods for working briefly with complex problems that have traditionally been addressed in long-term treatment. Thus, intervention models will need to be developed for working briefly with clients with chronic health problems, personality disorders, dysthymia, severe and persistent mental illness, and multistressed families. This will require social workers to be able to critically assess current practice theories and current modes of service delivery to determine if the assumptions inherent in them are still valid or whether new models need to be developed.

Rationale for Brief Treatment: Empirical Support

Brief treatment has emerged as a treatment of choice for reasons other than just cost containment. Studies attest to the efficacy and utility of brief treatment approaches. Most significantly, in outcome studies in which clients were randomly assigned to either time-limited or time-unlimited treatment, there was no reliable difference in the effectiveness between these two treatment modalities regardless of diagnosis. In addition, studies on the effectiveness of a variety of brief treatment approaches in which control groups received no treatment found that individuals receiving brief treatment functioned more effectively than control group members (Pekarik, 1996). Several decades of rigorous evaluation of the task-centered model of brief social work practice have consistently demonstrated the effectiveness of this model for resolving a variety of problems in living (Reid, 1992). Finally, even though studies have shown that clients continue to benefit over the full length of long-term treatment, it is also nevertheless true that the greatest improvements in functioning occur in the early sessions (Howard, Kopta, Krause, & Orlinsky, 1986).

Managed care organizations have relied on such research findings for developing practice guidelines, while in the fields of mental health and social services there has been an increasing push toward empirically based practice for both accountability and client satisfaction purposes. Research studies on the utilization of mental health services and outcome studies have also found that brief treatment was a closer fit with clients' expectations and actual use of services and that brief treatment was their treatment of choice. The idea that brief treatment might actually be the treatment of choice for many clients is bolstered by several metaanalyses of large numbers of clinical studies that found that in actual practice most treatment was unplanned brief treatment, even if the original plan had been for long-term treatment. That is, the average actual number of sessions attended was six to eight, even if long-term therapy had been planned (Koss & Butcher, 1986; Smyrnios & Kirkby, 1993).

Several hypotheses have been offered to explain the fact that most treatment is unplanned brief treatment. A possibility is that there are differences between therapists and clients in expectations about the length of treatment, with therapists generally feeling the need for long-term work and clients expecting and wanting short-term treatment. One study of the expectations of therapy of 70 clients in an outpatient clinic found that "over a third thought the therapy sessions would last 30 minutes or less, 73 percent anticipated some improvement by the fifth session, and 70 percent expected treatment to last 10 sessions or less" (Garfield, 1994, p. 202).

Other investigations on continuation in therapy have found that planned short-term treatment is associated with a reduction in the dropout rate. In a study of 149 new patients at a community mental health clinic, the attrition rate for patients in planned time-limited therapy was half that of patients in long-term, open-ended treatment. Brief therapy approaches are thought to minimize some of the factors associated with dropout because they are a closer match with client expectations that treatment be brief and problem focused (Sledge, Moras, Hartley, & Levine, 1990).

Brief Treatment and Culturally Relevant Services

Studies on continuation in therapy have also documented that ethnic minority and poor clients tend to underutilize mental health services and to drop out earlier and more frequently than white, middle-class clients (Rogler & Cortes, 1993). Since the 1970s, when these findings began informing the delivery of services to poor and minority people, efforts have been made to make services more culturally relevant. As a result, the disparity in dropout rates between ethnic minority and white clients has been reduced, although the overall dropout rate for poor and minority clients is still considerable, up to 50% (Sue, Zane, & Young, 1994). A strategy suggested for making therapy more culturally sensitive and thereby reducing attrition rates has been the replacement of exploratory, open-ended treatment approaches with structured, focused, problem-solving, time-limited interventions. The structured, brief approaches are seen as more congruent with how many minority clients understand and use mental health and social services (Koss & Shiang, 1994; Sue & Sue, 1990). In addition, several research studies have supported the effectiveness of structured, time-limited treatment with low-income clients and have documented the clients' preference for this treatment approach (Reid, 1978).

Community-based programs are also seen as a way to make services more accessible and relevant to poor and minority clients (Delgado, 1998). Recently, the rationale for developing community-based programs has come to be based on public health and managed care models of service delivery. That is, community-based mental health services are considered an important component in meeting the behavioral health care system's goals of delivering efficient, effective treatment in a cost-effective way. Community and family-based services are thought to be a more effective, more cost-efficient, and less stigmatizing form of mental health service than agency-, clinic-, or hospital-based services because of their focus on prevention, early intervention, and long-term maintenance. A community-based service approach addresses the fact that for many people, particularly ethnic minority individuals, the "help-seeking path-way" begins with and may end with primary and secondary group members. That is, in many communities the majority of care is provided by members of the community—by parents, relatives, neighbors, and naturally occurring, informal social networks—rather than through professional help organizations (Rogler & Cortes, 1993; Adams & Nelson, 1995).

Social Work Values and Time-Limited Practice

In addition to assessing the empirical support for the efficacy of brief treatment, it is also important to determine whether brief treatment tenets are consistent with social work values and standards for ethical practice. The following tenets (summarized here and expanded upon in Chapter 2) are representative of the primary common characteristics of brief treatment: (1) client-determined, circumscribed goals, (2) focus on current stresses, (3) competency-based practice, (4) collaborative worker-client relationships and active client participation, and (5) worker as catalyst for change.

Several of these tenets are consistent with social work beliefs about the dignity and worth of clients and the right to self-determination as well as with valued social work preferences in practice methods. For example, the emphasis in brief treatment on collaboration, active client participation, and client-determined goals is equivalent to the value placed in social work practice on mutual participation in the professional relationship: the right of clients to make decisions and have input into the helping process. Likewise, the emphasis in brief therapies on building on client strengths and competencies has also been a long-standing approach to practice that is valued in social work. As Hepworth, Rooney, and Larsen (1997, p. 8) assert, "[S]ocial worker interactions with people . . . should enhance their dignity and individuality, enlarge their competence, and increase their problem-solving and coping abilities." Finally, the brief treatment principle that the worker's role should be a catalytic one is similar to the value placed on empowerment in social work practice. "Worker as catalyst" means that the worker does not seek to cure pathology but instead provides resources and skills that enable clients to begin working toward their preferred goals.

The compatibility of social work values and brief treatment principles stems in part from the contributions that social work has made over 50 years to time-limited practice and crisis intervention theory. For example, the functional school of social work 60 years ago advocated a "time-limited helping process [in which] the client and social worker would attend only to the client's immediate issues" (Dorfman, 1988, p. 14). The principles of "starting where the client is" and client self-determination are well-known social work principles that are derived from the functional school's emphasis on client capability and responsibility for making changes in his or her life. Similarly, in brief treatment the client's definition of the problem is viewed not only as legitimate but also as the necessary starting point in treatment. Brief treatment models also share with the functionalist model the active participation of the client in the treatment process through such devices as homework assignments (Hoyt, 1995).

An emphasis on the client's strengths and resources is another fundamental principle of brief treatment that was also a tenet of the functional school. The idea of optimizing existing strengths followed from the functional school's recognition of the client's capacity to find creative and positive ways of making changes in his or her life. The strengths perspective has continued to be an important organizing principle for many models of social work practice. It is seen as a more effective and empowering approach to clients' difficulties than traditional social work models based on dysfunction or pathology (Saleeby, 1992).

In functional theory, the helping relationship was considered central to the change process. As in brief treatment, the focus in treatment was on the here-and-now interactions between worker and client rather than on the origins of the transference dynamics. The different phases of the relationship—the beginning, middle, and end—were considered to have specific characteristics that needed to be understood and used to facilitate change. Time, then, was viewed as being a significant variable in the therapeutic process. Moreover, placing time limits on the relationship was seen as a way of mobilizing conflicts and defensive maneuvers within the relationship that would lead to the client making needed changes (Dorfman, 1988).

In addition, social work has also made significant contributions to the empirical basis of time-limited practice and to the development of focused, structured strategies of intervention. One of the earliest studies on time-limited work found comparable outcomes between open-ended and time-limited casework (Reid & Shyne, 1969). This study, along with the 1973 Beck and Jones continuation study, provided early evidence that the majority of treatment is brief, even if it is planned to be long term, because clients are satisfied with pragmatic, circumscribed goals. Based on this empirical evidence of the efficacy of time-limited work, Reid and Epstein (1972) developed the task-centered model, which offered a brief, focused, structured approach to problem solving. Reid (1992) has continued to refine the task approach to practice, developing a systematic sequence for task implementation, then extending the applicability of the model to a greater array of problems and supporting these strategies empirically.

The work of Parad and colleagues (1965) on crisis intervention also was an early and significant contribution to the literature on planned short-term treatment. In this work, the nature of crisis and the typical sequences in crisis resolution were delineated, and intervention strategies based on that understanding were developed. Golan's work extended the concept of crisis to normative transitions and the stages and tasks involved in the resolution of crisis (Golan, 1981). Crisis intervention strategies have been incorporated into the lexicon of social work direct practice, although until recently they were more often seen as the preliminary stage of an intervention rather than a complete intervention in and of themselves. As the number of crisis situations social workers deal with has increased, and the utility of crisis intervention has been accepted, social workers have been instrumental in developing practice theory and skills for an expanded number of crisis situations—for example, Roberts (1984) on domestic violence and Lukton (1982) on psychotic breaks.

Summary

The major restructuring of the health care and social service delivery systems under managed care has resulted in significant changes in job performance expectations for clinicians. In moving from long-term, fee-for-service, self-monitoring care to a service delivery system in which there are restrictions on length and type of care based on the criteria of efficiency, effectiveness, and accountability to an external organization, clinicians are having to develop different sets of skills and types of knowledge. Consequently, clinical social workers today need to be knowledgeable about the principles and procedures of managed care and about brief, problem-focused treatment. However, becoming competent in brief treatment can require a major paradigm shift for individuals trained in long-term treatment. To aid in this transition process, the rationale for using brief treatment was presented, including the empirical evidence supporting the effectiveness of brief interventions, the positive impact on attrition rates, and client preference for and satisfaction with time-limited work.

Recommended Reading

Cummings, N., & Sayama, M. (1995). *Focused psychotherapy: A casebook of brief, intermittent psychotherapy throughout the life cycle.* New York: Brunner/Mazel.

Hoyt, M. (1995). *Brief therapy and managed care: Readings for contemporary practice.* San Francisco, CA: Jossey-Bass.

BRIEF TREATMENT PRINCIPLES AND TECHNIQUES: THEORETICAL FOUNDATION

Introduction

The following client situations are typical of the cases that clinicians present in case consultations as being difficult for them to consider working with in a limited time frame.

> Heather, a 28-year-old mother of two, was referred for outpatient treatment following her fourth suicide attempt and hospitalization. She is diagnosed as bipolar and is on Depakote. Periodically, she stops taking her medication and is eventually hospitalized. The current hospitalization was precipitated by a breakup with a boyfriend and going off her medication. The client has a history of substance abuse and problematic relationships with men. She has been steadily employed for 7 years as a nurse and has been in recovery for 9 months. Her two children appear to be well taken care of, although the older child has assumed a caregiving role.

> Toni is a 5-year-old girl referred for oppositional behavior, temper tantrums, and aggressive behavior. In the classroom she is easily distracted and demands a lot of the teacher's attention. Toni lives with her 18-year-old mother, teenage uncle, and grandmother. Although the grandmother is alcoholic, Toni's mother leaves her for long periods in the grandmother's care. Mother and grandmother have failed to keep most of Toni's medical, psychological, and educational evaluation appointments, and she is frequently absent from school. Family life is chaotic and crisis-ridden, with household needs often going unmet.

> Mr. and Mrs. B were referred by a hospital social worker for outpatient social services following Mr. B's hospitalization for complications associated with chemotherapy for esophageal cancer. The couple, who are in their late forties, have three children: two teenage daughters and a 10-year-old son. The prognosis for Mr. B is poor, with palliative care in a hospice setting the probable next step. The referral was made to provide the couple with financial and medical assistance and support around this medical crisis and the depression that their older daughter was already experiencing. Mr. B

had recently left his employment with a large corporation to start his own business.

While social workers have frequently dealt with these types of complex, severe, and persistent problems in the past, the introduction of externally imposed time restrictions under managed care is creating uncertainty and anxiety for many workers. They are concerned that there may not be enough time to adequately meet clients' needs or for such serious problems to be sufficiently resolved. There is also concern that any changes clients make will be ephemeral, since only a few problems will be worked on and clients will not have time to come to an understanding of how their problems originated. However, many of these concerns tend to diminish when workers are provided with a conceptual framework of principles and procedures that naturally lead to shorter, more efficient, and more effective therapy. One of the aims of this chapter is to present such a conceptual framework. The anxiety of workers is also reduced when they are provided with a systematic, strategic way of formulating a treatment plan. A structured approach to treatment planning ensures that clients' pressing needs will be met and that the managed care requirements of medical necessity and specificity of intervention will also be met. Therefore, this chapter will sketch out the fundamental tenets and features of the brief treatment perspective and will describe a model of intervention planning that will aid in prioritizing problems and arriving at the appropriate level of care.

Basic Principles of Brief Treatment

Several authors (Friedman, 1997; Cummings & Sayama, 1995; Pekarik, 1996) have noted that becoming competent in brief treatment requires that clinicians accept several paradigm shifts about the nature of practice. Friedman (1997, p. 3), for example, describes this as a letting go of

> time-honored assumptions we have accepted as true—for example, that more therapy is better; that emotional catharsis, in and of itself, is healing; that exploration of the past is necessary for change to occur; that "real" change requires time; that one "symptom" will replace another if the "core" issues are not resolved; and that "digging deeper" means better therapy. Although these traditional ideas have been with us for a long time, there is no empirical support for their validity. In fact, some of these assumptions have been responsible for unnecessarily prolonging the process of therapy.

Shifting the treatment paradigm can be difficult for many clinicians and even for students, because the changes involve values and assumptions that are at the heart of clinical social work. This paradigm shift cannot occur until workers have had repeated exposure to the principles and techniques that have come to define brief treatment, as well as hands-on experiences in applying the tenets of brief treatment to case exercises and then to actual case situations in their own practices.

Mastery of the tenets of brief treatment tends to lead to treatment abbreviation whatever the clinician's theoretical orientation (Pekarik, 1996). These tenets reflect certain assumptions and values about the nature of psychopathology and the therapeutic change process that are conducive to working briefly and efficiently with clients. First is the belief that clients can benefit significantly from therapy that focuses on current stresses and on narrowly defined problems in functioning. Not every problem of the client needs to be addressed, nor do all areas of dysfunction, let alone the developmental origins of the problems or dysfunctions. Selecting a narrow focus is considered to be key to abbreviating treatment in all brief treatment models, although the process of arriving at a focus varies across models. Some practitioners (Fisch, 1994; Friedman, 1997) arrive at a narrow focus by reducing the assessment data to descriptions of current behaviors, particularly interpersonal interactions that indicate how the problem is played out in the client's life. They also deemphasize the collection of data on the developmental origins of problems or explanations for problems based on personality characteristics, as this type of focus expands treatment time. Other practitioners, such as Pekarik (1996), start with a broader database, then prioritize problems according to a hierarchy based on the degree of likelihood of resolution, while others (Budman & Gurman, 1988) suggest selecting a focus on the basis of what is most meaningful and motivating to the client.

Goal specification and goal orientation are two other central tenets that help abbreviate treatment. Goals in general define what the preferred outcomes are for the selected problems to be worked on, while in brief treatment discrete goals that narrow the focus and clarify what will be the scope of treatment are essential (Pekarik, 1996). The preferred goals are limited to those that are relevant to the present stress and are achievable—for example, relief from distressing symptoms, a return to previous levels of functioning, or improvement in coping skills (Hoyt, 1994). Well-constructed goals (i.e., those that are clear, specific, and realistic) and an orientation toward goal achievement ensure that client and clinician will know when to stop and make it more likely that both will be satisfied with the outcomes of the treatment (Fisch, 1994).

Client participation in the formulation of goals is a central principle in brief treatment. Clients are most likely to work quickly and steadily toward goals that are consistent with their belief systems and that they have identified as being important to them and within their capacity to achieve. In addition to collaborating on treatment goals, the client is encouraged to participate throughout the treatment process when strategies such as regular client feedback are built into the treatment structure, when intersession tasks are negotiated rather than assigned, and when sessions remain focused on the client's experience of a situation. In the brief treatment framework, therapists see their roles as catalytic or facilitating rather than curative. Through questioning, solicitation of viewpoints, and in-session and intersession task assignments, the therapist actively engages the client in reflection and action (Cooper, 1995).

Clients participate most actively when their strengths, resources, and competencies are actively identified and become the basis for change. While deficits and problems in function are not ignored, the emphasis shifts from uncovering pathology to "building on and amplifying the client's own solutions, ideas, and successes" (Friedman, 1997, p. 66). Passivity, helplessness, and hopelessness (for both client and worker) tend to diminish when attention is paid to past and current instances of coping and resiliency. Brief treatment is predicated upon the assumption that change is inevitable, that it takes place largely outside of therapy, and that clients have strengths and healthy strivings that can be drawn on to facilitate the change process (Cooper, 1995).

While the expectation of change is inherent in brief treatment approaches, the anticipation of cure is not. Instead it is assumed that treatment may be intermittent and occur across the life cycle. Treatment focuses on mastery of current stressors rather than lifetime mastery; that is, there is an expectation that as an individual confronts new life stage challenges, or biologically based disorders reoccur, he or she may reenter treatment. Also within this lifespan perspective is an assumption that psychological growth is possible throughout the life span and that an important aspect of brief treatment should be environmental interventions that support positive lifespan development (Koss & Shiang, 1994). Thus, an ecological perspective informs the brief treatment assessment and intervention process. All parts of the client's system need to be evaluated, because the most effective and time efficient point or points of intervention might be at the individual, family, kinship, or community level. Consequently, interdisciplinary cooperation is emphasized in implementing the biopsychosocial treatment plan (Hoyt, 1995).

Common Brief Treatment Techniques

In addition to essential principles and beliefs, there are several practice techniques and intervention strategies that are characteristic of brief treatment models. The following techniques are considered useful ways of abbreviating treatment:

1. A positive working alliance is quickly established in order for goals to be achieved within a limited time frame. Engagement strategies that promote rapport, optimism, and a sense of safety and that increase motivation are employed as soon as possible, preferably within the first phone call.
2. Assessment is rapid but thorough enough to develop a well-crafted treatment plan. The treatment plan includes the client's strengths, resources, and capacity for change and specific, realistic goals (Hoyt, 1995).

3. Time is limited and used judiciously. The client is seen promptly after request or referral; intervention begins early in the treatment process, preferably in the first session; and sessions are scheduled in a flexible manner according to the client's needs.
4. The early interventions usually involve the introduction of novel ways of thinking, feeling, or doing.
5. A language of hope and expectation of change predominates in the dialogue so that the client's problem-saturated, self-denigrating stories are reframed[1] in a way to generate new perspectives and solutions (Friedman, 1997).
6. Interventions are structured and focused. The therapist guides the session so as to maintain the organization and focus of each session and between sessions. Problems are prioritized, a clear direction articulated, and changes in focus negotiated (Cooper, 1995).
7. Therapy is action-oriented. Clients are encouraged to engage in tasks (both cognitive and behavioral) that prepare them to make changes or help them to take action toward goals (Friedman, 1997).
8. Progress is monitored from session to session. Ineffective interventions are discontinued and replaced with new strategies.
9. Eclecticism in technique and flexibility in the use of modalities (individual, family, and group) are generally employed because of the need to quickly find what will work for a client in resolving a problem.
10. Empirically proven techniques are preferred and form the basis for the selection of intervention strategies (Hoyt, 1994).

Brief Treatment: A Conceptual Framework

An eclectic approach to practice is particularly suitable for time-limited work because it allows the clinician to select strategies and techniques from a variety of practice models that are most likely to be beneficial to a client (Koss & Shiang, 1994). In crisis intervention, pragmatism led to an early adaptation of eclecticism since no single theory could address all clinical situations, and clinicians needed to be able to respond rapidly with the technique that best matched the problems at hand. This has also been true of brief treatment, particularly in the managed care environment, where the treatment of choice is not determined by theory or therapist inclination but by empirical evidence of the efficacy of particular methods with particular problems (Corcoran & Vandiver, 1996).

---

[1] *Reframing* is a technique that is essentially a relabeling or recategorizing of an event, behavior, or motivation so that it has a positive connotation or so that the latent healthy striving is thereby revealed. The reframe offers clients an alternative perspective, one that accurately fits the facts but leads clients to a different interpretation. Such a reinterpretation may then enable them to try solutions that are alternatives to their previous counterproductive attempts.

Without knowledge of the empirical literature or a conceptual framework to guide intervention selection, though, eclecticism can result in a scattershot approach to practice, that is, a random trying out of methods in the hope of finding something that will work. While most brief therapies are eclectic in technique, each approach has identifiable theoretical foundations that support its practice methods or a conceptual framework for matching techniques and strategies to problems or to client coping style. For example, constructivist, solution-focused, and problem-solving theories of practice inform Friedman's (1997) Time-Effective Psychotherapy, and Beutler and Clarkin (1990) have developed a decisional model for differentially applying techniques and strategies.

Systematic Time-Limited Work: Theoretical Foundation

This book draws on several behavioral theories and practice models in formulating a time-limited social work practice approach. The major influences for this brief treatment approach are object relations, constructivist, and trauma theories, and cognitive-behavioral and crisis intervention practice models. The social work ecosystemic and strengths perspectives were also significant in this formulation of time-limited work.

Object relations theory and attachment theory, in particular, provide a way of conceptualizing and working with the interpersonal factors that influence the formation of the helping relationship. The establishment of a good working relationship is associated with positive outcomes in all forms of treatment but is particularly critical to achieving positive results in time-limited work. Therefore, an understanding of the nature of the alliance and the factors that facilitate or present obstacles to the establishment of the alliance is important to practicing effective brief treatment. The components of the therapeutic bond have been identified as "(1) the patient's affective relationship to the therapist, (2) the patient's capacity to purposefully work in therapy, (3) the therapist's empathic understanding and involvement, and (4) patient–therapist agreement on the goals and tasks of therapy" (Lambert & Bergin, 1994, p. 165). In addition, the therapeutic bond is influenced by the therapist's and client's expectations (based on personal and cultural norms) of how they should relate to each other. These expectations in turn affect their interpersonal behaviors, which can either promote or hinder the formation of the alliance (Orlinsky, Grawe, & Parks, 1994).

Object relations theory was selected because it provides insights into the transference aspect of the therapeutic relationship—that is, the negative and positive expectations of relationships derived from the individual's relationship history. These insights are useful for devising strategies for overcoming obstacles to the establishment of a therapeutic alliance. Attachment theory identifies the cognitive-interpersonal schema as the source of the expectations clients have of relationships. That is, on the basis of childhood experiences, individuals develop internal working models of how relationships will develop and there-after process information about relationships through these cognitive sets. In-dividuals with adverse early relationship experiences are often inclined to see relationships as threatening or difficult to obtain, while individuals with more positive early experiences tend to see relatedness as attainable and have the in-terpersonal skills to foster relatedness (Bowlby, 1979; Safran & Segal, 1990).

Safran and Segal (1990) and Butler, Strupp, and Binder (1992) have de-veloped brief treatment models based on cognitive and object relations theo-ries. The treatment focuses on patterns of negative expectations of others and maladaptive interpersonal relationships that interfere with the establishment of the therapeutic bond and with the formation of satisfying interpersonal re-lationships in general. Both models emphasize the here-and-now transference and countertransference interactions as a medium of assessment and thera-peutic change. The therapeutic relationship is used as a corrective relationship experience. The client becomes aware of self-defeating patterns of relating and learns an alternative view of relationships through disconfirming experiences with the therapist. Unsatisfying interpersonal interactions outside therapy are explored, and between-sessions experiments are introduced as ways of re-structuring maladaptive beliefs and changing dysfunctional patterns of relat-ing. The short-term practice model presented in this book will draw selectively from the models of Butler, Strupp, and Binder and of Safran and Segal in work-ing with problems in engagement and in the change process.

Cognitive-Behavioral Problem-Solving Interventions

Because of their proven efficiency and efficacy, cognitive-behavioral interven-tions have increasingly come to be the treatment of choice for clients with de-pressive and anxiety disorders and behavioral problems. Cognitive-behavioral interventions are aimed toward assessing and resolving client-selected current problems. These empirically derived techniques of intervention have been shown to promote rapid change and improve client sense of efficacy. It is a prac-tice model that is structured, focused, and short-term and has limited goals. That is, the goals are closely related to the client's reasons for requesting help and aim to reduce symptoms and interpersonal conflicts and improve the client's coping strategies (Berlin, 1983). These characteristics of cognitive-behavioral therapies are a good fit with the managed mental health care treatment goals of rapid symptom relief and improved functioning. Many preferred practice procedures thus are cognitive-behavioral interventions (Hoyt, 1995).

The cognitive therapy component of cognitive-behavioral interventions ad-dresses the client's "ideas and expectations and symbolic representations of real-ity [that] are simplistic and inaccurate and thus lead to dysfunctional responses" to the environment (Berlin, 1983, p. 1097). A variety of cognitive restructur-ing techniques lead to modification of the client's problems in information processing—that is, the faulty beliefs and assumptions that result in behavioral and emotional problems. In addition to problems stemming from faulty beliefs, clients may also have difficulty coping with their life situations due to lack of knowledge or skills. Therefore, part of the treatment plan for improving coping and problem-solving skills includes behavioral strategies in which alternative behaviors are introduced, modeled, practiced, and reinforced. Within-session behavioral enactments and between-session task assignments are used to help clients take needed and desired actions. Behavioral and cognitive interventions are today often combined to address the mediating interactions between thoughts and actions and to increase the effectiveness of each treatment method. For example, behavioral tasks are often assigned to provide clients with cognitive disconfirming experiences that will lead to shifts in the client's dysfunctional automatic thoughts and assumptions (Ackermann-Engel, 1992). At the same time, negative expectations and beliefs are carefully examined at each stage of the change process (planning, execution, and maintenance).

Cognitive-behavioral interventions are among the preferred practice methods in the new behavioral health care environment because managed mental health care companies are looking for concrete changes in symptoms and problems in functioning (Friedman, 1997). In this proposed practice model, cognitive-behavioral interventions are suggested for every stage of the intervention process, from engagement to relapse prevention and follow-up. Cognitive-behavioral interventions are particularly useful for providing the early gain in treatment that helps to quickly establish a positive working alliance. Because cognitive-behavioral strategies are useful for quickly reducing distressing symptoms, stabilizing chaotic situations, and assisting clients in making decisions, they are particularly useful for clients in crisis or at risk. Cognitive-behavioral interventions will also be the treatment of choice for clients who want rapid problem resolution or where deficits in skills and in information processing are central to the client's problems. In this brief treatment approach, cognitive-behavioral strategies are also recommended for the middle and termination stages of treatment, when the major tasks are learning lifetime problem or symptom management and relapse prevention skills.

Constructivism

Constructivist therapies have added significant new dimensions to current conceptualizations of the treatment process and have increased the effectiveness of time-limited work. Constructivist perspectives have contributed to a better understanding of how to engage clients, sustain a therapeutic alliance, and facilitate change when treatment is time limited. Although there are several constructivist therapies, only the cognitive-behavioral and narrative constructivist approaches will be discussed here. There will be some reference to solution-focused therapy, which shares several tenets with constructivist therapies and which has grown in influence as a brief treatment approach.

The cognitive and narrative constructivist therapies emphasize examination of deeper core beliefs beyond the discrete dysfunctional cognitions or units of behavior dealt with in cognitive-behavioral therapy. The focus is instead on clients' interpretative and meaning-making processes—the personal narratives by which individuals construct and know their lives. These personal meaning systems are explored in therapy because they influence behavior and because clients may pay an emotional and personal price for the narratives they tell themselves (Meichenbaum, 1996). The goal is to help clients move beyond the "bleak self-portrayals, inexorable plots, narrow themes, and demoralizing meanings that are well rehearsed, backed by selective negative evidence, and so persuasive that the person does not judge them to be stories at all, but real slices of life. Such people need alternative narratives that are also compelling but more viable and adaptive" (Ford & Urban, 1998, p. 519).

All constructivist therapies emphasize a collaborative approach to treatment. In narrative constructivist therapy, client and therapist co-construct a new, more adaptive narrative. Clients are encouraged to become more aware of all aspects of their self-experience, including their strengths, unrecognized survival strategies, and unconscious self-beliefs. Negative personal stories are reframed as predictable responses to past stresses or situations in which they were powerless. Clients are given the opportunity to reassess the beliefs or assumptions held about their degree of personal responsibility for the event, the amount of danger or uncontrollability in their lives, their self-image as victims, their ability to cope with stressful events, and their beliefs about reactions of others to the event or to themselves. Clients are then encouraged to formulate a healing story of their past, one in which they used the resources and strengths available to them at the time in order to survive and one that offers an alternative version of what happened to them and why (White & Epston, 1990). These personal narrative treatment approaches are particularly useful in middle- to late-stage interventions with clients struggling to come to terms with the sequelae of stressful events or with the aftereffects of childhood trauma (Schwarz & Prout, 1991). This approach is also useful when a client is at the stage of doing identity or self-work, although this work is not likely to be a part of most clients' brief treatment experiences as it of necessity comes after the crisis-intervention, symptom-relieving, problem-solving phase of treatment.

Constructivist tenets of practice usefully inform all stages of the treatment process (i.e., engagement, assessment, and intervention) even when the constructivist therapeutic approach is not the immediately appropriate response for a particular client (e.g., one in the early stages of a crisis or in need of concrete services). The constructivist emphases on collaborating with clients on goals and tasks, identifying and building on existing strengths, empowering clients to devise their own solutions to problems, and healing personally from within aid the therapeutic process because these techniques foster trust, optimism, and motivation to change (Dejong & Miller, 1995).

The emphasis on collaboration and empowerment has also proven useful in cross-cultural situations. In constructivist practice, the therapist's authority and power are deemphasized in favor of working with clients' views of their situations. The sociocultural context of the clients is considered to be highly significant for the way that they interpret events, perceive the implications of events, and ultimately construct the narratives of their lives. Therefore, the therapist takes a stance of "not knowing" the cultural or personal meanings by asking questions rather than making interpretations or diagnostic statements. This minimizes the possibility that the therapist's personal and theoretical biases and assumptions may create obstacles to the formation of a working alliance (Combs & Freedman, 1994). Such an approach to practice is less likely to result in the miscommunications and misunderstandings that are destructive to the establishment of rapport and trust.

Constructivist theoretical principles are also consistent with social work values and practice perspectives, among them the strengths and ecosystemic perspectives. For example, the preeminence given to client-centered practice, self-determination, and support of client capacities echoes fundamental social work practice principles. As Saleeby noted (1992), the strengths perspective, which is a view that people have an inherent power or transformational capacity for coping with problems, shares with constructivism the implicit assumption that professional knowledge is not inherently superior to the client's personal knowledge. Likewise, the emphasis in constructivism on the importance of the sociocultural context is akin to the emphasis in social work ecosystemic models on assessing person–environment transactions. Building on a client's strengths, assessing the client's sociocultural environment, and using multisystem interventions are central values and practice techniques in most time-limited practice models and will inform all the interventions described in this book. The solution-focused approach to time-limited treatment, for example, has led to the development of several interviewing techniques that uncover and promote client strengths and that promote collaboration between worker and client.

Solution-Focused Therapy

Several of the assessment and intervention strategies proposed in this book draw on the solution-focused approach to practice. It is an approach that is especially useful in setting the change process in motion even before sessions begin, developing appropriate goals, and increasing and maintaining the motivation to make changes. Solution-focused therapy is based on the notion that change is inevitable and that focusing on pathology and locating resistance within the client rather than in the interaction between worker and client can impede change. Instead, an emphasis in treatment on constructing solutions promotes change and empowers clients. Change in solution-focused therapy is facilitated primarily by two sets of interviewing techniques: "The first is the development of well-formed goals with the client within the client's frame of reference; the second is the development with the client of solutions based on 'exceptions'" (Dejong & Miller, 1995, p. 730).

Several types of interviewing questions are used to enable clients to arrive at concise, specific, and personally meaningful goals and to pay attention to exceptions to problem occurrence. Among these are the "miracle" question, scaling questions, and coping questions. The "miracle" question asks clients to imagine that by a miracle their problem has disappeared and then express in what ways their situation would be different. It directs clients' attention to what goals to work toward in order to bring about a desired change. Use of scaling questions, in which clients are asked to assign a number from 0 to 10 to "where they are" with regard to a problem or concern, helps keep them motivated to work toward goals. Scaling questions do this by making concrete the small steps involved in changing and helping clients keep informed of their progress. Coping questions in solution-focused therapy are designed to help clients uncover their own strengths and resources in the face of adverse life situations (Berg, 1994).

Trauma Interventions

As Roberts (1996) noted, there is an increasing number of clients who have been exposed to acute crisis events (family and community violence, substance abuse, sexual abuse, etc.) and who require short-term help in coping with these events. Over the past decade, trauma theory and techniques for treating trauma have evolved in response to the needs of professionals serving individuals with acute or chronic stress reactions. The therapeutic strategies that have been developed are based on an understanding of how individuals process trauma and are in part derived from existing therapy methods. Thus, cognitive-behavioral interventions have been found to be useful in dealing with the acute symptoms of trauma reactions and with the initial psychosocial and concrete tasks of trauma or crisis management, when the individual may be having difficulty coping with the daily tasks of living and with making necessary decisions. Constructivist therapeutic approaches can be helpful in the early stages of treatment in reducing emotional distress and restoring diminished self-esteem through normalizing stress reactions and identifying strengths. Both cognitive-behavioral and constructivist techniques are employed in the important later-stage task of altering the negative beliefs that victims of trauma can develop about themselves and their future. In addition, important strategies in the treatment of trauma include psychodynamic techniques such as encouraging catharsis and using the therapeutic relationship to provide a sense of safety and control. Family therapy and group work approaches are considered particularly useful for reducing shame, guilt, and isolation because they can be used to mobilize a support network (Schwarz & Prout, 1991).

Over time, there has been a convergence among these therapeutic approaches in how trauma reactions can be resolved and what strategies are most effective in enabling that resolution. Among the points of agreement among trauma treatment models are the following: (1) Therapy should occur sooner rather than later, (2) therapy generally should be brief and focused, and (3) certain strategies are particularly useful in assisting traumatized clients to achieve an adaptive resolution. These strategies are supporting adaptation and coping skills, normalizing stress reactions, decreasing avoidance, altering meanings given to the event, and facilitating integration of the self (Schwarz & Prout, 1991).

Saunders and Arnold (1993) also found that there has been a growing consensus that a stage approach is necessary to treat trauma. The stage approach is based on an understanding of the phases that individuals tend to move through in normal and problematic responses to stressful life events. In the Horowitz model of stress reaction, for example, the typical responses to stress include being initially overwhelmed and panicked, followed by a stage of denial and avoidance. Thereafter, alternating states of avoidance of and flooding of thoughts and feelings associated with the trauma eventually are worked through to the point that the trauma can be recalled without distress (Horowitz, Field, & Classen, 1993).

There is a general recognition that trauma treatment needs to be matched to the stage where the individual is in the trauma recovery process. Thus, in the early stage of treatment, where acute symptoms such as panic, flooding, and self-destructive behaviors predominate, there is a need for ego-supportive interventions such as teaching specific coping skills, normalizing post-traumatic symptoms, and increasing tolerance for painful feelings. The middle stage involves a "reconstruction and integration of the memories and meaning of traumata" (Saunders & Arnold, 1993, p. 199), grief work about the loss of assumptions and former self-identity, and a shift in the client's orientation from the past to the future. The final stage is the working through of the trauma, the reintegration of the self that includes the traumatic event, and construction of a narrative that makes sense and fosters adaptation.

The phased approach to treating trauma and stress reactions is also a model that can inform intervention planning in general; in time-limited work it is important to assess problem severity and the degree of risk to the client, and then to prioritize the problems to determine the appropriate level of intervention. Significant safety risks, severe to disabling symptoms, substance abuse problems, or a significant degree of distress and impairment in functioning will always be high priorities, and more protective, structured, or directive levels of care are indicated (Goodman, Brown, & Dietz, 1992). Thus the stabilization and symptom relief interventions of the first stage of trauma treatment would

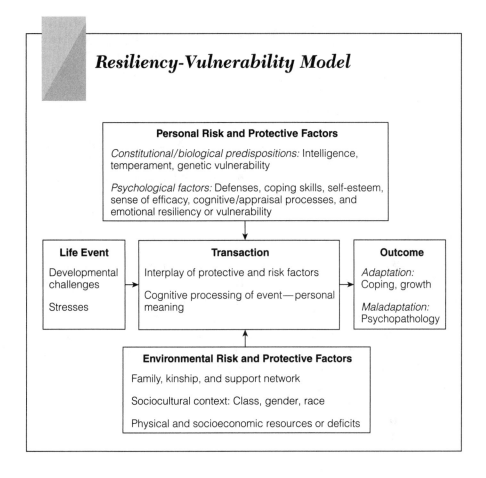

Resiliency-Vulnerability Model

Personal Risk and Protective Factors

Constitutional/biological predispositions: Intelligence, temperament, genetic vulnerability

Psychological factors: Defenses, coping skills, self-esteem, sense of efficacy, cognitive/appraisal processes, and emotional resiliency or vulnerability

Life Event

Developmental challenges

Stresses

Transaction

Interplay of protective and risk factors

Cognitive processing of event—personal meaning

Outcome

Adaptation: Coping, growth

Maladaptation: Psychopathology

Environmental Risk and Protective Factors

Family, kinship, and support network

Sociocultural context: Class, gender, race

Physical and socioeconomic resources or deficits

be the appropriate level of intervention for clients who are dealing with an immediate crisis or whose symptoms indicate a severe or prolonged reaction to stress. However, personal variables, such as individual coping styles, and environmental variables such as the quality of the social support network, need to be factored into the determination of the level of intervention. The Resiliency-Vulnerability model presented below is one means of arriving at a rapid but comprehensive assessment of the risk and protective factors that determine an individual's response to stress.

The Resiliency-Vulnerability Model

The Resiliency-Vulnerability model is one way of conceptualizing the process by which individuals adapt or fail to adapt to stresses or life challenges. In this model, the response to a stressor is seen as a function of the severity and duration of the stressor, the personal characteristics that shape the individual's appraisal of the stressor, and the social context within which the event occurred. It is a useful model for brief treatment because it requires that the clinician adequately assess both individual strengths and limitations and the adequacy or limitations of resources in the recovery environment. All relevant biological, psychological, and social resiliency and vulnerability factors are evaluated in order to understand why a client has arrived at the meanings attributed to the event and how that meaning system is contributing to the adaptive or maladaptive coping response (Rutter, 1989; Green, Wilson, & Lindy, 1985). It is a model that promotes the biopsychosocial, holistic perspective needed in brief treatment to arrive at the appropriate level of care and the most promising points of intervention.

Summary

The focus in this chapter was on the conceptual framework for time-limited practice, the general principles, assumptions, and procedures that define brief treatment today, and the behavioral and practice theories that guide the time-limited approach employed in this text. The tenets of brief treatment were reviewed in order to orient the reader to an alternative way of conceptualizing practice that naturally leads to shortening the length of treatment. An outline of theories and models that guided the practice approach taken here was presented so that the reader could examine how decisions about problem definition, assessment, and intervention planning were made.

Recommended Reading

Friedman, S. (1997). *Time-effective psychotherapy: Maximizing outcomes in an era of minimized resources.* Needham Heights, MA: Allyn and Bacon.

Pekarik, G. (1996). *Psychotherapy abbreviation: A practical guide.* Binghamton, NY: Haworth Press.

CHAPTER 3

LEVELS OF INTERVENTION: THE ENGAGEMENT AND ASSESSMENT PROCESS

Introduction

The emphasis in Chapter 2 was on developing a conceptual framework and a perspective on practice that would lead naturally to the development of effective abbreviated treatment. The focus in this and the next three chapters is on the specific steps of the helping process in time-limited work—that is, on the techniques and intervention strategies that enable one to apply brief treatment techniques to complex problem situations. At the beginning of Chapter 2, three client situations were presented as being typical of the type of complex and challenging cases found in agency and clinic practice today that clinicians find difficult to think of in brief treatment terms. These cases will now be restated here and discussed in order to illustrate how a systematic, strategic approach to assessment and case conceptualization can aid in the development of a brief treatment plan.

> Heather, a 28-year-old mother of two, was referred for outpatient treatment following her fourth suicide attempt and hospitalization. She is diagnosed as bipolar and is on Depakote. Periodically, she stops taking her medication and is eventually hospitalized. The current hospitalization was precipitated by a breakup with a boyfriend and going off her medication. The client has a history of substance abuse and problematic relationships with men. She has been steadily employed for 7 years as a nurse and has been in recovery for 9 months. Her two children appear to be well taken care of, although the older child has assumed a caregiving role.

> Toni is a 5-year-old girl referred for oppositional behavior, temper tantrums, and aggressive behavior. In the classroom she is easily distracted and demands a lot of the teacher's attention. Toni lives with her 18-year-old mother, teenage uncle, and grandmother. Although the grandmother is alcoholic, Toni's mother leaves her for long periods in her care. Mother and grandmother have failed to keep most of Toni's medical, psychological, and educational evaluation appointments, and she is frequently absent from school. Family life is chaotic and crisis-ridden, with household needs often going unmet.

Mr. and Mrs. B were referred by a hospital social worker for outpatient social services following Mr. B's hospitalization for complications associated with chemotherapy for esophageal cancer. The couple, who are in their late forties, have three children: two teenage daughters and a 10-year-old son. The prognosis for Mr. B is poor, with palliative care in a hospice setting the probable next step. The referral was made to provide the couple with financial and medical assistance and support around this medical crisis and the depression that their older daughter was already experiencing. Mr. B had recently left his employment with a large corporation to start his own business.

Each of the three client situations presented above, in addition to being complex, could also be described as a crisis or at-risk situation. The clients in these vignettes are at risk: for self-harm, for placement out of home, or for loss of family stability and functioning. These client situations might cause concern and doubt even among seasoned clinicians about how to devise an appropriate treatment plan. One of the central premises of this book is that complicated clinical situations are most effectively managed in brief treatment when the clinician has an intervention planning model or triage system for arriving at treatment decisions. Brief treatment is most likely to show a successful outcome when there is a systematic assessment that leads to a precise treatment plan targeted toward resolution of specific problems. A systematic assessment involves the prioritizing of problems and goals and the strategic selection of interventions according to the client's level of functioning and particular set of needs and based on best practice methods for the identified problem areas.

As noted in the last chapter, the Post-traumatic Stress Disorder (PTSD)[1] model of phased interventions can serve as a guide for intervention planning in brief treatment. Intervention planning in both models involves assessment of risk and client needs, prioritization of problems, and selection of treatment focus and precise goals. The PTSD stage model then suggests what the appropriate methods of intervention would be, based on an assessment of the severity of problems, degree of instability and dysfunction, and client need. This guide for making initial treatment decisions and for altering the treatment approach as problems become less severe and clients develop coping skills is useful in ensuring that the most pressing issues are addressed first. The PTSD model of treatment is also useful in assuring that a treatment plan will meet managed care requirements, that treatment necessity will be demonstrated, and that the appropriate level of care and best practice methods have been selected.

---

[1] Acronyms introduced in this chapter: PTSD, Post-traumatic Stress Disorder; AA, Alcoholics Anonymous; RAI, rapid assessment instrument; BDI, Beck Depression Inventory; MAST, Michigan Alcoholism Screening Test; DSM-IV, Diagnostic and Statistical Manual of Mental Disorders, 4th ed. (American Psychiatric Association, 1994); GAFS, Global Assessment of Functioning Scale; GARF, Global Assessment of Relational Functioning; SADS, Schedule for Affective Disorders and Schizophrenia; MCMI, Millon Clinical Multiaxial Inventory; CAI, computer-assisted instruments; QOLI, Quality of Life Inventory; I-D-E, Interpersonal-Developmental-Existential (model).

The Levels of Intervention Model

The Levels of Intervention model that is introduced here and elaborated on in the section on treatment planning is offered as a tool for tackling the kinds of complicated problems described above. As with any stage model, the Levels of Intervention model can serve only as a guide for thinking about a case, not as a prescription for action. Each stage in this model is not discrete; client problems might fall within two or more stages. Linear progression from one stage to the next is not assumed, and in fact a recycling back through earlier stages at points of stress or points of change is to be expected. The utility of such a model is that it offers the equivalent of a triage system: a way of ensuring that issues of safety, structure (internal and external), substance abuse, and stability are identified and attended to first. Thus, the client—and the managed care organization—are assured that the client's most pressing, troubling problems will be addressed within the time restrictions.

The Levels of Intervention model is a synthesis of treatment strategies derived from PTSD phased treatment approaches; systematic treatment selection (Beutler & Clarkin, 1990); differential family intervention strategies (Kilpatrick & Holland, 1995); and early intervention strategies with clients with borderline personality disorder (Corwin, 1996). In this model, the nature and severity of the presenting problems and the client's coping styles, strengths, resources, and preferences are matched to the intervention strategies that have been proven clinically and in empirical research to be the most effective for resolving those difficulties. There are three levels of assessment and intervention, which are briefly described here. Clients presenting with problems in which their safety or the safety of others is at risk, or who have substance abuse problems, severe psychiatric symptoms, unstable living situations, and lack of social supports, and who report being in a state of crisis, are best served by Level I interventions. Level I interventions are more structured, problem-solving, and psychoeducational in nature and include substance abuse treatment, medication, and case management methods to provide needed resources and stabilize the client's life situation. For clients who are not in crisis and who are not significantly impaired in functioning, assessment would center on such issues as interpersonal conflicts, academic and occupational difficulties, unresolved losses, and moderate levels of mood disturbance. These types of difficulties indicate the second level of intervention, in which more exploratory, expressive, and interpersonal techniques are employed. Medication and lifetime management skills training may also be used in conjunction with these methods. When clients present with problems that are primarily adjustment difficulties related to developmental challenges or typical life stresses, or when clients have resolved more serious difficulties (within Levels I and II), the appropriate treatment choices are Level III interventions. These interventions are directed toward uncovering deeper core beliefs and meaning systems, insight development, and narrative reconstruction.

Levels of Intervention Model

Level I

A. Problems involving safety, self-care, severe symptoms, stability, and substance abuse issues. Families at this level have difficulty meeting basic needs of food, clothing, or shelter, or minimum level of nurturance, health care, etc.

B. Interventions: crisis intervention, case management (advocacy, mediation, and referral), psychoeducation, problem-solving models (e.g., cognitive-behavioral), addictions treatment, family preservation techniques, guidance, maximizing personal strengths and support network.

Level II

A. Problems with conflicted, confused, or misidentified thoughts or feelings; interpersonal conflicts; work and/or parenting functioning. Families are sufficiently organized to provide minimal structure, limits, and safety, but maintaining authority and boundaries or setting limits are problems.

B. Interventions: exploratory (insight) and expressive therapies; interpersonal and coping skills development; bereavement work; cognitive restructuring; solution-focused, structural, and family systems interventions.

Level III

A. Problems of selfhood: self-esteem, identity, and self-evaluation. Client has made the movement from a focus on past and worry about future to present, or there is an emphasis in treatment on consolidation and maintenance of therapy gains. Desire for greater intimacy, connection, and self-actualization.

B. Interventions: narrative constructivist and object relations (individual and family) approaches. Reconstruction of a personal narrative that moves the individual or family from a passive to an active role and from negative self-evaluation to an appreciation of his or her or family strengths.

(Derived from Beutler & Clarkin, 1990, and Kilpatrick & Holland, 1995)

If the Levels of Intervention model were used as a guide in assessment and intervention planning for the three client situations, the clinician would gather data on risks, strengths, and resources to begin the differential assessment– intervention planning process. In the first case vignette of Heather, who was recently hospitalized after going off her medication and making a suicide attempt, the model would direct one to evaluate the risk for self-harm, relapse, treatment noncompliance, and family dysfunction. Other personal strengths besides steady employment and capacity for nurturance might be identified, or family or community resources sought, but initially one would be thinking in terms of Level I structuring and stabilizing interventions. In the second vignette of 5-year-old Toni, who is exhibiting aggressive and impulsive behaviors, the risk assessment would center upon the family's capacity to meet all of the family members' basic needs—in particular, their capacity to meet Toni's attachment needs. Evaluation of extended family and community resources would be an essential part of this assessment because of the likelihood that several Level I interventions would be needed to increase the level of family functioning. Finally, in the third vignette, a risk assessment reveals that the B family is in the midst of a medical crisis that is complicated by, and complicates, other stresses the family is experiencing (financial stress and adolescent depression). Again, the presence of a crisis would indicate that Level I interventions initially would be the appropriate level of care. However, with all of these clients, a complete assessment of coping capacities might reveal areas of resiliency or resources that might make the need for Level I interventions only a brief initial response, so that some combination of Level I and II interventions might prove most helpful.

The discussion of the three cases demonstrates how the Levels of Intervention model can aid in making the rapid assessment required in brief treatment by providing guidance as to the essential data that will need to be collected and processed. While an actual thorough assessment of each of these cases might lead to a different plan than the initial impression of crisis and limited family resources would indicate, the model makes it more likely that essential data will not be overlooked and that the client will receive an adequate level of care. The rest of this chapter will describe in more detail the assessment and treatment planning process in time-limited work. The description of the process will begin with a section on engagement, since the establishment of rapport and a positive working alliance is a necessary first step in completing an accurate assessment.

Although tasks of the engagement-assessment stage and strategies of intervention will be described in separate chapters, in actual brief treatment practice they often overlap because of the need to use time effectively. In general, brief treatment models follow a structured approach to practice in which phases of treatment are distinguished and specific tasks are to be accomplished in each session. However, the need to maximize the amount of time available for problem resolution means that the intervention process should begin in the first session. Developing rapport, gathering information, and responding therapeutically are linked or may even be identical in brief treatment.

Engagement and Assessment

The first session is very important in brief therapy because of the number of tasks to be accomplished in one session and because the first session can affect positively or negatively the whole course of treatment. Research on dropout rates and outcomes in treatment has found that the positive perceptions and reactions of clients in the first sessions are strongly associated with continuation in treatment and positive outcomes (Garfield, 1994). In addition, the first session is also the point at which therapists have maximum therapeutic leverage. It is the point at which there is the strongest push toward change, due to the novelty of the situation; the client's motivation is heightened due to the pressure of problems; and the therapist's ascribed credibility and influence may be greatest (Budman & Gurman, 1988). Therefore, it is important to examine in detail what needs to be accomplished in the early sessions and the techniques that will aid in the establishment of a sound working alliance.

The following tasks are prescribed for the first session in most brief therapy models: (1) establishing a safe and comfortable environment in which a positive working alliance can develop; (2) assisting applicants to become clients through exploration of the referral process, elicitation of clients' expectations of help, and orientation to the use of therapy (Hoyt, 1994; Reid, 1992); (3) evaluating the client's difficulties, resources, and level of motivation to engage in therapy and to work toward change; (4) collaborating with the client and contracting on goals, methods of treatment, and outcome expectations; (5) determining a focus or organizing theme of treatment; (6) providing an early gain in treatment through the introduction of a novel way of thinking, feeling, or doing; (7) eliciting feedback from clients about their experience of the session; (8) negotiating with the client about homework and issues to be discussed in the next session; and (9) establishing baseline criteria for evaluation of outcome (Cooper, 1995; Hoyt, 1994).

There are several strategies used in brief treatment to rapidly establish a working alliance. One such strategy is to use the intake or appointment telephone call to begin building the alliance and discovering the theme or focus around which treatment will be built. For example, involuntary or mandated clients may express their reluctance to enter treatment in the very first phone call, in the setting up of an appointment time, as in the following case example.

> Ann was referred by her employee assistance program for a substance abuse evaluation after episodes of coming in late and smelling of alcohol. When Ann called to make an appointment, she angrily found fault with each proposed appointment time. The worker responded empathetically to the client's

distress about having to accept a referral in order to keep her job and then tried again to find an appropriate time. Ann was then able to accept an appointment and kept all subsequent appointments.

This vignette illustrates the technique of moving with the resistance, a technique that is useful for enabling reluctant applicants to become clients. It is based on the recognition that resistance is motivated behavior, that it is interpersonal in nature, and that resistance can be utilized to promote understanding and change (Cummings & Sayama, 1995; Shea, 1998). Thus, negative feelings such as anger, resentment, shame, fear, or anxiety are understood as normative reactions to the loss of freedom and the loss of control in being an involuntary client. Excessive anxiety, in particular, inhibits engagement and motivation. The clinician engages the client by uncovering the source of the anxiety (e.g., fear of being misunderstood or negatively judged, or fear that the clinician cannot or will not help) and then by directly or indirectly addressing these fears. The clinician can reduce defensiveness by normalizing the client's reactions, making the covert resistance overt, and respecting the client's fears and need to reassert control (Shea, 1998). In this instance, the clinician did not react to the client's angry, uncooperative behavior but instead addressed the client's distress about the referral while being flexible about the appointment time.

The initial telephone call can be used to help the client sort out what he or she would like to see happen in therapy. Particularly with involuntary and mandated clients, it is important to hear what they see as problems and as possible solutions to their problems, and how that might be different from what the referral source might say. De Shazer's (1985) "formula first session task" is especially useful when a child is the identified patient, but it is also useful in general for shifting the client's perspective from a total focus on problems to one on unrecognized strengths and resources. This therapeutic task directs the client to take notice between the initial call and the first session of "what is happening in your family that you would like to continue to happen" (de Shazer, 1985, p. 137). In the first session, this approach can be expanded upon to include the parents' vision of the kind of parents they would like to be and what kind of children they want to raise. This continues the shift in perspective away from entrenched problems to goals and solutions.

In brief therapy, time is used more effectively and therapeutic leverage is easier to establish if the intake and assessment tasks are completed by the same person who will be seeing the client. Since many agencies still divide up these tasks among different clinicians, pretreatment tasks will then have to be completed in the first session. Another time-saving strategy is to gather as much information before the first session as possible and to have the client complete a history form before the first session. Gathering information before the first session enables the worker to learn what worked in the past and what did not and what strengths or resources the client possesses, thereby increasing the likelihood that the client's initial perceptions of therapy will be positive (Berg, 1994).

Engagement Strategies with Involuntary or Mandated Clients

Other strategies in addition to the technique of moving with the resistance are useful for rapidly establishing a working alliance with involuntary and mandated clients. One such technique is "joining"[2] with clients by entering into their worldview and learning their perspective on their situation. Clarity and honesty about the referral process and the problematic behaviors for which the client was referred is another important first intervention with referred clients. Mandated clients, in particular, need to know which goals are nonnegotiable and where they have freedom of choice in the helping process (Rooney, 1988), as is illustrated in the following case vignette.

> Rose was a young woman who had been ordered to receive counseling by a court as part of her probation after she was convicted of making death threats against a former therapist. The client was angry, belligerent, denigrating, and demanding and at times sat in hostile silence. Exploration of what the court experience had been like for her, and how she felt about the mandate to seek counseling, revealed how damaging this experience had been to her self-esteem. She considered herself a hard-working middle-class person, unlike the criminal "low-lifes" she felt she had been forced to associate with in court. Rose feared that she would be disdained and rejected because she had been adjudicated and mandated to come for treatment as part of her probation. Acceptance of her anger about being tried and forced to come for treatment and her fear of being misjudged enabled her to negotiate the treatment goals. Although she didn't want to be forced into treatment, Rose was able to contract around the goal of lifting the court mandate that she would receive counseling and refrain from threatening anyone. She also accepted that alternative ways of handling stresses and interpersonal conflicts were necessary objectives toward reaching her goal.

Outcome studies have shown that clients are more likely to engage in and remain in treatment when goals are realistic, achievable, and desirable to the client. Thus, as is illustrated above, there is a need to take seriously what is causing the greatest distress for the client and address those concerns, while at the same time maintaining clarity about the purpose and direction of treatment, including the role the client will play in this process (Rooney, 1988). Taking time in the first session to clarify mutual expectations of treatment and pro-

---

[2]*Joining* is the stance the clinician takes to establish a positive working relationship with a client or family. It involves careful listening and observing, reflecting back an understanding of the family's viewpoint, and conveying respect for the family's rules of communication and engagement.

vide information about treatment options, the therapy process, and length of treatment (Cooper, 1995) can in the end save time that might otherwise be lost later on dealing with resistance and therapy ruptures.

Most clients enter treatment in a demoralized state, whether or not they are in agreement with the problem as defined by the referring source. That is, they may be resistant to therapy because of a general state of hopelessness and helplessness. Therefore, inspiring optimism or providing an early gain in therapy can provide motivation to engage in treatment. Two intervention strategies that can be used in this way are normalizing for clients their reactions to stresses and educating them about the course of illness. A third technique, reframing, is useful for reducing demoralization and resistance, particularly if the reframe incorporates the client's "healthy striving" behind problematic behaviors or the client's unrecognized strengths that can be drawn on for resolving current difficulties (Berg, 1994; Selekman, 1993; Waters & Lawrence, 1993).

Finally, the models of the change process that Miller (1983) and Prochaska, DiClemente, and Norcross (1992) developed for understanding addictive behavior and for enabling problem drinkers to change their drinking behavior also offer useful insights into how to engage reluctant clients. Miller sees motivation as a balance between opposing viewpoints: "One side favors doing something about the problem, the other side favors avoidance." The task for the therapist is "to help the individual in this motivational struggle [by] tipping the balance in the right direction" (Miller, 1983, p. 154). Miller terms this process "motivational interviewing." It is an approach that emphasizes the need to first enhance self-esteem and sense of efficacy to enable people to examine problem behaviors, as well as consciousness-raising rather than confrontation. Clients become motivated to engage in the change process through an increasing awareness of the discrepancy between their stated goals and their actual behaviors.

In motivational interviewing, clients are not confronted about their problem behaviors, nor must they accept the referral source's definition of the problem. Instead, the worker uses strategies that enable clients to make the internal shifts necessary for problem recognition and to gain the motivation to resolve their problems. Strategies such as reflective listening, in which the clinician reinforces the client's statements about the negative consequences of his or her behaviors, or slightly restructures the reflection to offer another perspective, are used to decrease defensiveness and increase self-awareness and reappraisal (Miller, 1983).

The Stages of Change Model

The techniques employed in motivational interviewing are similar to the consciousness-raising strategies that Prochaska and DiClemente (1986) suggest in their Stages of Change model. Consciousness-raising strategies are deemed

Prochaska-DiClemente Stages of Change Model

I. Precontemplation

A. Individual does not see behavior(s) as a problem or does not see it as problematic as others see it. Reluctance, resistance, rationalization, or resignation may be present.

B. Interventions: motivational interviewing, consciousness raising, experiencing consequences, environmental shifts, and catharsis.

II. Contemplation

A. Client open to information and to weighing decision to change. Ambivalence, fear of change, and interest, but not commitment, are characteristic of this stage.

B. Interventions: same as precontemplation with movement toward self-reevaluation, assessing how one feels and thinks about oneself with respect to problem. Education, bibliotherapy, and confrontation may be useful.

III. Preparation

A. Client determined to take action and may make serious attempt at change. Shifting levels of commitment and ambivalence are present.

B. Interventions: commitment-enhancing techniques, summarizing pros and cons of taking action, considering options for making changes, negotiating a plan, setting meaningful, realistic goals.

IV. Action

A. Implementation of a plan; client uses therapy to obtain confirmation of his or her actions and goals, seeks support, and gains greater sense of self-efficacy.

B. Interventions: positive reinforcement of successful actions, support and enhancement of social support network, devising alternatives for problem behaviors, restructuring environment and daily activities, cathartic relief, and increasing rewards.

V. Maintenance: Relapse and Recycling

A. New behaviors become firmly established; preparation for maintenance through assessment of conditions under which problems might reappear.

B. Interventions: relapse prevention techniques—for example, plan for risk situations, plan for recovery from setback, and schedule booster contacts.

(Derived from Prochaska, DiClemente, & Norcross, 1992)

to be the appropriate methods for assisting clients who are unaware of problems or are unprepared to make changes in their behaviors. In their research on addictive behaviors, Prochaska and DiClemente found that people enter treatment with differing degrees of readiness to make changes and that effective treatment requires that there be a match between interventions and the client's level of readiness. Prochaska and DiClemente's (1986) model consists of five stages of degree of readiness for making changes. Each stage is indicative of the kind of maneuvers that people go through in reacting to stresses and in resolving conflict in order to maintain a sense of safety and predictability in their lives. First there is the exclusion of certain aspects of the problem from awareness, with an overreaction to other parts of the problem and an avoidance of action. Then, after weighing the consequences of action or inaction, a decision is made for action. After action is taken, there is an assessment of the effectiveness of the action, and the efforts are then reinforced or redirected, perhaps with recycling through the previous stages (Beutler & Clarkin, 1990). Prochaska and DiClemente (1986) termed these five stages of change precontemplation, contemplation, preparation, action, and maintenance.

An awareness of where a client is in the change process enables the clinician to make an intervention that matches the client's level of motivation. Clients in the precontemplation and contemplation stages will need opportunities to become more comfortable with the idea of change. In the precontemplation stage, the individual does not recognize a problem or is ambivalent about doing anything about a problem. An individual in the contemplation stage recognizes a problem, considers doing something about it, but then rejects the idea. The most productive interventions at these stages are educational interventions that provide information and feedback to the prospective client about the nature of his or her problem and supportive and empowering strategies. In subsequent sessions, after the client has accepted the need to do something about the problem behaviors, the therapist employs strategies that promote dissonance between actual behaviors and stated goals. The therapist also prepares the client to take action and, when the client is engaged in the change process, introduces relapse prevention strategies (Prochaska et al., 1992). In the case briefly described here (the treatment will be presented in more detail in Chapter 9), the client was in the contemplation stage but was motivated to take action when he could see that valued goals would be impossible to achieve without giving up drinking.

> Dave, a 34-year-old single man with an 18-year history of alcohol abuse, was seeking treatment after he had been turned down for medical insurance. Dave recognized that family and friends believed he had a drinking problem, but he was not committed to treatment except to be able to qualify for insurance. However, he had agreed to accept counseling for other issues he was concerned about. These issues were his failure to achieve goals that his

contemporaries had achieved, such as home ownership and marriage. Since these failures were tied to his drinking problems, cognitive dissonance could be created between his stated goals and his behaviors. He could then accept the necessity of getting treatment for his addiction and consider treatment options.

Engagement Issues with Culturally Diverse Clients

Many of the client-centered engagement strategies described above are useful for working with culturally diverse clients to address the problem of high dropout rates among ethnic minority and poor clients. Misunderstandings stemming from differences in value systems and concepts of help and the helping relationship between worker and clients create a greater risk of these clients failing to engage and dropping out quickly. Such individuals may have different interpretations of distress, problem definitions, and ideas of what constitutes a positive outcome, as well as where one turns for help (Rogler & Cortes, 1993). Legault (1996), in a study of the difficulties encountered by social workers working in multicultural and multiethnic contexts, found several typical situations of intercultural misunderstanding. "The most significant incidents of culture shock between workers from a developed western-type society and clients from developing non-western societies relate to a different notion of the role of social services, different ways of bringing up children, unequal relationships between men and women, a different concept of the family and to a different concept of physical and mental health" (Legault, 1996, p. 49).

Intercultural misunderstandings or instances of "culture shock" between worker and client tend to occur because differences in worldview—that is, differences in beliefs, assumptions, and values in key areas of social behavior—are largely unconscious. Thus, workers first need to develop an awareness of their own cultural background. Being aware of aspects of one's cultural background that were previously taken for granted increases the likelihood that one will recognize when there are significant differences in perspective with clients. The constructivist stance of "not knowing" (a way of learning the client's perspective that is as free as possible from the clinician's biases) is also a good beginning position to take in conducting a cross-cultural assessment (Anderson & Goolishian, 1992).

The family therapy technique of "joining" is particularly useful with ethnic minority clients because it helps to develop trust and a level of comfort for clients who may have doubts about the effectiveness of therapy for solving their problems. The technique of "moving with the resistance" can also be useful because, for many minority clients, seeking Western professional help may be their choice of last resort. In "moving with the resistance," the clinician attempts to understand the origin of the resistance, validate the underlying fears or tensions, and try to decrease the resistance by resolving those tensions. It is a recognition that the resistance in these situations may be an expression of conflicting goals and expectations stemming from cultural differences in perspective (Shea, 1998; Berg, 1994). Thus, acknowledging that it may have been difficult for them to seek help or to accept a referral for help can help reduce the fear, anxiety, or shame fueling the resistance. The process of discussing this fact and normalizing it may reveal cultural beliefs about emotional problems and methods of problem resolution that are in conflict with Western mental health beliefs (Rogler & Cortes, 1993).

Another engagement strategy that can foster a positive working alliance when working with ethnic minority clients is to provide clear and explicit information about the referral and treatment process. Therapy may be both unfamiliar and threatening to many of these clients; therefore, taking time to explain the process and present a rationale for it can reduce any discomfort and anxiety they may be experiencing. In addition, treatment is more likely to make sense for many ethnic minority and low-income clients when there are early gains in treatment, as this matches their expectations that they will get help in the first session. Interventions in the first session aimed at alleviating the client's distress or beginning the problem resolution process can help the therapist gain credibility with clients who are doubtful about the value of Western treatment methods (Sue & Zane, 1987), as demonstrated in the following vignette.

Soon was a female graduate student from Korea who presented with the signs and symptoms of major depression. She had become increasingly anxious and depressed after being accused of plagiarism, but she had refused her roommate's suggestion that she get help because she was already overwhelmed by feelings of shame and did not want the additional stigma of being considered mentally ill. Exploration of the plagiarism charge revealed that Soon had not intended to plagiarize. That is, she had followed a style of citing references that she had learned in Korea that was not acceptable in this country. She experienced great relief when her explanation of the situation was accepted and from the psychoeduational intervention of providing information about depression. She also responded well to the normalization of her stress reaction and to concrete assistance, such as interceding with the department chair to postpone the hearing on the plagiarism charge until she was sufficiently recovered from the depression to mount an adequate defense. Soon was also able to accept the suggestion that she reconnect with the Korean student organization once she was able to recognize that the other Korean students were not rejecting her and in fact were offering to help her fight the plagiarism charge. Even though Soon initially had indicated that she was only intending to come in for one session, she readily agreed to another appointment and then for six more sessions.

Summary of Engagement Issues

The formation of a positive working alliance is essential in time-limited work. Therefore, the brief therapist needs to understand the factors and therapeutic techniques that foster rapport, trust, confidence, and cooperation and that enhance motivation, as well as those factors that lead to or increase resistance. Anticipating obstacles to engagement when clients are involuntary, have a history of adverse interpersonal relationships, or are at the precontemplation level of change, or when there are cultural differences between worker and client, will enable the worker to begin to deal with these issues before they short-circuit the establishment of a working alliance.

Assessment in Brief Treatment

Assessment is "the process of gathering, analyzing, and synthesizing salient data into a formulation" (Hepworth, Rooney, & Larsen, 1997, p. 193) that makes clear the nature of the client's problems or needs and the appropriate goals and interventions. Under the managed care utilization review process, in order for services to be authorized, the assessment must also achieve other aims. The assessment should present a clear picture of the client's level of impairment in functioning so that treatment necessity is proven. In addition, an accurate diagnosis and the appropriateness and cost-effectiveness of the treatment plan must be documented (Corcoran & Vandiver, 1996). Assessment in time-limited work can be challenging because it must be both rapid and thorough. A broad-based inquiry, using as many sources of information as is feasible, is necessary before goals can be narrowed to those that are specific, attainable, and meaningful to the client. By the end of the first session or shortly thereafter, a working case formulation and treatment plan should have been developed, with the expectation that additional information or the client's responses to treatment, particularly a lack of positive response, may indicate a need for reevaluation and a revised treatment plan (Cooper, 1995).

For clinicians accustomed to taking several sessions to complete an assessment before beginning treatment, doing an accurate assessment and beginning the intervention in the first session may seem like a daunting task. Certainly, having a wide-ranging, solid clinical knowledge base can make the assessment process less intimidating. It is also helpful to have a conceptual framework to provide structure and guidance to the assessment process. The following examination of the evaluation and assessment process is intended to serve as a framework for understanding, gathering, and organizing the information from a time-limited perspective, rather than as a comprehensive guide to assessment and differential diagnostic issues. It is a conceptualization of assessment that draws on the basic principles and values of time-limited work, such as the need for a multisystem assessment and for the identification of the client's competency capacities, motivation level, and meaning system. Included in this conceptualization of assessment and intervention planning is the Levels of Intervention model. As previously described, this model uses a triage perspective in which stresses, personal strengths and vulnerabilities, and environmental risk and protective factors are evaluated. The balance between the degree of risk or impairment and the protective factors determines the issues that will need to be addressed first and the type of intervention strategies that should be selected.

Risk Assessment and Level of Impairment

The first objective in a time-limited assessment is to gather the information that will ensure that clients receive the appropriate level of care. In this model, the highest priority task is to assess the degree of risk that the clients' problems are presenting for themselves and others and the severity of impairment in functioning. Assessing substance abuse problems, stability of living situation, and a family's capacity to meet basic needs are also high priorities, as addressing these issues takes precedence over other presenting problems. In determining whether a client is in crisis, is at risk for harming self or others, is deficient in self-care, or is incapacitated by symptoms, the worker needs both guiding hypotheses and crisis and risk assessment tools. Developing a hypothesis or hypotheses about the central problem and what factors are creating and maintaining it is a helpful strategy for any time-limited assessment, but is especially important in crisis or risk assessments. Hypotheses provide structure and direction so that valuable time is not lost gathering information that is not the most salient to understanding the client's difficulties. Hypotheses help the interviewer to sensitively focus the interview without the mechanical or rushed feeling that standardized interview forms sometimes give. In addition, a guided inquiry helps to quickly establish the interviewer's professional credibility, which is an essential part of the engagement process (Shea, 1998).

Working hypotheses can be developed from a number of sources—for example, from history gathered prior to the first session, the client's initial verbal and nonverbal presentation, practice wisdom, or clinical theory. If the initial focus has been on getting the details of the client's experience of his or her situation or problems, the interviewer should reach a tentative understanding of what is most significant or pressing for the client in the first 15 minutes of the session. This segment of the interview should be more open and less structured than the remainder of the session (Shea, 1998). This data, combined with the clinician's knowledge of responses to stress or trauma and of the factors influencing adaptive or maladaptive responses, can lead to the development of a hypothesis that will guide the expansion of information in the more structured final 30 minutes of the interview. A working hypothesis allows the interviewer to tailor the subsequent inquiry into history and mental status specifically to the client's problems so that the inquiry should feel more natural and responsive to the client's story. The following examples illustrate the development and use of hypotheses to guide the assessment interview.

An interviewer may begin to develop a hypothesis that a past and current history of painful interpersonal relationships is significant. This hypothesis may emerge from the client's initial interactions with the clinician and from the type of presenting problems for which the client was referred, such as depression and substance abuse. Careful attention will be paid to the use of self as an assessment tool, and a careful history of interpersonal relationships will be necessary. The second part of the assessment interview would then focus on the details of the historical and current "behavioral incidents" and the client's interpretation of these events (Shea, 1998). The following case example illustrates how a focus on the interpersonal perspective can lead to valuable information about self-care or safety issues. Using clinical theory and practice wisdom about the association of the client's particular social history with problems with self-care, the clinician follows this hypothesis in eliciting details of how the client responds to interpersonal difficulties.

> Tom was a 38-year-old man who was referred by his internist for stomach pains and symptoms of major depression. Tom was a Vietnam vet who had been treated for Post-traumatic Stress Disorder (PTSD) in the past and still occasionally experienced flashbacks and nightmares. He had also been treated for alcoholism but had experienced 10 years of sobriety with Alcoholics Anonymous (AA). In the first part of the intake session, there was an air of tension because of Tom's tendency to quickly avert his eyes whenever he made eye contact and because of the guilt-laden content of his presentation of his concerns—for example, guilt about leaving his first wife and children, the suicide of his brother, and his experiences in Vietnam. He also expressed concern about his relationship with his second wife, who could be quite volatile and demanding. A careful examination of the details of their encounters and of his social history (he had been physically abused by his alcoholic father) revealed a pattern of outbursts of violent anger that were always turned against himself. He expressed relief when concern was expressed about the possibility of his hurting himself. He agreed to set up a written plan for how he would manage the conflicts with his wife so that he would not get to the point of explosive rage.

In the case of a medical crisis (e.g., a diagnosis of a life-threatening illness), the worker will need to respond quickly and in an informed way to reduce the client's distress and to foster coping responses. By developing a hypothesis about what this crisis might mean to the client, the worker will be able to intervene more quickly and effectively, as is essential in medical social work when there are only a few opportunities to connect with the client. With a crisis of medical illness there are predictable adjustment issues and known factors, such as past coping style and family or community supports, that influence how the client will adapt to the demands of the illness. Among the predictable adjustment issues are (1) the loss or feared loss of control of one's life, (2) alteration in body image and self-image, (3) adjustment to dependency, (4) stigma management, (5) fear of isolation or abandonment, (6) emotional upheaval, and (7) expectation of death (Taylor & Aspinall, 1993; Pollin & Kanaan, 1995).

The final example of the use of a hypothesis is a case of assessing the degree of danger that a client presents to others. Here, knowledge about the association of social phobia and alcohol abuse, as well as careful observation of the quality of the client's interactions with the therapist and information about client strengths, led to a hypothesis about the origin of voyeurism that structured the remainder of the risk assessment.

> Peter, a 23-year-old man living with his parents, was referred by his mother following his arraignment on a charge of stalking and spying on a female acquaintance. The mother and family doctor expressed concerns about Peter's potential for violent acts against women. The initial impression of the client was that of a shy, awkward man who was very uncomfortable being with a female therapist. Discussion of this discomfort and ways of ameliorating it led Peter to connect his shyness with females to his alcohol abuse. He recognized that the stalking incident was one of several problem situations he had gotten into as a result of drinking heavily and that he was most inclined to be involved in heavy drinking in social situations. Peter expressed a strong commitment to AA, which he had joined following his arrest. This desire for sobriety then served as an impetus to working on his social phobia.

Precipitating Factors and Personal Meaning

In crisis assessment, important objectives of the first session are determining the nature of the crisis events, the precipitating factors that have led to the client's distress, and the significance or meaning of the events (Hoff, 1995). Understanding the stresses or other forces that may be motivating the client to seek treatment at a particular point in time is also an important objective in brief therapy because of the importance of accessing and enhancing motivation. As Budman and Gurman (1988, p. 28) note, "[E]ntrance into therapy is *not* a random event. Rather, it usually occurs in the context of interpersonal, existential, and developmental changes." Therefore, assessment must include questions about the recent changes in the client's life circumstances that might be propelling the client into treatment at this point, as well as questions about the personal and family or community strengths that enabled the client to cope or function adequately prior to the change in circumstances.

Information from this inquiry may prove valuable for determining the focus of the therapy. This is because the focus is selected from the most accessible problem areas, the most affectively laden issues, or from difficulties that are stressing the client's usual coping capacities (Hall, Arnold, & Crosby, 1990). The "existential-developmental" crises that are motivating the client to seek treatment are frequently out of the client's awareness or incompletely understood by the client. If the crisis is identified in an empathic and empowering way, it can also become a motivating force for engagement. One of the fundamental tasks of assessment, then, is to explore with the client why the client is seeking help now rather than at other times in the past when the same or similar problems existed.

Some examples of possible unconscious "existential" crises are unresolved losses, current experiences that resonate with past traumas, anniversaries, fear of the future or of the long-term negative consequences of current behaviors, developmental impasses, and alterations in basic assumptions about life as a result of a traumatic or stressful event (Budman & Gurman, 1988). The "why now?" question encourages the client to think about personal goals and to become aware of feelings and values that may be unconscious and highly motivating forces. These overt or covert forces can then be mobilized to provide the motivation and sustaining power for the processes of change, particularly when they have been reframed as healthy strivings and worthwhile goals, as in the following case illustration.

> Alberta, a 15-year-old girl, reluctantly came to the intake session with her adoptive parents. They were very concerned about her long disappearances and probable sexual activity and drug use after they had found her several times with known drug dealers. At home Alberta had become defiant and hostile toward her parents, a marked change in their relationship. The initial question for Alberta was a variation of the "why now" question: Why would her parents need to bring her in for counseling at this point? Alberta at first insisted that they were only trying to control her, but further exploration revealed that she had a lot of questions about her parents' ability to be committed to her in view of the fact that they had "real" children of their own and that her biological mother had given her up for adoption. Noting that her mother had been 15 when she placed Alberta for adoption and that her mother's substance abuse problems made it impossible for her to keep and raise her, Alberta's defiant, acting-out behavior was reframed as a healthy desire to find out who she was, where she came from, and where she belonged.

Assessment Instruments

The assessment of risk and of substance abuse and the determination of level of impairment can be expedited through the use of assessment instruments (e.g., diagnostic screening, problem screening, rapid assessment, and computer-assisted instruments). These standardized tools have the benefit of ensuring that all of the significant diagnostic assessment factors relevant to a particular problem are reviewed. They also offer standardized norms against which the client's difficulties can be evaluated and objectively reported for prospective utilization review to prove treatment necessity. The scores can also serve as baseline data to monitor treatment progress and evaluate the effectiveness of the treatment. Again, such data is useful for providing the evidence, for concurrent and retrospective utilization review, that the interventions selected are helping the client and in a timely, cost-effective manner (Corcoran & Vandiver, 1996).

There are a number of rapid assessment instruments (RAIs) that can aid the clinician in arriving at an accurate diagnosis quickly and that will simultaneously provide proof of medical necessity. Instruments such as the Beck Depression Inventory (BDI) and the Michigan Alcoholism Screening Test (MAST) have become popular because they are easy to use. The Beck Depression Inventory is a 21-item questionnaire that asks clients to rate the severity of depressive symptoms and attitudes experienced in the past week. Dimensions such as mood are measured by responses to statements such as "I don't cry any more than usual" (scoring 0, absent) and "I used to be able to cry, but now I can't cry even though I want to" (scoring 3, severe) (Beck, Rush, Shaw, & Emery, 1979). A shortened 13-item version of the BDI is also available. The Michigan Alcohol Screening Test is a 25-item questionnaire that assesses the extent of the client's drinking problem on the basis of the social, legal, health, and vocational consequences of drinking. Questions such as "Have you ever lost friends or girlfriends/boyfriends because of your drinking?" help to determine the presence of interpersonal problems stemming from alcohol abuse (Selzer, 1971).

In spite of availability and ease of administration, practitioners have not routinely used standardized measures in the assessment process (Wakefield & Kirk, 1996). Agencies, though, are increasingly employing standardized assessment and mental status interview forms as a way of ensuring the thoroughness and reliability of their assessments and in response to the demands of managed care and employee assistance programs for a clear delineation of the presenting problem and an accurate DSM-IV diagnosis (American Psychiatric Association, 1994; Corcoran & Vandiver, 1996). Readers interested in reviewing the instruments listed below can consult the two volumes of *Measures for Clinical Practice* (Fischer & Corcoran, 1994) and the *Handbook of Depression* (Beckham & Leber, 1995).

The assignment of a DSM-IV diagnosis is required for third-party payment and fourth-party review and has become a part of the practitioner's routine. In the past, typically only the Axis I clinical disorders and Axis II personality disorders ratings were reported. The Axis V rating of the client's psychological, social, and occupational functioning was less frequently recorded. Again, however, under the impetus of outside review, this axis is becoming another means of documenting the need and planning for treatment and evaluating its progress. This rating is arrived at through the use of the Global Assessment of Functioning Scale (GAFS), a scale that ranks the client's current functioning along a continuum from the healthiest level of functioning to the most impaired and symptomatic. The scale can also be used to rank the client's highest level of functioning for the previous year in order to determine the likely outcome; for example, a higher level of functioning before the onset of an illness tends to indicate a better prognosis. Also available in the DSM-IV manual is the Global Assessment of Relational Functioning (GARF) Scale. It rates the functioning of families or other "relationship units" in the areas of problem solving, organization, and emotional climate. The GARF and the Defensive Functioning Scale can be used to augment the less detailed ratings in the GAFS on Axis IV (American Psychiatric Association, 1994). In general, the clinician's job of convincing the managed care reviewer that treatment is necessary and the diagnosis is accurate is made easier when a score from a standardized instrument is available to support his or her clinical judgment (Corcoran & Vandiver, 1996).

Diagnostic screening instruments such as the Schedule for Affective Disorders and Schizophrenia (SADS), the Millon Clinical Multiaxial Inventory (MCMI), and the Addiction Severity Index have not routinely been employed by practitioners, even though they have been found to lead reliably to accurate differential diagnoses. Clinicians have not found them practical to use because of the expense and the amount of time required to administer them. However, they have become easier to use because of the development of computer-assisted instruments (CAIs). Among the CAIs currently available are the Brief Symptom Inventory, MCMI-III, Symptom Checklist 90-R, and the Quality of Life Inventory (QOLI) (Corcoran & Vandiver, 1996).

Multisystem Assessment

The assessment instruments listed above largely evaluate the nature and severity of psychological problems, although the MAST does evaluate the social and vocational consequences of problem drinking for the client. There are several rapid assessment instruments that address the quality of the interpersonal context—for example, the Index of Family Relations, the Index of Marital Satisfaction, and the Dyadic Adjustment Scale (Fischer & Corcoran, 1994). Students in a brief treatment course have reported each semester that such instruments have enabled them and their clients to identify and focus on the central interpersonal difficulties, and that they thought their use resulted in better problem resolution and greater client satisfaction with treatment.

Even though there is considerable emphasis in the managed care model on determining level of impairment and an accurate DSM-IV diagnosis, effective time-limited work is predicated on "capacity building," that is, on optimizing internal and external resources and connections to community. Therefore, there is also a need for a thorough review of the client's social support network and environmental resources. The ecomap (Hartman, 1978) is especially helpful in this regard because it is easy to administer and provides a vivid picture of the important components of the client's system and the stresses and strengths in the social support network. The ecomap is a graphic assessment tool that maps the number and quality of the client-family-environment transactions. The transactions between the client and the components of his or her social network can be depicted as strong, tenuous, or stressful. The ecomap directs attention to where the resources and deficits are in the client's system for intervention purposes. It can be administered again midway and at the end of treatment to chart the progress of interventions (example in Chapter 4).

Assessment of Interpersonal Dynamics

In addition to assessing the degree of support or stress that an individual or family is experiencing in interpersonal relationships, it is also important to evaluate the client's interpersonal needs and characteristic styles of interaction. The client's characteristic ways of viewing relationships (his or her internal working model of relationships) and characteristic interpersonal patterns will influence how he or she experiences the treatment process and interacts with the therapist (Butler, Strupp, & Binder, 1992). A client's expectation of being hurt, ignored, criticized, rejected, or of experiencing some other negative reaction in relationships can make the formation of a working alliance a more difficult process. Therefore, accurate assessment of interpersonal dynamics is a priority in brief treatment because of the need to quickly establish this positive working alliance.

Information about cognitive-interpersonal style can be gathered from the client's social history and from a detailed report of current interpersonal interactions. However, direct observation of interactions in a multiperson modality (couple, family, or group) will yield more accurate information faster than a self-report. Participant observation is another way of gaining quick insight into the client's characteristic interpersonal patterns, although this method is subject to distortion that can result from the therapist's countertransference reactions. Participant observation is a method whereby clinicians use themselves as an assessment tool. The therapist monitors his or her emotional and behavioral responses to interactions with the client, examining the "strong pull for a complementary response" that repeats interactions that the client is likely to have with other people (Safran & Segal, 1990, p. 80).

CULTURAGRAM

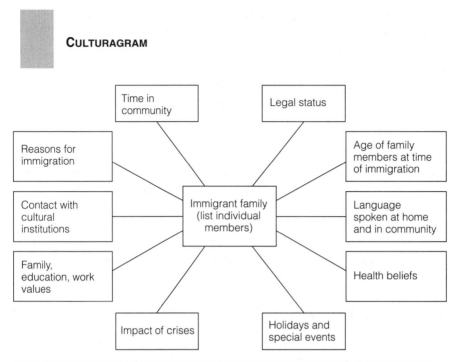

Source: Adapted from "The Use of Culturagrams to Assess and Empower Culturally Diverse Families," by E. P. Congress, 1994, *Families in Society, 75*, (9) 531–539. Copyright © 1994 Manticore Publishers. Adapted with permission.

Culturally Informed Assessment

A multisystem assessment is particularly important when working with culturally diverse clients and families whose relationships with extended family, kin, and community members are relatively interdependent. In addition, there are likely to be particular psychosocial stressors associated with the ethnic minority experience, for example, migration, acculturation strains, communication difficulties, poverty, environmental deficits, and experiences with prejudice or discrimination. The ecomap is also a useful tool for evaluating the social context of culturally diverse families because it allows for an evaluation of a fluid, inclusive sense of family and community that could be overlooked by clinicians from the dominant culture.

The culturagram developed by Congress (1994) for the assessment of families from culturally diverse backgrounds is another useful tool, as it provides a framework for reviewing ten significant cultural domains. The culturagram assesses the family's migration experiences; ethnic identity, including language usage; values regarding family, education, and work; rituals; and the impact of crisis events.

Ramirez (1991) offers another model for determining the significance of cultural differences for a client. This model is useful for evaluating the family's level of acculturation, comparing and contrasting traditional and modern cultures along seven cultural dimensions. These seven dimensions are gender role definition, family identity, sense of community, time orientation, age status, deference to authority, and spirituality and religion. For example, gender roles in a traditional culture are described as being more sharply distinguished, while in modern cultures there is greater gender role flexibility. Accordingly, as the family confronts the immigration-acculturation experience, gender roles can become redefined. Harrison, Wilson, Pine, Chan, and Buriel (1990, p. 352) noted that among the strategies that ethnic minority families employ to adjust to a changed social status is "social role flexibility." Family roles become more flexible in terms of expectations and performance; for example, the breadwinner role is shared among all the adults in a household.

The following case illustrates the utility of a culturally informed assessment in intervention planning.

> Mrs. P, a 34-year-old woman, requested help with her 14-year-old daughter, Yolanda, whom she described as being increasingly defiant and as getting into fights with everyone. The mother and her two children had moved in with her sister's family, which included their mother. Yolanda was very unhappy with this move, which had come about when her father was sent to jail for allowing drugs to be sold from his bodega and the family lost their business and home. Yolanda was close to her father, whom she described as more American and more relaxed and fun-loving than her mother and the mother's family. Mrs. P was born in Puerto Rico and had moved to the mainland as a teenager. Mrs. P's mother spoke only Spanish, so Spanish was spoken in the home, annoying Yolanda, who, like her father, did not speak much Spanish. The interview revealed major differences in the levels of acculturation between mother and daughter that were contributing to the marked disagreements between them about what was appropriate behavior and who were appropriate friends for her. Mrs. P and her mother wanted Yolanda to conform to the more sheltered existence of teenage girls in Puerto Rico, and Yolanda wanted to be able to do what her friends could do after school and on weekends. Therefore, an intervention plan was designed to assist mother and daughter to become more bicultural in their expectations of each other.

Assessment of Strengths and Resources

The tools discussed in the previous section represent a few of the many culturally sensitive approaches to assessment that have been developed in recent years. They are meant to augment the standard models for assessing individual and family functioning. The models that have been developed for assessing strengths and resources also fall into this category of adjunct assessment tools. In the process of making the paradigm shift in clinical practice from a focus on deficits and pathology to a focus on competencies and coping capacity, the purpose and function of the strengths assessment has sometimes been misunderstood as negating the need for a full, standard assessment of a client's or family's functioning (Saleeby, 1992). Assessment of strengths is not a substitute for a risk assessment or mental status review, nor can dysfunction or pathology be ignored. The strengths perspective also does not ignore clients' pain or their focus on their problems. Rather, the medical model and the competency models are complementary, each providing information that will have greater significance at different parts of the intervention process (Saleeby, 1996).

The standard assessment models serve the function of gathering information about what is creating and maintaining a problem and what forces will potentially aid or impede efforts made at resolving the problem. This approach to assessment is most useful for finding a focus and in determining goals. The assessment of strengths and resources, on the other hand, is useful in the treatment planning stage, when the task is determining what can be done about problems—that is, formulating intervention strategies. These strategies are based on the client's previous or current coping capacities and on the resources available in his or her social support network (Cowger, 1992).

There has been a shift in focus in the assessment of culturally diverse clients. In the past, assessment focused more on identification of areas of need, family and community deficits, and the impact of oppression or victimization, while the adaptive strategies and inherent strengths and resources of ethnic minority families were not recognized. Among the adaptive strategies that "promote the survival and well-being of the community, families, and individual members of the group . . . in response to ecological challenges" that have not been recognized and drawn upon by social workers are "family extendedness and role flexibility, biculturalism, and ancestral world views" (Harrison et al., 1990, p. 350). The extended family often enables its members to cope with the stresses of acculturation and discrimination through emotional support, guidance, and material or tangible help. It can also increase the resources of the nuclear family—for example, by providing child care when parents must work long hours to survive financially or enabling the purchase of a needed household item through the pooling of financial resources. Spirituality, collectivism, respect for elders, natural healing practices, and traditional healers, and a strong work ethic are also ethnic minority strengths that can be utilized in planning interventions (Lum, 1996).

Cowger (1992, 1994) offers a framework for assessing personal and environmental strengths in which he provides guidelines for both the content to be covered and the process of collecting this data. The areas of personal competency to be evaluated include (1) *cognition:* adaptive ways of viewing the world and of processing information from the environment; (2) *emotion:* ability to recognize, tolerate, and express emotions in a productive manner; (3) *motivation:* acknowledgement of problems, seeking to resolve them, and perseverance;

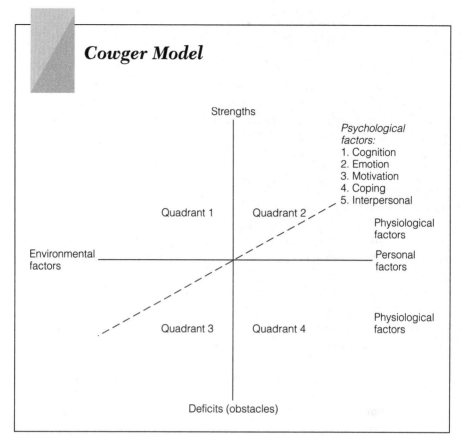

Cowger Model

Strengths

Psychological
factors:
1. Cognition
2. Emotion
3. Motivation
4. Coping
5. Interpersonal

Quadrant 1   Quadrant 2

Physiological
factors

Environmental
factors

Personal
factors

Physiological
factors

Quadrant 3   Quadrant 4

Deficits (obstacles)

Source: From D. Saleeby, *The Strengths Perspective in Social Work Practice,* Fig. 11-2, p. 144. Copyright © 1992 by Allyn & Bacon. Reprinted by permission.

(4) *coping:* flexible, resourceful, planned responses to stresses and problems; and (5) *interpersonal relationships:* the capacity for reciprocal, caring, cooperative, supportive, stable relationships.

Focus Selection

The final step in the assessment process in brief treatment is the development of a case conceptualization, which is the therapist's understanding of the nature and cause of the client's difficulties. The case conceptualization contains the clinician's rationale for the focus, goals, and intervention strategies selected. Thus, after gathering the relevant information about the client's past and current functioning, the clinician develops a hypothesis as to why the client is entering treatment and what will be most motivating for the client to work towards. This then serves as the basis for the selection of a focus (Pekarik, 1996).

There are several models of focus selection, one of which is the Budman and Gurman (1988) Interpersonal-Developmental-Existential model. The I-D-E model offers five typical reasons for people to enter treatment; these can serve as the organizing foci for treatment. The five types of reasons are (1) loss issues, (2) developmental dyssynchrony (a discrepancy between the client's life situation and his or her age-related expectations), (3) interpersonal conflicts, (4) acute symptoms, and (5) personality disorders or long-standing character pathology. The I-D-E model is easy to use because there are only five categories, and these categories encompass the majority of presenting problems. Each of these foci represents an area of disturbance or dysfunction in the client's overall biopsychosocial system and as such they are interlocking states. Thus, regardless of the focus selected, change in one area will bring about change in all other areas of the client system; therefore, there is no one correct focus. The selection of the focus is instead dictated by that which is propelling the individual to seek treatment at that point and that which is most compelling or motivating to the client to resolve. However, Pekarik (1996) suggests that there is a hierarchy for identifying a problem focus in terms of number, severity, and pervasiveness. Problems get progressively more difficult to resolve in brief treatment as one moves down the hierarchy from a single, circumscribed problem to life crises, to behavioral and emotional disturbances, and finally to personality-related problems.

Another approach to focus identification is the behavioral excess or deficit model, in which problem behaviors are selected to be the focus of treatment on the basis of the degree of negative impact they have on adaptive functioning. Thus, one or two behavioral problems of excess or deficit (behaviors that are engaged in too much or too little for adequate functioning) become the focus of treatment depending on the degree of severity, duration, and frequency of occurrence of the problem behavior (Pekarik, 1996).

Summary

This chapter introduced the Levels of Intervention model of assessment and intervention planning as the conceptual framework for organizing evaluative data and formulating treatment plans. The particular challenges of rapid engagement and the rapid completion of a comprehensive, biopsychosocial assessment were addressed, and techniques for accomplishing these tasks were described. Methods for gathering information from multiple systems, including data about personal and environmental risk and protective (strengths) factors, were presented. Particular attention was paid to the challenges of working with involuntary, culturally diverse, and at-risk clients.

Assessment Exercise: Donna

Use the following vignette to answer the questions in this exercise.

> *Donna, a 32-year-old single woman, called to request an appointment after having been referred to the clinic by her EAP counselor. She felt that she needed to see someone because "I'm not coping very well anymore." She described herself as tense and tearful, having trouble sleeping, and as "messing up" at work. Donna worked as an accountant and was afraid that if she continued to make mistakes, she would lose her job. She stated that she had been feeling overwhelmed by her parents' serious medical problems, her favorite uncle's terminal illness, and her brother's long-term drug addiction problems. After work she rushed between her parents' and her uncle's homes, returning to her own home exhausted. With the declining health of her parents, they expected her to handle all of the legal and health problems of her brother, which she resented but acceded to doing.*
>
> *Donna reported that until the past month she had always been able to cope well with the various stresses in her life. Her parents had always relied upon her to be the responsible, emotionally stable member of the family, particularly in the face of the stresses that her brother's addiction had created for the family. Until recently, Donna had been very active as a volunteer emergency medical technician in her town and had been honored for her leadership of the squad. The squad had been the center of her social life and social support system, but she felt too overwhelmed at this point to continue working as a volunteer and didn't enjoy socializing anymore, either.*

1. *Assess Donna's level of motivation to change.*
2. *What interpersonal dynamics might affect the quality of the helping relationship?*
3. *What rapid assessment instruments might be employed to quickly arrive at a working diagnosis?*
4. *Select a focus, using the I-D-E or behavior excess or deficit model.*
5. *Identify the individual strengths and family or community resources that can be mobilized to help buffer stresses and reduce symptoms of anxiety and depression.*
6. *Develop a treatment plan that includes a definition of the problem to be worked on, discrete goals and behavioral objectives, and strategic methods of intervention.*

Answers to this exercise appear in the Appendix.

Recommended Reading

Congress, E. P. (1994). The use of culturagrams to assess and empower culturally diverse families. *Families in Society, 75*(9), 531–540.

Cowger, C. D. (1994). Assessing client strengths: Clinical assessment for client empowerment. *Social Work, 39*(3), 262–269.

Prochaska, J. O., DiClemente, C. C., & Norcross, J. C. (1992). In search of how people change: Applications to addictive behaviors. *American Psychologist, 47*(9), 1102–1114.

LEVELS OF INTERVENTION: CASE CONCEPTUALIZATION AND TREATMENT PLAN

Introduction

By the end of the first session in brief treatment, the clinician should strive to have reached a working understanding of the nature of the client's difficulties and a tentative plan of action for resolving these difficulties. The ease with which a clinician can arrive at an accurate case conceptualization and an effective treatment plan is a function of the adequacy of the biopsychosocial data that has been collected. If sufficient information has been collected on the client's experience of his or her problems, emotional status, current stressors, coping capacities, personal strengths, past functioning, social support network, risk factors (including biological vulnerabilities and environmental deficits), readiness to change, interpersonal dynamics, cultural framework, and expectations of treatment, the therapeutic process becomes one of integrating and analyzing the significance and meaning of the information collected (Jongsma & Peterson, 1995).

Case Conceptualization

The case conceptualization represents the clinician's understanding of the nature, origin, and contributing factors to the difficulties that the client is experiencing. It is an estimation of what is the balance of risk and protective factors in a particular client's life and what the balance of personal and environmental strengths and limitations means for the client's ability to resolve his or her problems. It is the clinician's working hypothesis of the case, and it provides the rationale for the treatment plan. The case conceptualization is essential to a systematic, coherent approach to treatment because it is the linkage between the selected problems to be worked on and the means for resolving them. As Freeman, Pretzer, Fleming, and Simon (1990) note, the presence or absence of a case conceptualization will be apparent in the treatment process. "If the various interventions used during the session seem to 'hang together,' make sense to the observer, and appear to be 'on target,' this suggests that the therapist is basing interventions on a coherent and adequately correct view of the client's problems. Without a coherent conceptualization to provide a framework to guide intervention, the session is likely to appear disorganized, interventions are likely to appear disconnected, and the session is less likely to be productive" (Freeman et al., 1990, p. 324).

The case conceptualization represents both the clinician's synthesis and analysis of the information collected about the client's functioning in his or her life situation and the interpretation of this information based on the clinician's theoretical orientation toward personality development, psychopathology, and the change process (Pekarik, 1996). Throughout the treatment process, the case formulation remains a work in progress subject to modification as additional data emerge or hypotheses about what is creating or maintaining a problem are confirmed or rejected. Nevertheless, at the beginning of the intervention process the clinician should strive to have a complete and accurate understanding of a client's situation that resonates with and makes sense to the client.

Treatment Plan

The treatment plan is derived from the case conceptualization. It is the translation of the understanding of the nature of a client's problems into a plan of action. In the case conceptualization, the biopsychosocial assessment data have been analyzed and synthesized. This should allow identification of the problems that are most central to the client's current dilemma, are most likely to be resolvable within the given time frame, and are most meaningful to the client. This selection and narrowing of the list of problems to be worked on is the first step in the construction of a treatment plan. The next step is to individualize the plan by providing a description of how each of the selected problems is being manifested in the client's life (e.g., the DSM-IV symptoms or the impairments in functioning) and the impact of these difficulties on the client's life. For example, for a client suffering from depression, the treatment plan would specify which symptoms are present and whether the physiological, psychological, or interpersonal signs and symptoms of depression are the most distressing or disabling to the client. Using these client-defined and DSM-IV diagnostic criteria of problem selection, goals and objectives are prioritized, and the desired positive outcomes of treatment and the proposed means for achieving the goals are stated. The final steps of the treatment planning process are the selection of targeted interventions and the assignment of a diagnosis (Jongsma & Peterson, 1995).

The treatment plan is a means by which the clinician can convey to clients an understanding of their problems that is "more organized, less punitive" than the views that most clients present with in their demoralized states. It is a way to transform the "global, amorphous nature [of their problems] into specific components that can be dealt with," thereby engendering hope that problems can be resolved (Berlin, 1983, p. 1102). In the treatment plan, the therapist conveys to the client what has been learned about the client's problems and concerns as well as his or her strengths and competencies. The client's wishes and hopes for the future should be reaffirmed during the presentation of the plan, while alternative paths to reaching worthwhile goals are offered. The process of collaborating and negotiating about goals and methods of intervention begins the process of restoring or building the client's sense of efficacy and competency.

The treatment plan also provides an opportunity to educate the client who appears to be suffering from a discrete clinical problem as to the nature of the particular disorder. For example, a client suffering from panic disorder would be given information about the nature of panic attacks, including the role of anticipatory fear and cognitive distortions in the onset and maintenance of the attacks. In addition the client can be given a handout describing the physiology and psychology of fear and anxiety that precipitate and maintain the panic attacks, thereby reducing the sense of uncontrollability of symptoms (Meichenbaum, 1996).

Feedback from the client should then be elicited about the assessment findings, so that corrections can be made and negotiations around differences in goals can take place. As Cooper (1995) notes, the research evidence and clinical experience indicate that a positive outcome in brief therapy is associated with the client's investment in the goals of the therapy. Clients are more invested in goals that match what they consider to be reasonable solutions and that are specific, manageable, and achievable. In the goal negotiation process, clients should be encouraged to state goals in terms of what they want so that they have a vision or direction about where they would like to go in treatment. Finally, stating goals in terms that incorporate the client's coping strategies and that indicate the role the client will play in accomplishing them is an empowering intervention (Friedman, 1997).

The goals also need to be stated in behavioral terms and be measurable, so that progress toward the goals can be monitored and the outcome evaluated at termination by the client and by the managed care organization. The treatment plan is the means by which the therapist demonstrates to the utilization review team the need for treatment through a concise case formulation that includes level of impairment and a DSM-IV diagnosis, specific, measurable goals, and intervention strategies that logically relate to the case formulation.

Writing a treatment plan that documents medical necessity and contains a convincing plan of action is probably a new skill for most clinicians. There are several recent books that can assist clinicians in learning how to write treatment goals and objectives in precise, measurable, behavioral terms and how to link intervention strategies to those goals and objectives. These books present a step-by-step approach to writing treatment plans and provide sample treatment plans for a variety of clinical problems and populations. Examples of helpful planners from the J. Wiley & Sons treatment planner series are (1) Jongsma, A. E., and Peterson, L. M. (1995). *The Complete Psychotherapy Treatment Planner;* (2) Perkinson, R. R., and Jongsma, A. E. (1998). *The Chemical Dependence Treatment Planner;* and (3) Jongsma, A. E., Peterson, L. M., and McInnis,

W. P. (1996). *The Child and Adolescent Psychotherapy Treatment Planner.* Clearly these treatment planners need to be used in a thoughtful manner; that is, they should be used as guidelines for how to write behavioral goals and design intervention strategies rather than as prescriptions for treatment. An effective treatment plan is one that is individualized for the client rather than copied from a treatment planner.

The selection of appropriate intervention strategies begins with the client's definition of problems, views on acceptable resolution of these problems, and preferences for treatment methods. The case conceptualization also guides the process of intervention selection. The treatment planning process described above requires strategic selection of interventions—that is, interventions that have been found on the basis of empirical evidence or clinical practice to be the most effective ones for a particular type of problem.

Practice guidelines and models such as the Levels of Intervention model can be used as guides in that decision-making process. Under the impetus of managed mental health care and other forces for accountability, the mental health field has been actively involved in identifying best practices. Clinical practice guidelines are sets of standards and protocols that reflect the current consensus on the best practices for managing a particular disorder (Clinton, McCormick, & Besteman, 1994). The American Psychiatric Association, for example, has published guidelines for treating major depressive disorder, bipolar disorder, substance abuse disorders, and eating disorders, and for the psychiatric evaluation of adults (American Psychiatric Association, 1994). Practice guidelines help clinicians convey to a managed care organization the specific steps that will occur in treatment to resolve the client's defined problems. Authorization is more likely to occur when a step-by-step protocol based on preferred practices is submitted as the treatment plan (Corcoran & Vandiver, 1996).

Levels of Intervention Model

As previously stated, the Levels of Intervention model is an assessment and intervention planning model. It is a model in which the determining factors for the selection of interventions are the nature of the stressors, the quality of the client's or family's coping style, the availability of family and community resources, the degree of impairment in functioning, and the client's personal meaning system. There are three broad categories of intervention ranging from the more direct, problem-solving, educational, and skills-enhancing ones to the more insight-oriented and meaning-restructuring interventions.

The first level of intervention would be indicated when a client is experiencing stresses that are overwhelming his or her personal and social support system's coping capacities, or when safety and substance abuse issues are preeminent, or when the client is acutely symptomatic. The interventions at this first level are aimed at ensuring the client's safety, providing stability and structure at times of crisis, and reducing severe symptoms, overwhelming affects, and substance dependence. Structured intervention approaches such as psychoeducational, cognitive-behavioral, and case management ones are the treatments of choice because they provide the client with needed support and resources and promote coping capacity (Beutler & Clarkin, 1990). Referral for medication evaluation is an important Level I intervention for clients who meet DSM-IV criteria for major psychiatric disorders. Included in this first stage are the full range of crisis interventions: normalization of distress and dysfunction, education about the impact of stress or crisis, teaching of stress management skills, dosing, desensitization, interpersonal and affect regulation skills, anticipatory guidance, and role-playing used within the context of a supportive relationship to help the client find ways of coping with overwhelming affects (Schwarz & Prout, 1991). Social support network enhancement, case management, and linkage with community-based services are important treatment approaches for meeting the objectives of safety and stabilization in this stage.

Client preferences and personality styles are also a part of the treatment selection process. Thus, Level I intervention strategies would also be the treatment of choice for clients with what Beutler and Clarkin (1990) term "externalizing" and "cyclic" styles of coping. Individuals with externalizing defensive styles characteristically attribute the source of their difficulties to external forces. Individuals with cyclic coping styles tend toward ambivalence, stereotypical reactions to events, rigid defensiveness, and cycling between overcontrol and undercontrol, with intense behavioral and mood swings. In general, individuals who externalize their problems or exhibit a cyclic coping style do better with approaches that focus on dysfunctional cognitions and behavioral excesses or deficits, as in cognitive-behavioral, task-centered, or solution-focused therapies. Individuals in the precontemplation and contemplation stages of the Prochaska-DiClemente model process—that is, those who have not accepted the need for change or are just contemplating making changes—would benefit from the educational, supportive, and cognitive therapy approaches of Level I interventions.

Contemplators who are ready to examine their thoughts and feelings about their problems and the impact of these problems on their lives, and those in the preparation stage, can make use of the exploratory Level II interventions. Thus, psychodynamic and constructivist techniques that foster self-awareness, such as interpretation and confrontation, or that foster values, such as reexamination and emotional release, can help such clients move past their ambivalence to prepare for change. In the Levels of Intervention model, expressive, exploratory, or constructivist treatment approaches are considered to be more appropriate treatment choices for clients who are troubled by mild to moderate symptoms and whose functioning is mildly to moderately impaired, or when substance abuse or problems of "excessive or insufficient behaviors" are not preeminent concerns. These approaches are also likely to be more effective with clients who are not in crisis and who have a sufficient degree of support from their families and communities.

Level II therapy interventions focus on the exploration of unidentified or misidentified feelings or on unconscious conflicts and motives. Expressive or exploratory techniques are most appropriate with clients who tend to internalize their distress or who employ repressive rather than externalizing coping mechanisms. Therefore, psychodynamic, gestalt, constructivist cognitive therapies or insight-oriented family or group therapies, which are designed to "magnify and expose the affective and sensory levels of awareness," are the treatments of choice with these clients (Beutler & Clarkin, 1990, p. 246). These treatment approaches are particularly useful with clients when conflicts about feelings and thoughts are compromising their ability to cope with stresses such as losses, changes in personal circumstances, or developmental challenges. In addition, when clients are moving into the action stage, that is, when they have reevaluated themselves and their situations and are working to make changes, expressive therapies can provide the kind of cathartic experience that can amplify clients' motivation to take action (Prochaska, DiClemente, & Norcross, 1992).

Issues of unresolved loss or complicated bereavement are typical of the kinds of problems in which insight into the meaning of the event, awareness of incapacitating self-evaluations, and the opportunity to express disavowed feelings can lead to reduction in symptoms of anxiety and depression and to improved functioning. Once any disabling, neurovegetative signs of depression and risk of suicide have diminished and maladaptive coping strategies (e.g., substance abuse) have been replaced with Level I interventions, then clients are able to make use of the more exploratory and discovery-oriented Level II interventions. They will be better able to tolerate examination of painful aspects of their developmental history, particularly conflicted relationships with the deceased, once they are not so overwhelmed by feeling states and once they have alternative ways of managing tensions. Clients at this stage are more ready to make use of insights gained about the "behavioral impact, emotional toll, and personal price" of holding onto core beliefs about self and relationships (Meichenbaum, 1996, p. 18). For example, a client who had reported having symptoms of severe depression, acute suicidality, and irrational guilt about having caused her brother's death was ready to explore core beliefs about her self-worth (e.g., a conviction of her badness stemming from a childhood of abuse and neglect) once the severe symptoms had subsided and she had taken actions to begin the mourning process (bringing in newspaper clippings and visiting the grave site).

Interventions at the Level II and III stages are designed to help clients become aware of the impact of psychological vulnerabilities in their lives—for example, the role that cognitive distortions or core beliefs play in their experiences of distress. Level III interventions, in particular, are useful for individuals who have developed a greater self-awareness and now are looking to consolidate a more positive identity based on a more constructive narrative of their lives and future. Where Level I interventions focused on skills and self-efficacy issues and Level II interventions promoted self-discovery and awareness of interpersonal dynamics, Level III interventions emphasize the consolidation of self-esteem and identity issues. Individuals who are in the maintenance stage of the change process are most suitable for the deeper discovery techniques of Level III.

Selection of Modality

Brief treatment is characterized by flexibility of intervention not only in technique but also in modality. Psychosocial and medical or somatic modes of treatment are frequently used in combinations or sequentially. Individual, family, marital, and group modalities are also employed according to client need and shifting treatment dynamics. The managed mental health care demand for effective practice has reinforced the need for flexibility in practice. Treatment plans that include an assessment and, when indicated, the use of medication and that incorporate family and social support networks are generally viewed more favorably by utilization review organizations, because they represent best practices (Browning & Browning, 1994).

The selection of modality must also be based on client preference and feasibility factors. For example, a client may prefer to be seen individually, even though the presenting concerns involve others, or a client may wish a partner or family members to be involved, but those significant others decline to participate. Thus, if a client still elects to be seen alone, even after having been encouraged to view the problem and solution in an interpersonal context and to involve his or her spouse or family in therapy, then the treatment should begin on the client's terms (Duncan, Solovey, & Rusk, 1992). In addition, if other family members are not "customers for change," using Berg's (1994) term for precontemplators, and do not choose to attend, then the work begins with the client who is seeking help. One could work individually but use a family systems perspective to help clients understand the interpersonal nature of their difficulties.

Selection of Time Frame

Selection of the appropriate or optimal number of sessions is a dimension of brief therapy that has been less developed than selection of practice approach or modality. Time limits are rarely discussed in the literature except in terms of general rules, such as that it is better to assume that therapy can be brief unless proven otherwise (Budman & Gurman, 1988). In this approach, neither duration nor number of sessions is specified in setting time limits, but instead the therapist works to make the treatment shorter rather than longer. Another general approach to setting time limits is to "set the date of termination but leave the number of sessions open, allowing for more frequent sessions earlier in therapy and less frequent sessions later" (Bloom, 1992, p. 315). In some cases the number of sessions is predetermined by program policy, as in capitated managed care organizations such as HMOs, EAPs, or crisis intervention centers.

With the advent of managed mental health care, another approach to limiting the number of sessions has become more common. This is the utilization review process, by which the number of sessions is determined on a case-by-case basis by a managed care organization. The clinician members of the individual provider association or preferred provider organization submit each case on a prospective, concurrent, or retrospective basis for approval of the treatment plan and authorization of services. The utilization review team determines the number of sessions based on treatment guidelines or protocols (in-house or published) that outline the preferred methods of intervention and expectable time frames for restoration of functioning (Corcoran & Vandiver, 1996). In the absence of predetermined effective-service plans, the clinician must show that progress is being made toward treatment goals (Strom-Gottfried, 1997).

To function well in this managed care environment, therapists will need to use time in a planned, goal-focused, but flexible manner. Whether the clinician has autonomy in selecting the length of treatment or is constrained in number of sessions by outside forces, treatment is likely to be more effective if the therapist bases the appropriate length of contact on information derived from the assessment and case conceptualization. Thus, in determining the number of sessions, the factors to be considered should include (1) the client's priorities in treatment and level of motivation for change, (2) severity of symptoms and impairments in functioning, (3) severity of stressors, (4) the presence of risk or safety factors, (5) the quality of coping strategies and of personal and environmental resources, (6) potential for improvement in key problem areas, and (7) the suggested time limits provided by practice guidelines for the treatment of particular disorders. The aim in taking all of these factors into consideration is to arrive at a cost-benefit analysis, that is, an analysis of the optimal benefit that can be achieved with the most parsimonious use of time. This analysis is, of course, predicated upon prioritizing problems, narrowing the focus of intervention, and devising a treatment plan that builds on existing strengths (Pekarik, 1996).

The time parameters stipulated in treatment manuals or in practice guidelines are based on research on the effectiveness of a particular therapeutic approach with specific problem areas. As an example, the treatment protocol for the cognitive-behavioral treatment of panic disorder is 12–15 sessions (Craske & Barlow, 1993). The time-limited (6–12 sessions), task-centered model has been adapted for use with a variety of problems in living, population groups, and treatment modalities. For example, it has been used with a variety of problem situations, with all age groups, and in group and family therapy modalities (Reid, 1992). A recent compendium of current psychotherapy treatment manuals (Lambert, Chiles, Kesler, & Vermeersch, 1998) lists 66 manuals by problem area, treatment orientation, and modality, with the majority of the manuals specifying a time-limited approach, such as 12-session CPT (cognitive processing therapy) for Post-traumatic Stress Disorder (Calhoun & Resick, 1993).

Weighing all of these factors, the limits selected should represent the most parsimonious treatment plan for each client. If a single session will effectively address a client's needs even though the client has a 12-session plan benefit, stopping at that one session will both empower the client and demonstrate to the managed care organization that the clinician is a cost-efficient, time-effective provider. Implicit in this approach to selecting a time frame for treatment is the recognition that problems will need to be prioritized and that not all problems will be addressed in any one course of treatment; that is, treatment will occur on an intermittent, across-the-life-cycle model. The client whose pressing concerns were addressed in a few sessions may well return to treatment at a future point when he or she is interested in mastering different problems or resolving different issues (Lebow, 1995).

Accountability

The demands of managed mental health care for efficiency and efficacy have meant that practice is being monitored through case record reviews, prospective and retrospective utilization forms, surveys of consumer satisfaction, and institutional and cross-institutional studies of service outcomes. In the interest of staying economically viable, agencies, community mental health centers, and medical centers are also interested in determining and documenting that clients are receiving adequate, appropriate care and that consumers are satisfied with the services offered (Wakefield & Kirk, 1996; Lyons, Howard, O'Mahoney, & Lish, 1997). Therefore, among the tasks to be accomplished at the first session is the determination of the means by which changes in the targeted problems will be assessed. This can be done using a single-subject design, which entails the prospective gathering of baseline data with planned repeated measurements, or informally through a retrospective review by worker and client of the degree to which goals were accomplished.

Social work practitioners have been hesitant to use single-system designs and standardized instruments routinely in their practices, in part because there is a concern that this will be experienced as an imposition by the client and thereby impede the formation of the working alliance, thus benefiting the agency but not the client. There is also concern about the length of time it would take to complete an evaluation of outcome in agency or clinic settings where high caseloads are the norm. The following case summary is an example of use

PRETREATMENT ECOMAP

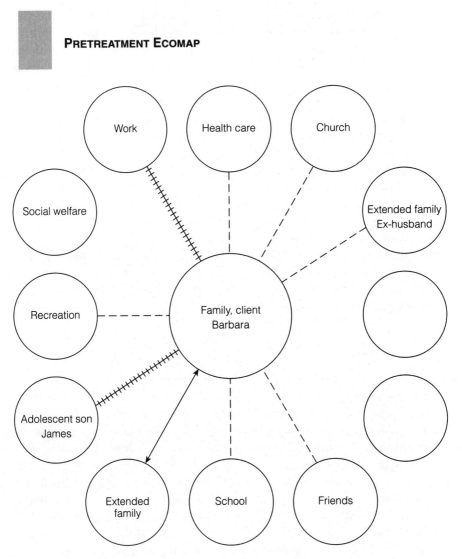

Instructions: Fill in connections where they exist. Indicate nature of connections with a descriptive word or by type of line: —— strong; — — — tenuous; ++++++ stressful. Draw arrows to signify flow of energy, resources, etc.: →, ←→. Identify significant people and fill in empty circles as needed

of a simple AB design (baseline condition plus intervention) that was non-intrusive and readily executed in a high-volume outpatient mental health clinic. It was designed to evaluate progress toward three primary goals: reduction of depression symptoms, reduction of psychosocial stressors, and increase in social supports. The case formulation and intervention process for this case will be discussed in more detail in Chapter 7 in the section on brief treatment of depression.

POSTTREATMENT ECOMAP

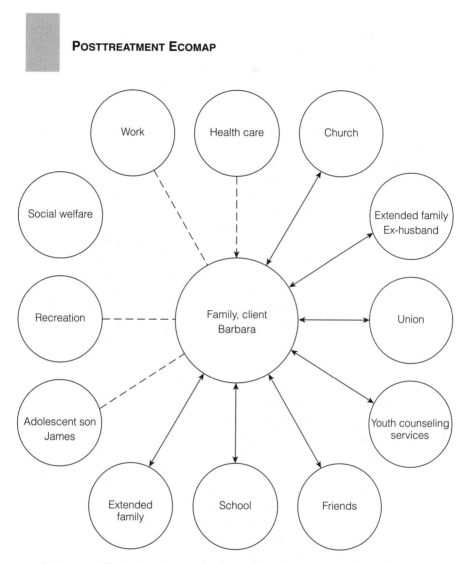

Instructions: Fill in connections where they exist. Indicate nature of connections with a descriptive word or by type of line: ———— strong; — — — tenuous; ┼┼┼┼┼┼ stressful. Draw arrows to signify flow of energy, resources, etc.: →, ←—→. Identify significant people and fill in empty circles as needed

Barbara, a 35-year-old single parent, was seen on an emergency basis because of her concern that she might harm her teenage son and that she might lose her job. At presentation, Barbara looked angry and depressed. She complained of tension, irritability, and feeling overwhelmed and unable to manage her new position at work or to cope with her teenage son. The two were in constant conflict over his unwillingness to clean his room, do his homework, and come home on time. Barbara reported problems with concentration, memory, and decision making, as well as fatigue, early-morning awakening, headaches, and decreased appetite. She also had passive suicidal thoughts. Her score on the Beck Depression Inventory was 41, indicating a severe depression (scores of 24–63 are in the severe depression range). Three psychosocial stressors appeared to have been contributory to the onset of the depressive episode: discord with her son over adolescent behaviors, a stressful work situation, and a diminished social support network. The ecomap was used to chart the progress toward reducing psychosocial stressors and increasing her social support network.

Barbara was seen individually for 12 sessions. The interventions used for the treatment of the depression were medication, psychoeducation concerning the nature and management of depression, and cognitive-behavioral treatment for the development of interpersonal and problem-solving skills. The conflict with her son was addressed through education and guidance on parenting a teenager and reestablishing counseling for her son. The problems of workplace stress and lack of social support were addressed through the empowerment techniques of providing information, guidance, and support around accessing resources and helping her to reestablish social supports. At the end of treatment, Barbara and her son had established a workable parent-adolescent relationship, and she had moved to a less stressful job assignment and had been able to make use of help from her ex-husband, union, and church (see postintervention ecomap). Her BDI score was 2, which is in the nondepressed range.

The process of evaluation of treatment outcome begins with the selection of discrete, measurable goals and objectives and of targeted intervention strategies for each short-term goal or objective. If the worker elects to measure a problem or goal attainment formally, he or she may use a specific rapid assessment instrument (e.g., the Parent Child Relationship Survey), an instrument that measures more global functioning (e.g., the Compass Mental Health Index), client self-anchored scales for monitoring thought and feeling states, or through goal attainment scaling (Corcoran & Vandiver, 1996; Lyons et al., 1997). Progress can also be informally monitored through discussion of the targeted symptoms or problems and of the progress being made toward goals at regular intervals in the treatment and then in a more comprehensive way in the final session.

Goal attainment scaling is a fairly simple and efficient way of monitoring progress toward treatment goals. It is also flexible enough to reflect individual goals in a family or goals set by different parts of the client system as in the following example. A fuller description of the case will be found in Chapter 6, Brief Treatment with Children and Families.

James G, age 6, had been referred by his school for academic and behavioral problems. The primary areas of difficulty were low academic performance due to inability to complete assignments, refusal to accept directions or abide

GOAL ATTAINMENT GUIDE

Focus	Scale 1 Peer Relationships	Scale 2 Extracurricular Activities	Scale 3 Academic Performance	Scale 4 Classroom Comportment	Scale 5 Anger and Frustration Management
Best outcome [5] [4]	Makes one friend**	Goes on field trip without mother**	Completes most assignments without direct supervision**	Routinely meets and follows rules**	Controls anger, waits turn, plays by rules**
Some success [3] [2]	Plays well in supervised play group	Goes on one trip without mother	Completes one assignment per day	Listens and follows teacher's requests 50% of time	Calls names but doesn't hit
Most unfavorable outcome [1]	No one will play with him*	Excluded from all class trips*	Does not complete work or pay attention*	Ignores teacher's requests; refuses to follow rules*	Hits other children and takes their things*

* = level at beginning of treatment; ** = level at end of treatment.

Source: From Steven Friedman, *Time-Effective Psychotherapy,* Table 10-2, p. 238. Copyright © 1997 by Allyn & Bacon. Adapted by permission.

by class rules, inability to stay in his seat, annoying and hurting other children, and social isolation (other children avoided him, and he was excluded from all extracurricular and after-school activities). James's goals for himself were to go on a field trip and play with friends. James's mother and teacher wanted him to be able to complete his class work, listen to and follow directions, abide by rules, and get along with other children. James also met the diagnostic criteria for Post-traumatic Stress Disorder (PTSD), so another therapeutic goal was to reduce his level of disorganizing anxiety. The primary methods of intervention were play therapy for reducing anxiety, parental guidance and support in applying behavior modification strategies, coordination of home and school approaches to managing behavioral problems, and placement in a small-group after-school program to develop social skills. The goal attainment guide charts the progress made toward the goals.

The use of formal clinical measurement tools has the advantage of facilitating communication with managed care organizations. Proving medical necessity and effectiveness of intervention is easier because quantification makes it possible to chart the course of the treatment. However, many clinicians still find the introduction of measurements into the treatment process to be cumbersome and intrusive. Therefore, they may find it easier to begin or stay with more informal methods of monitoring progress. Although single-subject designs cannot determine whether a particular intervention was effective, they do show if positive changes have taken place in the targeted problem behaviors (Wakefield & Kirk, 1996). Therefore, data from clinical measurement tools in conjunction with measures of client satisfaction contribute to the knowledge base that "provides guidance regarding which consumers benefit from what services, in what amounts, and from which providers" (Lyons et al., 1997, p. 13).

Contracting

Sufficient time should be set aside at the end of the first session to carefully review the treatment plan with the client. In brief treatment, it is very important that the client fully understand and be in agreement with the stated goals and methods of treatment and not just be complying with the therapist's assessment. This is especially important with involuntary and mandated clients and with clients who have been involved with social service or mental health agencies where they were expected to sign treatment plans without significant involvement in their planning. Taking the time to be certain that there truly is agreement on the assessment findings and the treatment plan reinforces the notion that treatment is a collaborative process and that clients' views are essential to resolution of their difficulties. The objective here is to create a dialogue, an exchange of ideas and feelings that can be built on for the change process.

Reviewing the treatment plan with clients is also an opportunity to offer them alternative perspectives on their presenting problems, perspectives that draw on overlooked strengths and the "healthy strivings" that lie behind symptomatic or problematic behaviors (Waters & Lawrence, 1993). This kind of reframing of the clients' view of their problems, coupled with the offering of a vision of how the clients' goals or their unconscious healthy strivings could be achieved by alternative methods, may make clients more receptive to trying different solutions to problems than the ones they had been using without success (Duncan et al., 1992). Professional credibility is enhanced if the clinician can provide some evidence to clients that the solutions being offered are methods that have led to satisfactory outcomes for other people with similar problems or for other people at a similar level of readiness for making changes (Budman & Gorman, 1988).

Contracting Illustration

Returning now to the case of Peter, the 23-year-old man who was mandated to receive treatment for voyeuristic activity, the following dialogue illustrates the process of treatment plan review and contracting with a client following the first session. The case conceptualization on which the treatment plan was based centered on the possible roles that biological vulnerabilities for depression, substance abuse, social phobia, personality disorder, and interpersonal conflicts might have played in the nature of Peter's presenting difficulties. In view of the fact that the presenting problems were criminal behavior and substance abuse, a risk assessment was a priority. The assessment revealed that there might be a risk of aggressive behavior toward women, given the degree of conflict in his relationships with his sister and mother. However, the social history and interpersonal interactions in the evaluation session did not point to the presence of Antisocial Personality Disorder, and he did not fit the DSM-IV criteria for Voyeurism. Ruling out the potential for violence and the presence of an Antisocial Personality Disorder would require additional evaluation through psychological testing. Peter did, however, meet the DSM-IV diagnostic criteria for Dysthymic Disorder and Social Phobia. Peter's chronic depression appeared to be related to the stress of chronic family conflict and a genetic vulnerability to depression and alcohol abuse (his father was withdrawn and anhedonic and had a long-term alcohol abuse problem). There were several areas of strength, including steady employment, pursuit of a college degree, and strong friendships. Most importantly, following his arrest, Peter had moved into the action stage with regard to his alcohol abuse. He reported that he had joined AA and was attending daily. The review of the assessment findings, the proposed treatment plan, and the contracting took place as follows:

> **WORKER:** *First, before we go over what I've learned today and what might be done about the problems you've identified, I wanted to say that I realize that this has not been easy for you. Having to come to see me and then having to talk about behavior that you said you are very ashamed of must have been difficult, especially talking to a woman.*
> **PETER:** *It was hard at first, but I feel okay now.*
> **WORKER:** *Well, I'm glad to hear that. One of the things you will have to take a look at is whether you think you will be able to work with me or whether you would prefer talking with a male therapist. We can discuss that after we have had a chance to talk about what brought you here today and how I see your situation. You said that you saw your drinking as the root of your problems. You thought that you wouldn't have spied on this girl if you hadn't been drunk. I agree with you that your drinking has become very problematic for you and that it is very important to do something about this. So in taking the step of going to AA, you have already taken a big step toward dealing with the behavior that got you arrested. I think that any therapy that you get involved in should support your efforts to stay sober. When we discussed your drinking history, you noticed that you had started drinking heavily as a teenager because you felt so uncomfortable in social situations, particularly around females. You also said that you feel extremely awkward in any interaction with*

females on your job or in school and that this makes you really unhappy. It would seem, then, that it would be a good idea to deal with this problem in therapy since it does create pressures for you to drink. I wonder if this makes sense to you?

PETER: *It makes sense to me. I haven't been going anywhere but AA meetings, which is okay for now, but I wondered whether I would ever be able to do anything else. There's a party every Friday at school that I haven't gone to for three weeks. I thought about going this week, but I don't think I will. I can't even talk with a girl in my class who wanted me to help her with an assignment.*

WORKER: *So one of the things you would like to get out of treatment would be feeling more comfortable talking with women?* (Peter nods his head yes.) *We can take a look at what about AA makes that a comfortable experience for you and see if you can replicate that experience in other social situations. The other thing we talked about today that also seems to be tied into your desire to drink is your depression, which you think you have had since at least age 13. Your shyness with women is one thing that you associate with being depressed. The other thing seems to be the kind of day-in, day-out conflicts you have with your mother and sister. You seem to feel that they don't treat you like an adult. Is this how you see your situation?*

PETER: *Yeah, I've got to figure out how to get them to stay out of my life. I'm going to have to live there until I finish college, but sometimes I don't think I can stand to do that.*

WORKER: *Would another goal be, then, to improve your depressed mood and that one way to do that would be to find a way for you to assert yourself in your family?*

PETER: *Yeah, I really would like to figure that one out. I just want them to leave me alone and let me manage my own life.*

WORKER: *Well, we can't change what they do unless they want to change, but we can talk about ways that you can feel more in control of your life even if they don't want to. I can see that this situation makes you very angry. I'd like to understand better what effect all of this anger is having on you and that is one reason I would like to refer you for psychological testing. I think the testing would help me to have a better understanding of your depression, and in addition the testing would meet the court requirement that you receive a psychological evaluation and counseling. How would you feel about that?*

PETER: *That would be okay with me. I'd be interesting in learning more about me. I took a psychology course and I was always trying to apply the stuff to my life.*

WORKER: *Good. When I have made the appointment, we can talk more about what's involved in the testing. We've decided on a couple of goals here, but it will be difficult to make progress toward any of them if you don't feel comfortable talking with me. What I would like to suggest is that we use the next session to focus on sorting out what we can do to make this a good working relationship. We can try to figure out what makes you feel tense when you are talking to a woman, what I might be doing to make you tense, and what I can do to reduce that tension for you. We would still be discussing your concerns, but we would be taking the time periodically to examine how things are going between the two of us and then taking steps at these points to do things that could help you feel more comfortable. How does that strike you?*

PETER: *Well, I feel a lot more comfortable now than I did at the beginning, but you're right, I'm still feeling a little tense. I guess it would be a good idea to talk about this some more, but I think I would like to see you again and not see someone new.*

This excerpt from the contracting phase of a first session illustrates several brief treatment principles. It highlights the importance of taking a strengths perspective, doing a risk assessment, prioritizing, and focusing. The assessment of the degree of risk for violence and the impact of substance abuse on Peter's life were the top priorities in the evaluation. The working hypothesis at the end of the first session was that the voyeurism for which he had been referred by the court for treatment was the result of Peter's intense social anxiety and the use of alcohol to cope with this anxiety and chronic depression. However, this hypothesis would have to be carefully tested to gain a greater degree of certainty that the risk for violence was low. Therefore, a referral for psychological testing was indicated. The treatment plan centered upon Peter's strength in taking action about his alcohol abuse, with goals being devised to support that commitment. The initial focus of treatment had to be on reducing the severity of his symptoms because of the potential of Peter's acute social anxiety to disrupt treatment and to undermine his commitment to abstain from alcohol. Thus, the initial interventions were designed toward immediately reducing his social distress through the use of in-session modification of perceptions and responses to females and the development of social skills. Once Peter was able to tolerate the therapy session without undue anxiety, treatment could shift to helping him find alternative ways of coping with the stresses of his family situation and toward transferring his new interpersonal skills to actual social situations. The following is the formal treatment plan.

Problem Definitions

1. Court-ordered treatment of voyeuristic behavior.
2. Alcohol abuse in remission 1 month after 6-year history of binge drinking in social situations.

3. Chronic depression with feelings of low self-esteem, low self-confidence, and a tendency toward self-criticism.
4. Social phobia as evidenced by fear of and avoidance of encounters with females and severe anxiety (blushing, stammering, and extreme self-consciousness) when interacting with females.
5. Frequent family conflicts with mother and sister over issues of autonomy and privacy.

Goals and Objectives

1. Control voyeuristic activity by:
   a. evaluating risk of aggressive acting-out and the origins of impulse disorder
   b. resolving the contributing factors of alcohol abuse, social anxiety, and displaced anger
2. Maintain sobriety by:
   a. monitoring and supporting AA attendance
   b. using the therapeutic relationship and AA group experience to develop confidence in interpersonal interactions with females
   c. developing client awareness of the role of social anxiety and family stress in triggering substance abuse and relapses
3. Reduce social anxiety by:
   a. developing awareness of beliefs and assumptions underlying fears of social interactions with females
   b. learning means for controlling anxiety through cognitive and behavioral strategies
   c. providing graduated exposure to social anxiety-producing situations beginning with in-session experiences
4. Improve dysthymic mood by:
   a. increasing confidence and enjoyment in social situations
   b. reducing number of attacks on self-esteem in family interactions
   c. redirecting client's attention to many areas of strength and accomplishment
5. Decrease level of current conflicts with mother and sister by:
   a. increasing awareness of the possibility of alternative reactions to family dynamics and conflicts
   b. expanding social support network and extrafamilial sources for approval and satisfaction of attachment needs
   c. developing assertiveness skills

Interventions

1. Referral for psychological evaluation of potential for violence toward women

2. Referral for psychiatric evaluation of need for antidepressant and anti-anxiety medications
3. Relapse prevention through a functional analysis of relapse triggers and introduction of alternative coping strategies in stressful situations
4. Cognitive analysis of sources of social anxiety
5. Psychoeducation about social phobia and alcohol abuse
6. Introduction of cognitive-behavioral strategies for managing anxiety, including relaxation training, attention redirection, and thought stopping
7. Cognitive restructuring of dysfunctional beliefs about self (being helpless, ineffectual, uninteresting, etc.) and self in relationship with others
8. Altering destructive interactions with mother and sister through development of assertiveness and conflict resolution skills

DSM-IV Diagnosis

Axis I: 300.23 Social Phobia
           305.00 Alcohol Abuse Early Full Remission
           300.4   Dysthymic Disorder
Axis IV: Criminal Justice System Involvement
                      Family Conflict
Axis V: GAF = 55

Summary

This chapter detailed the importance and functional utility of a clear, concise case conceptualization and treatment plan in effective brief treatment. A structured approach to treatment planning was presented that began with integration of the biopsychosocial data gathered in the assessment. This was followed by an analysis of the exact nature of the client's problems and the impact of these problems on the client's functioning. A step-by-step approach to the formulation of the treatment plan was then presented.

Treatment Plan Exercise: Janet

Use the case vignette below to answer the treatment planning questions.

> Janet, a 17-year-old white female, was referred by her primary care physician for evaluation of a possible eating disorder. She had recently lost 15 pounds, which had put her weight close to the danger point of less than 85% of normal for her height and age, because she was slender when she began dieting. She had amenorrhea and intermittently exercised compulsively. Janet did not exhibit an intense fear of gaining weight. However, she was insistent on maintaining the weight level that she had achieved. She attends a vocational high school where she is doing well and has friends, but she has been

more socially withdrawn in recent months. Janet lives with her mother, who is employed doing clerical work. Her mother suffers from dysthymia, has recurrent episodes of major depression, and is on an antidepressant. Her father, who is a factory worker, is alcoholic and unreliable in providing child support. Janet's older brother lives at home and attends community college.

Janet's anorexia began at the age of 13, when she developed transmandibular joint disorder following an automobile accident. The pain frequently prevented her from eating solid food. Six months prior to the referral, she broke up with her boyfriend. After that, she became less interested in social activities and more dissatisfied with her appearance. Three months later she began dieting.

1. Select and prioritize the problems to be worked on in brief treatment.
2. Provide behavioral definitions of the selected problems.
3. Name long-term goals and short-term objectives.
4. Select interventions that are targeted to meeting the goals and objectives.

Answers to this exercise appear in the Appendix.

Recommended Reading

Jongsma, A. E., & Peterson, L. M. (1995). *The complete psychotherapy treatment planner.* New York: J. Wiley & Sons.

Pekarik, G. (1996). *Psychotherapy abbreviation: A practical guide.* Binghamton, NY: Haworth Press.

CHAPTER 5

THE INTERVENTION PHASE

Introduction

The intervention phase proper begins when the case conceptualization and treatment plan have been completed and so can guide the intervention process. However, as noted in the last chapter, in brief treatment the engagement, assessment, and intervention phases typically overlap in the first session. Therefore, many of the intervention strategies discussed here may also be employed during the assessment period. This chapter will review the intervention strategies that help make therapy brief and effective and explore some of the common challenges and concerns that clinicians encounter in doing brief treatment. Challenges such as maintaining a focus in treatment when multiple problems exist or when crises erupt, or dealing with concerns about termination of therapy will be addressed. The intent of this chapter is to present intervention strategies common to many brief therapy models, rather than to survey the treatment techniques of one particular model.

To illustrate the brief treatment intervention process, the case of an adolescent in crisis will be presented throughout the chapter. The first part of the case presentation will highlight the brief treatment aspects of the engagement, assessment, and early intervention stages. After a discussion of the tasks and intervention strategies of the middle and final sessions, excerpts from representative sessions will be presented to illustrate the brief intervention process.

Case Illustration: Doreen, An Adolescent in Crisis — Assessment and Treatment Planning

Mrs. S came directly to the clinic from Family Court with her 14-year-old daughter, Doreen. She had gone to the court to request supervision and possible placement out of the home because her daughter refused to obey any rules and was staying out all night, skipping school, acting angry and defiant toward her teachers, and refusing to do her schoolwork. Mrs. S was also concerned about Doreen's new friends, many of whom she suspected of using or dealing drugs. The social worker at the Family Court recommended that the S family begin counseling before the court heard Mrs. S's petition. The social worker indicated that he planned to continue to be involved with the family, but his role would be that of backup; that is, he would reinforce Mrs. S's disciplinary efforts and stand ready to provide emergency placement if Doreen continued to engage in high-risk behavior.

Doreen was the younger of Mrs. S's two daughters and was in the seventh grade. Mrs. S expected that Doreen, who had already repeated a grade, would also have to repeat the seventh grade. Her sister, Joanne, was 20 years old, lived at home, and attended college. Mrs. S, who had been divorced for 4 years, worked full time as a data entry clerk and part time as a sales clerk. The S family lives in an inner-city residential area that borders a high-crime area. Although they have strong ties to the community, Mrs. S is concerned about her daughter's safety there. Since the divorce, Doreen's father has maintained regular contact with her. However, recently, in an attempt to get her to behave, he stopped her weekly visits to his home until she started obeying her mother again. Doreen began having behavior problems after beginning seventh grade. She had been an average to below-average student in elementary school, but not a behavior problem. Over the course of the school year, Doreen had become progressively more rebellious and defiant at school, and then in recent months she began exhibiting the same behavior at home. She insisted that she wasn't going to let anyone tell her what to do and that everything would be fine if everyone just left her alone.

The first session was an hour and a half long, because the family presented in crisis. The interview time was divided as follows: 20 minutes individually with Doreen and 20 minutes with Mrs. S for the social and developmental histories, 20 minutes for the family assessment, 10 minutes for consultation with the Family Court, and 20 minutes with the family for the assessment and treatment plan review and intervention.

In her individual interview, Doreen at first kept her head down and was very reluctant to engage in the interview until her resentment was acknowledged and normalized as something a lot of teenagers feel when they are told they have to come for treatment. She then became animated and talked angrily about everyone trying to run her life. Asked for a recent example of this, Doreen described a run-in with a teacher in which the teacher reported her for talking back. Doreen felt justified in talking that way to her teacher because the teacher was "bothering" her about talking to a friend in class. Doreen had similar complaints about her mother and sister, but had no complaints about her father even though she missed spending weekends with him. She acknowledged that she was in danger of repeating seventh grade and that she didn't want to be held back a grade because she wanted to stay with her friends. When asked to describe other things that she enjoyed doing, Doreen talked about playing in the school band and watching music videos. However, when her mother and sister joined us for the family interview part of the assessment, Doreen quickly again became withdrawn and hostile.

Doreen's retreat back into sullen silence appeared to be in reaction to Mrs. S and Joanne immediately launching into a litany of complaints about Doreen. Mrs. S was very angry and denunciatory, but she was able to pull back from her anger when the focus was shifted to identifying what her worries about Doreen were and to specific details of worrisome events. When her anger was reframed as a desire to keep her daughter safe because of her love and concern for her, Mrs. S could talk about what it was like for her to sit home worrying about her daughter. Although they couldn't think of a recent time when they had enjoyed spending time together, they could remember many good times in the past. They all agreed that Mrs. S had been very close to both of her daughters until this past year. Mrs. S said tearfully that she had always thought they were a happy family. She wondered what she had done that was so wrong that Doreen could be acting the way she was now. In her individual-assessment session, Mrs. S could see that her own adolescence had been closer to Doreen's tumultuous struggles than to Joanne's uneventful passage. She came to realize that she was worried that Doreen could follow in her footsteps and become a teenage mother.

The case conceptualization centered upon the difficulty that Doreen and her mother were having mastering the developmental challenges of adolescence. Doreen appeared to need to break away from her family precipitously, perhaps because she had been so close to her mother, leaving Doreen without the support and guidance to keep her safe. Her acting-out seemed to have intensified after her father broke off contact. Doreen also seemed to be struggling with identity formation issues. She had a tendency to compare herself negatively to her high-achieving sister and may have been finding it easier to assume a negative identity than a positive one. In addition, Mrs. S was very reactive to Doreen's rebelliousness because she herself had regrets about having been a rebellious adolescent and a teenage mother. She wanted Doreen to have a better life but feared that Doreen was about to repeat her mistakes. There were many strengths in the S family, including strong attachment bonds, positive goals and goal-directed behaviors, a solid social support network, and capacity to make use of school and community resources.

After consulting with the social worker at Family Court over our respective roles in assisting this family, the following treatment plan review and contracting with the family took place.

WORKER: *I just spoke with Mr. Rivera from Family Court about what we could do to help you with the difficult situation you are dealing with. We both thought that this family could be helped with counseling, because we see a lot of positive things in this family. For one thing, we see how much love and concern you have for each other and how good your relationships were before you hit the speed bump of adolescence. We also understand, Mrs. S, that you have good reason to be concerned about Doreen's safety, and we want to assure you that we want to do everything we can to keep her from getting hurt. That is why Mr. Rivera will continue to be involved while you are coming to see me so that if we need to act quickly to get Doreen into a safe situation, we can do that. I know that you and Mr. Rivera discussed the rules about going to school and coming home by curfew time that Doreen is expected to follow. He will continue to meet with you regularly to make certain that Doreen is kept safe. How does that sound to you?*

MRS. S: *Well, I never really wanted Doreen to go away, but I felt like I didn't have a choice. If she won't listen to me, then I don't know what else I can do. I think it is a good thing that Mr. Rivera will still be involved, because Doreen seemed to listen to him.*

WORKER: *Doreen, what do you think about this arrangement? That you and your family will be coming to see me to work on getting along better?*

DOREEN: *(shrugs) If I have to, I guess I'll come.*

JOANNE: *I think it would be a good idea. I can't stand to see my mother so upset. If this will help Doreen to stop doing what she's been doing, then I'm all in favor of it.*

WORKER: *Well, there are a lot of hurt and angry feelings all around, and there are some things that can be done that will ease the stress some. I think the three of you need a break from so much anger and worry. I suggest that Doreen spend a couple of days with her grandmother until our next appointment, which we will set up for a few days from now. Is this a possibility?*

MRS. S: *Yes, we could do that, but my mother couldn't put up with Doreen running around the streets all night. She's too old for that.*

WORKER: *I know that Doreen is very fond of her grandmother and enjoys helping her out. Of course, the same rules that you worked out with Mr. Rivera would have to apply there, also. Doreen, do you think you could stay with your grandmother for a few days so that everyone can get some time out from the fighting? (Doreen nods her head yes.) Good. I think it would also be a good idea for me to meet with each of you separately for a while until the anger dies down enough that you can listen and talk to each other again. After that we will all meet together for at least part of the hour. The other thing I would like to do is to get in touch with Doreen's father to invite him in so that we will all be working together to return your family life to the way it was when you were all getting along.*

MRS. S: *I'm not sure that he will be able to come in, because he works at two jobs, but I'm sure he will be happy to talk to you. He tells Doreen not to give me such a hard time, but she doesn't listen to him, either. At least he doesn't blame me.*

WORKER: *That's good to hear, because you already blame yourself so much. I know you spend a lot of time thinking about what you must have done wrong and what a bad parent you must be for this to be happening in your family, but from what I've learned here today from you and from Mr. Rivera, I would see the situation differently. From what I can see, the problem isn't that you were a bad parent, but you were too good a parent. Sometimes, when a family is as close as your family was, the teenage years can be very trying. The family knows how to get along when everyone is close, but people aren't sure how they should relate to each other when one of them is pushing off and wanting to be more independent. This can be a confusing time for everyone. I know, Mrs. S, that you remember your own adolescence as being a tough time for you and your family. So I would like to suggest that one of the goals for our work here together could be figuring out how to be a family with a teenager in it.*

MRS. S: *I hadn't thought of it that way. I just thought Doreen was bad and it was my fault. I think we could use help here, because we just can't talk anymore without fighting.*

(Joanne agreed they needed help in communicating better. Doreen agreed that they fought too much, but she only shrugged when asked if she thought they should work on finding a different way of being with each other now that she was older.)

WORKER: *Doreen, it seems that you are not quite ready to meet together with your mother and sister, and since we are not planning to do that right away anyway, there are other things you and I could be discussing, like what to do about school. It's getting late in the school year, so we need to find out right away what can be done about your failing grades. I'd like permission from you and your mother to talk to your guidance counselor. Is that okay with you? (Doreen and her mother both agreed that this was a priority.)*

Early Intervention Strategies

Most brief treatment models recommend that the intervention process begin in the first session in order to make optimal use of time, capitalize on the motivation to initiate treatment, or increase therapeutic leverage. Therapeutic leverage is often present in the first session by virtue of the therapist's professional status. When the therapist uses that credibility in the first session to decrease the client's feelings of distress, pessimism, and sense of incompetence or failure, both therapist credibility and client optimism and motivation to continue to work toward needed changes are enhanced.

Early intervention strategies can take the form of concrete, direct assistance in accessing resources or help in solving problems through the use of cognitive-behavioral techniques that promote self-confidence or improve coping skills. For example, clients struggling with serious interpersonal conflicts might, in the first session, gain hope about being able to resolve these difficulties if they can try out, through role playing, alternative ways of thinking about and reacting to typical conflicts. Other consciousness raising interventions, such as those that assist clients in uncovering the meaning to them of their problems and stressful events or that reveal the healthy strivings behind problematic behaviors, can provide the change in perspective that clients need to begin to move away from stuck positions. As noted earlier, many early interventions are inseparable from the engagement, assessment, and treatment planning tasks of the first session in brief treatment. Most brief treatment models recommend that time be allotted at the end of the first session to review with clients the results of the assessment, negotiate the treatment goals and homework, and get feedback from them about how they experienced the session. This is because the end-of-session summary and negotiation process can be used to initiate change, particularly with clients who have had negative contacts with social service or mental health agencies.

Eliciting feedback from clients can uncover potential obstacles to successful brief treatment, such as failures in rapport, unspoken disagreement with the therapist's findings, misunderstandings, covert negative-transference reactions, or inhibiting fears and anxieties (Ackermann-Engel, 1992). Seeking feedback reinforces the collaborative nature of the work as well as conveying the message that the client's views and perceptions are important to progress in treatment. Many clients have had little experience with having their points of view respected or validated. Thus, taking the time to work through misperceptions or misunderstandings before proceeding with treatment can provide the client with a corrective relationship experience. That is, the client's negative expectations of relationships will be disconfirmed or at least challenged, which in attachment theory and cognitive-behavioral therapy is an essential step in altering dysfunctional beliefs about interpersonal relationships.

The excerpt from the first session of brief therapy with Doreen and her family illustrates the use of both concrete, direct interventions and indirect interventions that are embedded in the assessment and treatment planning process. The early interventions employed were (1) assistance to client in generating solutions for an immediate reduction of conflict and distress—for example, using family members to gain time out; (2) coordination of services with Family Court and an offer of guidance about mobilizing school and family resources; (3) positive reframing; (4) naming of the problem; (5) linking of the problem to unfinished business; and (6) normalizing of family reactions to developmental challenges. The crisis nature of Doreen's presenting problems (her dangerous acting-out behaviors, the threat of placement out of home, and imminent school failure) dictated employing the crisis intervention responses of immediate, practical help with overwhelming conflicts and linkage to family, community, and school resources. However, this excerpt also illustrates that early interventions can be subtle and a natural part of the treatment plan review. Thus, the process of identifying and clarifying the nature of the presenting problems, identifying coping strategies, and uncovering potential solutions can bring immediate relief. Clients often gain alternate, more helpful, and more hopeful views of their problems and of themselves in this process, thereby diminishing the sense of incompetence that arises from their previous ineffectual attempts to resolve problems (Frank, 1982).

The offering of interpretations and the use of reframing are ways of introducing a novel perspective to clients. In this case, Doreen's acting-out behavior was reframed for Mrs. S as a sign that she had been too good a mother and that her daughter was having to work extra hard to break away from what had been a very close and satisfying relationship. This reframing and the restatement of Mrs. S's rage as due to fear and concern for her daughter's well-being, as well as linking this fear to her own unfinished adolescent business and the identification of adolescence as the problem, appeared to have enabled the mother to regain some sense of efficacy as a parent and to invest in outpatient therapy rather than insisting on an out-of-home placement.

Other possible early interventions are (1) symptom or distress relief through the provision of information about the nature of particular problems and the teaching of specific coping skills; (2) normalization of clients' reactions to their situations; (3) provision of a coherent, reality-based understanding of problems and, in the case of clinical problems, information about the nature and course of an illness; (4) restatement of problems into desired outcomes and the cultivation of hope or a vision for the future; (5) provision of opportunities for ventilation or catharsis; and (6) introduction of novel ways of doing things that set the change process in motion through the use of in-session enactments or homework assignments (Budman, Hoyt, & Friedman, 1992). Each of these interventions is a Level I intervention that is designed to address the specific reasons that the client requested help or the problems that are having the most impact on the client's social, economic, or interpersonal functioning.

Early gains in treatment may be especially significant in working with ethnic minority clients, who may have a different conception of help than the traditional insight-oriented, exploratory approach of Western psychotherapy. Many immigrant ethnic minority clients may expect that treatment will focus on the presenting problem and that that problem will be alleviated in a short period of time. To achieve credibility with clients who expect help to be brief and action oriented, Sue and Zane (1987) recommend that, in the first or early sessions, clinicians employ strategies that will help clients to achieve an early benefit from the treatment. Early interventions that assist clients with pressing problems by drawing on family and community resources, that help them find direction at a time of confusion and demoralization, or that help them understand their symptoms as understandable responses to stressful situations are particularly useful with ethnic minority clients who are experiencing stresses related to migration, acculturation, or minority status.

Homework: Promoting Action

Certain components have become central to the brief treatment approach. These include the clinician's taking an active stance in the treatment and encouraging clients to take action in their lives. The pressure of developing culturally sensitive practice approaches, as well as the push from managed care companies to demonstrate concrete changes in clients' circumstances, has also meant a greater emphasis on in-session behavioral enactments and intersession task assignments. Just as in cognitive-behavioral therapy, where homework tasks are emphasized because of their usefulness in promoting and sustaining changes in behavior, so also in the brief treatment perspective, therapy is seen as a "laboratory for change" where new ways of behaving can be practiced, and homework assignments are likewise emphasized (Friedman, 1997).

Using the phased approach to treatment advocated in the Levels of Intervention model, the in-session rehearsals in the early sessions would take the form of social skills training rather than consciousness raising experiences in which conflicted feelings or disabling cognitions are uncovered. This phased approach to enactment interventions ensures that clients will have the tools to deal with their pressing concerns and the opportunity to develop strengths and to experience successes before dealing with more threatening material. An intervention at the end of the first session with Peter illustrates the use of an in-session, behavioral enactment. (Peter had been referred for evaluation after being arrested for stalking. The evaluation revealed that, in addition to alcoholism and social phobia, Peter was suffering from a dysthymia that was related to chronic conflict with his mother and sister.) Peter had become noticeably tense and angry when we were discussing the treatment goal of working on conflicts with his mother and sister. He related how angry he was to discover that morning yet another instance of what he considered an invasion of his privacy and his mother's infantilization of him. He dreaded going home because he knew that there would be another fight when he confronted her about what she had done. Peter was encouraged to try out in the session different ways of approaching his mother and then to consider trying at home the approach that got the result with the therapist that he would like to get with his mother. He quickly concluded that his usual way of dealing with this problem only prompted anger and defensiveness in his mother and that he wanted to find alternatives to their usual patterns of interaction.

Intersession tasks (homework assignments) are another way to introduce new perspectives and skills to clients. Homework also extends the in-session learning experiences to the client's life. Thus, before the end of the first session, the idea of homework is introduced and its purpose explained. Often, first-session homework assignments are used to expand upon the assessment by directing the client or family to observe and record the problematic behaviors and interactions. By so doing, they direct the client's or family's attention to overlooked details, which could result in a more accurate understanding of their situation, recognition of hidden strengths, or discovery of possible solutions (Wells, 1994). For example, asking a parent to do an ABC (antecedent, behavior, and consequence) assessment of problem behavior in preparation for setting up a behavior modification program directs their attention to what sets off the problem behavior, the context in which it occurs, the exact dimensions of the problem behavior, and people's reactions to the behavior. Similarly, asking the parents to keep track, in the week before the first appointment, of when the child is behaving in a way that the parents like is a way of helping parents to notice (and reinforce) positive behaviors at a time when they are likely to be preoccupied with the child's problem behaviors. It also directs their attention to the times when exceptions occur, which can then be analyzed to uncover the conditions that promote the desired behaviors (Berg, 1994).

Homework assignments should expand upon the client's usual coping style and meaning system. Collaboration with the client on the selection of tasks is important in order for the tasks to be experienced by the client as meaningful and "do-able." In fact, homework assignments are most effective when the ideas originate with the client and are then built upon by the therapist (Budman et al., 1992). The tasks selected should also be consistent with the client's level of motivation, development, or functioning. Friedman (1997) has devised a solution-focused approach to designing tasks, based on the client's readiness to take action, that is, on whether, in his terms, the client is a "customer," "complainant," or "visitor." In this approach, tasks are categorized along four dimensions: direct, indirect, behavioral, or nonbehavioral. Clients ready to take action are likely to respond to all four types of tasks—that is, straightforward task assignments or suggestions by the therapist to think about their situations in a different way, as well as the indirect methods. Clients not yet prepared to take action on their own behalf are likely to be more responsive to indirect, nonbehavioral tasks in which they are encouraged to find their own solutions to a problem or where story or metaphor are used to raise awareness of issues or point the client in the direction of change. Thus, clients at the precontemplation level of readiness to take action would be more likely to follow through with "passive" tasks such as bibliotherapy or tasks that lead them to take notice of exceptions to problem occurrence or think differently about problem situations. Someone in the action stage could be assigned an "active" task such as scheduling time for themselves in a busy day or working on anger management (Prochaska, DiClemente, & Norcross, 1992).

Brief treatment is geared toward helping clients to quickly take small steps toward problem resolution and thus experience success. Therefore, it would be counterproductive to assign tasks that are too complex or too demanding of time and energy or that do not match the individual client. Planning for the implementation of the homework and for potential obstacles to task accomplishment also increases the chances of the client following through on the assignment

(Reid, 1992). However, matching of tasks to client and client need is an inexact art, so it is possible that clients will not complete assignments and that tasks will need to be adjusted as additional information is gained about the factors perpetuating problems and about unforeseen obstacles. Alerting the client that adjustments may have to be made, particularly with behavior modification tasks for children, can diminish discouragement when the desired results are not quickly achieved or when there is a lack of cooperation among family members on task accomplishment.

Guidebooks to homework construction similar to those for treatment planning are now available. Two examples are (1) Hecker, L. L., Deaker, S. A., & Associates (1998), *The Therapist's Notebook: Homework, Handouts, and Activities for Use in Psychotherapy;* and (2) Schulteis, G. M. (1998), *Brief Therapy Homework Planner.* Guidebooks can provide useful suggestions for constructing homework assignments. However, it is important that tasks resonate with the client and reflect the therapist's personal style so that the client experiences them as authentic, meaningful, and worthy of the time spent on them.

The selection or construction of homework assignments is determined ultimately by what will initiate or maintain change in problem behaviors. For example, clients who are stuck in ineffective patterns of behavior will benefit from tasks that seek to interrupt unproductive patterns of behavior or cycles of interaction. The above vignette illustrates the use of a breaking-out-of-the-cycle task. In session, Peter practiced a way of asserting his rights with his mother that was different from the angry, confrontational, defensive, retaliatory interaction that had typified their relationship. This task was later elaborated upon in homework assignments to address other unproductive patterns of interaction that Peter had with women.

Examples of other homework assignments for commonly occurring problem situations are (1) tasks that implicitly give permission to self-sacrificing clients to take time for themselves, (2) relaxation-training or breathing-retraining homework assignments for clients with disabling anxiety, (3) gold-star charts that direct parents' attention to occasions when the child is engaging in desired behaviors, (4) tasks that reduce isolation and build on culturally approved help-seeking methods by asking clients to seek advice from family and friends in situations of bereavement or depression, and (5) tasks that promote positive interactions and restrict negative ones (Friedman, 1997).

Case Illustration: Doreen— Homework Assignment

Returning to Doreen's crisis situation, in which she was in danger of out-of-home placement due to her self-endangering behaviors, the following is an excerpt on the construction of a homework assignment with the mother at the end of the second session. The second session occurred three days after the initial session, in which it had been arranged that Doreen would spend the days between therapy appointments with her grandmother in order to defuse the anger and halt the negative interactions between her and her family. Telephone contact had been made with Doreen's father since the first session. He agreed that he needed to be involved with her again, but he didn't want to let her visit for the weekend unless she started listening to her mother. However, he agreed to stop by after work to talk with her during the week.

> WORKER: *Mrs. S, several times you have expressed your fear that even though Doreen came back from your mother's house less angry and more cooperative, she is going to go right back to hanging out on the streets with her friends and not listening to you. However, you also seemed to feel that Doreen was listening to Mr. Rivera about following the rules you set up on curfews and attending school, because she knows that he means business. So that is something that is different from the last time we met.*
>
> MRS. S: *Yeah, she listens to him. He made it very clear to her what was going to happen if she didn't come home on time or let me know where she is. Doreen told my mother that she doesn't want to go to a group home to live, but she hasn't said anything to me. She isn't talking to me.*
>
> WORKER: *I can hear the sadness now when you talk about your relationship with Doreen. The last time we met, you and Joanne were so worried and so angry that the sadness was kind of pushed to the back. I wonder, now that you have the backup of Mr. Rivera, and Doreen's father is getting involved again, if you would be willing to try something a little bit different with Doreen. Or actually, if you would be willing to go back to doing something that the two of you used to do together. You mentioned before that you and Doreen used to like to go shopping together, and the two of you liked to sit on the porch and watch what was going on in the neighborhood.*
>
> MRS. S: *I always kept a big bag of sunflower seeds. Doreen and I used to sit, crack seeds, and laugh about everything we saw. There's always so much happening on our street.*
>
> WORKER: *I know from talking with Doreen that she really is a keen observer of life and that she has a very interesting way of describing her observations. She's a born storyteller. I can see why you enjoyed your time sitting on the porch. What I would like to suggest is that you and Doreen do a little homework assignment together. We find that things get better faster if family members can keep working together in between our sessions. So between now and our appointment next week, I would like you to get another bag of sunflower seeds and spend some time on the porch with Doreen. This should be a time when you are just watching the neighborhood scene, rather than a time when you are telling her what*

you are angry with her about or what you want her to do. That discussion can take place when you are back in the house. Does this seem like something you would be able to do now?

MRS. S: *I can do that if she hasn't kept me up all night running the streets. It's been hell going to work after one of those nights. I don't even want to see her when I get home. I just want to go to bed.*

WORKER: *This has been so stressful for you, worrying about whether she's okay. I'm sure the last three days have been a welcome break from all of that. Would it be possible for you to spend some time sitting on the porch tonight while things are not so tense? It will still be light when you get home.*

MRS. S: *I could do that. I was just going to pick up take-out for dinner tonight, anyway. So, yeah, we could do that tonight if Doreen wants to.*

WORKER: *Well, let me invite her in for a few minutes to see what she thinks of this homework assignment. (Doreen was surprised, but accepted the assignment.)*

The negotiation around assignments is an essential part of the homework construction process because it can reveal potential obstacles to completing the task, and it reinforces the idea that therapy is a collaborative process. The discussion with Mrs. S over the proposed homework assignment revealed that there was a need to move quickly to capitalize on the lull in hostility between her and Doreen, because of the possibility that Doreen would act out again and then the homework might not be attempted. On the other hand, the fact that the homework was designed around existing family strengths and behaviors meant that the family was generally accepting of the assignment and comfortable with it. The objective of the homework assignment was to increase the opportunities for positive interactions, thereby changing the interpersonal dynamic. The subsequent course of treatment indicated that this objective had been met.

Clients frequently do not complete homework tasks even when they have participated in their construction and have agreed to try the task. Clinicians sometimes get discouraged or feel angry and resentful when clients fail to complete agreed-upon homework. It is unfortunate if they are then disinclined to assign further homework tasks, because homework assignments are very useful adjuncts to therapy in time-limited work. In actuality, failure to complete homework assignments presents an excellent opportunity to gain a more in-depth understanding of the client and, in the process, an opportunity to strengthen the therapeutic alliance. A careful examination of the reasons why the task was not carried out or why the results were not positive often will uncover negative beliefs and feelings that the client harbors about his or her ability to carry out the assignment. Since the client's low sense of efficacy or self-esteem is probably compromising other areas of functioning, identifying these feelings and modifying them around task noncompletion could improve functioning in general.

In addition, if the review of homework difficulties is conducted in a non-judgmental, matter-of-fact way, the experience can serve to disconfirm the client's negative beliefs about self and others. For example, for clients who expect criticism or rejection for failing to complete an assignment, a corrective experience can occur when they are not criticized but instead are encouraged to discuss their feelings and concerns about the assignment, and to adjust the task if necessary. Adjustments may indeed need to be made to adapt the assignment more closely to the client's motivational and functional level, particularly if it becomes apparent that deficits in skills or impulse and anger dyscontrol problems are interfering with task completion (Reid, 1992). In this process of opening up a dialogue about obstacles to task completion and about fine-tuning the assignment to fit the client, the worker is also modeling problem-solving and effective communication skills.

The Middle Phase of Treatment: Maintaining Treatment Focus

As noted before, establishing a narrow focus is considered the sine qua non of brief treatment (Pekarik, 1996). However, selecting an appropriate focus, one that will result in clients feeling that their most pressing needs are being met, is only the first challenge. Maintaining a focus with steady progress toward the treatment goals within the focal area is the central task of the middle phase of treatment. Homework assignments can also aid the therapist and the client to stay on course if homework tasks are designed to expand upon the themes or skill areas under discussion in a session. The discussion and negotiation around homework tasks can bring into sharper focus for the client what issues were worked on in that session and the progress that has been made. Intersession tasks serve as a bridge to the next session, since the client's experiences in doing the homework or the problems in completing the assignment will be a topic in the next session.

Another method for maintaining a focus and also monitoring the progress toward problem resolution that was developed in cognitive therapy is to take time at the beginning of each session to do a status check of the client's mood, symptoms, and life situation. This status check, in conjunction with a review of the work of the previous session and the homework, forms the background to the worker-client discussion of the focus and agenda for each session (Ackermann-Engel, 1992; Pekarik, 1996). Once this agenda has been decided upon, the worker may have to help maintain a focus to the treatment, as when the client's review and agenda setting become discursive or scattered in response to a crisis-ridden lifestyle. One way that this can be done is through defining and connecting the themes in the client's discussion that form a pattern reflective of the original goals and objectives (Beutler & Clarkin, 1990). However, this does not obviate the need to always remain attuned and responsive to the client's changing needs, as in the following case situation.

> Mrs. R, a 50-year-old woman who had been in open-ended treatment for more than a dozen years for treatment of depression and self-destructive behavior, was now being seen in brief, problem-focused therapy, with cognitive therapy as the primary method of intervention. It was initially difficult for her to stay focused because she tended toward a discursive and histrionic style of communicating, but by the middle of a 15-session therapy, she had responded well to the structure of each session, redirection when necessary, and cognitive therapeutic techniques. Her depressive symptoms had significantly diminished, when the accidental death of a child occurred. The treatment then became less structured, turning to grief work and the rapid shoring up of her social support network, especially the reworking of the husband-wife relationship to allow each to be supportive to the other. Although the focus shifted from interpersonal conflict to grief work, it was possible to connect her current reactions to the previous theme of her treatment, which was her conviction that she had always been unsupported in all of her relationships.

It is easier to maintain a focus in treatment if the focus selected accurately reflects the issues that are most compelling to the client, and the focus is stated in a way that uncovers the healthy striving behind the symptoms and problems and in a way that provides a hopeful sense of the future. Thus, when there is difficulty maintaining the focus in treatment or working toward an agreed-upon goal, it is useful to take the time to rethink the focus and goals that were selected. For example, a client may agree to work on a problem of substance abuse, for which she was referred, but instead may want to focus most of her therapy time on her anger with her mother, with whom her children are now living. Reformulating the focus from becoming clean and sober to one that reflects her loss issues and setting goals that reflect the healthy striving beneath her constant fighting with her mother—that is, her desire to reestablish her bonds with her children—might be more meaningful to her at that point in the treatment. In addition, her goal to reunite with her children and be a better mother to them could then be used in a motivational interviewing approach, since it is likely that she is not fully prepared to take action on her substance abuse problems.

Monitoring Treatment Progress: The Working Alliance

Renegotiating the focus of treatment, homework assignments that are not working, and treatment methods that are not producing desired results are all reflective of the brief therapy tenet that progress toward goals and the quality of the helping alliance must be constantly monitored. The therapist actively takes responsibility for treatment progress by checking with the client in each session about what appears to be working and what does not and then seeking to determine what might be more helpful (Winegar, 1992). Assessing the quality of the helping alliance is important throughout the treatment, but it is especially important in the early sessions, when the alliance is still in formation. Signs that the alliance may be weak include lack of progress in treatment, resistance to in-session and intersession work, cancelled or missed appointments, and increased anxiety about the therapy process.

In brief treatment, problems in the alliance are dealt with in a direct, here-and-now way. Attention is paid to all ruptures in the alliance and signs of resistance at the moment they happen in order to determine what can be done by both participants to work out a better working relationship. If there are real difficulties in forming an alliance, such as miscommunications and misunderstandings stemming from differences in cultural backgrounds, these underlying misunderstandings are examined or alternative ways of communicating are worked out. If unconscious fears and anxieties about the therapist or the therapeutic process stemming from past negative interpersonal relationships seem to be the source of alliance difficulties, then these negative expectations will need to be addressed in a supportive manner. As in long-term treatment, the negative transference or negative expectations are gently brought into awareness through exploration and interpretation. However, in brief treatment the focus is not on the transferential origins of clients' perceptions and reactions to the therapist, but on the here-and-now consequences of their characteristic patterns of relating for the client-therapist relationship and their other relationships. In addition to solidifying the therapeutic alliance, close examination of the relationship dynamics in a nonpunitive, nonjudgmental manner allows for a powerful disconfirming behavioral experience that can lead to restructuring of negative relationship beliefs and a reduction of interpersonal fears and anxieties (Butler, Strupp, & Binder, 1992; Hepworth, Rooney, & Larsen, 1997).

The strength of the alliance and client motivation can also be affected by the degree of gain or improvement the client experiences in the early sessions. If the client experienced some relief from the first session or was able to make some changes toward solving a problem, this change needs to be supported and built on to strengthen the alliance and sense of optimism. In this and subsequent sessions, it is important that clients recognize whatever changes have occurred and understand how they were able to make these changes. Thus, the details of initial changes such as a change in perspective or doing one thing differently should be examined in such a way that the client comes to take credit for the change (Meichenbaum, 1996).

On the other hand, if the client did not experience a gain in treatment, could not follow through with the homework assignment, or a negative transference persists, these issues will need to be addressed in the next sessions. The resulting disappointment or pessimism needs to be acknowledged and discussed in a way that models for the client how to problem-solve when things do not go as planned or desired. This may require the clinician to acknowledge misunderstanding or imperfectly understanding the client's needs or concerns. A retooling of the therapy process in this way generally strengthens the therapeutic alliance (Berg, 1994).

The regular monitoring of progress toward treatment goals is performed in brief treatment not only for reasons of accountability to managed care organizations or for determining when the current treatment approach is not helping and another approach should be tried. It is also a means of alerting the clinician to a client's changing treatment needs and a need to adjust the level of care. As the client makes progress, the level of intervention can also shift from less intensive to more exploratory, expressive, insight-oriented, or meaning-restructuring methods. When more severe feelings of distress have subsided and functioning has improved, the level of care can shift from an intensive, skill-building, problem-solving level of intervention to one that addresses other areas of difficulty that derive from the presenting problems or that make the individual vulnerable to reexperiencing the same problems. For example, depression takes a toll on an individual's interpersonal relationships, and, conversely, chronic interpersonal conflict can make the individual vulnerable to depression.

If rapid assessment instruments were used in the assessment session, then the clinician has a very useful means of measuring the client's movement toward treatment goals. These instruments are not only helpful in determining whether progress is being made in the targeted areas, but they can also help to fine-tune the interventions for the remainder of the treatment sessions. An instrument such as the ecomap, for example, provides the clinician and client with a quick visualization of the remaining points of stress or insufficiency in the social support network that will need to be addressed in the time remaining. The administration of a rapid assessment instrument midway in the treatment can also be used to remind clients of the progress they have made. This is a particularly useful intervention in situations of interpersonal conflict. An instrument such as the Conflict Tactics Scale (Straus & Gelles, 1990) that assesses the degrees to which reasoning, physical aggression, and verbal aggression are used in resolving conflicts can help members of the family see areas of improvement that might be obscured for them by their negative expectations of each other, based on long periods of unsatisfying relationships.

Lifetime Stress Management Skills

Implicit in all of the intervention strategies discussed thus far is the principle that each session should be treated as if it were the only session, and therefore in each session there should be a tangible gain; that is, there should be at least one beneficial intervention or interaction that advances the client's coping capacity (Cooper, 1995). In addition, because brief therapy is an intermittent, across-the-life-cycle approach to treatment, there is also an emphasis on the development of knowledge and skills for the lifetime management of the problems that brought the client into treatment. The coping skills developed are expected to result in a generalized ability to deal with subsequent problems in life, but there is no expectation that the individual will never again need treatment (Cummings & Sayama, 1995). Instead, the overarching goal is for individuals to develop sufficient self-knowledge and knowledge about their interpersonal relationships to recognize the personal stresses and vulnerability factors that would lead them to respond with distress or dysfunction to such situations, and to recognize when they are not coping and when they need to seek help.

Lifetime stress management skills are a component of relapse prevention strategies in cognitive-behavioral therapy. Such strategies were developed for individuals in recovery from substance abuse to help them remain abstinent, but they have come to be used more generally in therapy to assist clients in maintaining gains in treatment. While relapse prevention is a central task of the termination stage of treatment, in actuality the behavioral skills training, cognitive restructuring interventions, and lifestyle changes that are introduced early in the treatment process constitute relapse prevention interventions. Cognitive-behavioral treatment models tend to have specific, structured approaches to maximizing and maintaining treatment gains, but many other brief treatment models utilize similar strategies for maintaining changes. Among these shared strategies are anticipating stressful situations and reactions, normalizing stress reactions, planning for a return of symptoms or problems, developing specific skills for managing high-risk situations and relapses, altering self-defeating beliefs and assumptions, assigning homework tasks that address specific stress management issues, enlisting significant others in therapy and enhancing social support systems, and gradually reducing the frequency of sessions (Ludgate, 1995; Beutler & Clarkin, 1990).

The following vignette illustrates the use of homework in relapse prevention.

When Dave, a client who had been abusing alcohol for 18 years, achieved a period of sobriety, the focus in treatment shifted to relapse prevention. In particular, we examined all of the points of vulnerability that might lead to his resuming drinking. His first homework assignment was to chart the course of his day to find potential trouble points. There were many points, but the most troubling to him were the hours that he had spent every day in a bar, for which he had no substitute activities. The next homework assignment was to begin to fill those hours with the few pleasurable activities he could identify—for example, working out in a gym. Subsequent homework assignments combined pleasurable activities with activities designed to help him meet his other goals, such as learning how to relate to women when not drinking.

Dealing with Obstacles to Change

Resistance to change is a common occurrence in therapy, whether long term or short term. Clients may overcome their initial reluctance to enter into treatment but at a later point encounter external forces that can inhibit or sabotage their change efforts, or they themselves may become resistant to change. Much of the previous discussion about monitoring change, renegotiating goals, practicing homework, and maintaining the treatment alliance is applicable to managing these inevitable bumps in the road. In addition, a careful multisystem assessment, which includes an analysis of the forces promoting or inhibiting change or an ecomap of the points of stress and conflict in the client's environment, can provide clues as to why a client may be resisting doing homework or has become negative or pessimistic about making changes. Inviting in an extended family member, friend, neighbor, or community or religious leader to serve as a consultant is always a useful intervention, whether or not they are resisting the changes that the client is attempting to make. Most people relish playing the role of a consultant and readily give their views of the client's situation, past and present. If their contribution is acknowledged, they often are ready then to participate in problem solving or in the altering of problematic patterns of interaction, as in the following case situation.

> Mrs. E requested help because she was feeling exhausted and overwhelmed and was concerned that she wasn't able to keep up with the demands of her family and her job. She worked as a cafeteria worker in a public school and was the primary caregiver for her daughter's two children and for her elderly mother. In addition, her four siblings and her two other children frequently called upon her for help, but no one shared the care of her mother, who was crippled by arthritis. She was given a diagnosis of major depression and placed on an antidepressant. The focus of the treatment was on her interpersonal relationships, and the primary goal was developing her ability to set reasonable limits on sharing her time and energy with family members.
>
> Mrs. E had been making steady progress on setting limits with her daughter about the care of her children, and was beginning to work on being more assertive with her siblings, when her sister, Mrs. F, lost her babysitter and insisted on leaving her daughters with Mrs. E. When Mrs. E tried to protest, her sister became angry with her, and Mrs. E agreed to take care of them. Mrs. E came to the next session looking depressed and overwhelmed again. She reported for the first time that she hadn't done the homework and that she didn't see any point in ever attempting it, because things would never be any different with her family. She did agree to ask her sister to come in to serve as a family consultant to help provide a better understanding of the family relationships. When Mrs. F came in, she expressed surprise that her sister was receiving therapy. Mrs. F readily responded to the request that she describe the family relationships while they were growing up and how she

saw Mrs. E's role in their family then and now. She reported that Mrs. E had always been the sensible, reliable one in the family and that, when their father died, their mother turned to Mrs. E to help take care of the family. Asked to describe the current family relationships, Mrs. F on her own recognized that the pattern of dependence on Mrs. E continued and that this might be too much for her sister now. After this session, Mrs. E was able to return to working on assertiveness skills.

Inviting family or community members in for a session or two can also help when the treatment is not progressing for reasons other than external resistance. These individuals often provide another perspective on the client's situation, one that resonates with the client and allows them to think differently about problems that they may feel are beyond their ability to change. Members of the clergy, for example, can give clients permission that they are unable to give themselves to work on personal problems, and at the same time they can provide an enduring source of support while clients are struggling with their problems. In addition, family and community members can be particularly useful as cultural mediators when client and therapist are from different cultural backgrounds. They can provide insight into how differences in family structure, male and female roles, and child-rearing practices may be leading to misunderstandings between therapist and client, and they can marshal additional support for the client.

When outside factors are not interfering and treatment is not progressing, the therapist will have to determine whether the lack of progress is due to resistance or to inappropriate goals, or whether the therapist needs to modify the case formulation and selected treatment methods or modalities. As previously noted in the discussion of engaging with reluctant clients, the key to working with the resistance is to move with it rather than oppose it. Moving with the resistance involves respecting the client's reasons for resisting change while at the same time trying to understand the function that the resistance serves. Once the client's motivation is understood, it is usually possible to reframe the resistance in terms of the positive goals that the client has but is not aware of. For example, parents of acting-out adolescents often become locked into patterns of constant criticism and angry exchanges with their teenagers because they feel justified by their child's difficult or dangerous behavior. The parents' inability or unwillingness to change their behavior is often motivated by intense fear about their child's safety or future. Incorporating the healthy striving into the treatment goal can open up a conversation about alternative ways of reaching a desired goal. If the parents' goal is to keep their teenager safe, then brainstorming about all of the possible ways of accomplishing this can lead to movement away from the unproductive criticism and arguing.

It may be necessary to change goals or to break objectives down into smaller steps. This is frequently the case when working with children with behavior problems. Behavior charts, for example, frequently need to be adjusted to the child's actual level of ability to accomplish the task. Parents can become angry and discouraged or stop doing the homework assignment when the child's problematic behaviors seem to be changing too slowly or when there is actually regression in behavior. Some of these obstacles can be prevented if, at the beginning of treatment, parents are told to anticipate that there will be problems, setbacks, and times when the child will not want to carry out the homework assignments (Webster-Stratton & Herbert, 1994). Parents will need to be reminded of these predictions and be given a great deal of support and encouragement while they develop more realistic expectations of themselves and their children. This kind of support and encouragement is important for all clients when there is an impasse in treatment, as is the need to help clients recognize and give themselves credit for small areas of improvement.

The brief therapist must be prepared to determine quickly when the original assessment was inaccurate or incomplete and that, therefore, the treatment approach must be modified, as in the following case vignette.

> Mrs. D, a hospital administrator, requested help for feelings of depression following the breakup of her marriage to an alcoholic man. On evaluation, she met all of the criteria for major depression. An appointment was made with the psychiatrist for a medication evaluation at the end of the week. Mrs. D also agreed to let the worker call her mother before she left the session to get her some immediate help with the care of her children. The next appointment was 2 days later. In this session, Mrs. D was notably more anxious and agitated in addition to being seriously depressed. She accepted the suggestion that she have her parents stay with her for the time being and that they come in with her for her appointment with the psychiatrist so that we could all work together to help her through this difficult period. However, Mrs. D failed to keep this appointment. Her father, reached by telephone at Mrs. D's home, reported that she had not returned home the previous night after withdrawing a substantial amount of money. Several possibilities were explored, including the possibility of a disappearance related to substance abuse. A cursory substance abuse history had been taken initially, but the focus in the two sessions had been on the depression and anxiety. The parents did not know about her substance abuse but had had suspicions, which they had ignored until now. They agreed to come in with her after she returned home. They did this on the following Monday after they had confronted her with their suspicions. Mrs. D reluctantly acknowledged that she had been on a cocaine binge, but she was not prepared to take action or even to acknowledge that this was a problem that needed to be addressed. The focus of treatment changed to substance abuse issues, and the primary intervention strategy became one of motivational interviewing. The technique of developing discrepancy between her goals and values and her substance abuse was particularly effective with her because she had a lot to lose if she did not get treatment for her addiction. In addition, her desire to get relief from her

depression was a motivating force. Her parents were periodically involved to provide support and motivation for Mrs. D to begin working on her substance abuse problem.

Termination

Preparation for termination is built into brief treatment, beginning with the contracting on the number of sessions and followed by regular end-of-session reviews. These reviews are used to summarize what has been worked on and accomplished thus far and to learn from clients their views of their progress in reaching their goals. The end-of-session review is also an opportunity to remind clients of the time remaining and to set the direction for the remaining sessions.

The termination phase in brief treatment shares with longer term treatment approaches many of the same objectives and techniques for bringing treatment to a close. However, there are differences in emphasis related to the differences in the nature of the therapeutic alliance formed and differences in the conceptualization of treatment. That is, in brief treatment it is expected that the client may very well return at a future point, when different stresses or problems occur, as opposed to the expectation in long-term work that major issues and their causative factors will largely be resolved. Because the relationship in brief treatment is less intense than in open-ended therapy and because the treatment is centered on the client's strengths and the development of skills in living, there is less dependence on the therapist, and the feelings about the relationship ending are less intense.

While feelings about the loss of the therapeutic relationship are explored in the termination stage of brief treatment, particularly if the focus of treatment has been on unresolved loss issues, there is less emphasis on working through the stages of loss. Instead, the focus in the last sessions is on consolidating the gains in treatment, transferring these skills to the client's real life, and maintaining those gains or preventing relapse. Therefore, the typical tasks of termination in brief treatment include (1) exploration of thoughts and feelings about termination, (2) review of the course of treatment, (3) identification of what has been learned and accomplished and how this can be used in the future, (4) identification of areas for future work, (5) promotion of the client's role in making changes, (6) using this ending to promote a better management of losses, (7) setting up a follow-up or booster session for some time after termination, and (8) evaluating the outcomes of treatment (Lebow, 1995).

Relapse prevention in the termination phase of treatment involves providing the client with self-control and self-therapy methods for managing personal vulnerabilities and stresses in the future after therapy ends. From the beginning of treatment, clients are educated about the nature of their problems, their areas of strength and vulnerability, and the impact of certain stresses on their functioning. In the final sessions, clients learn about the relapse process and about the need to develop relapse prevention skills (Ludgate, 1995). Clients' subjective responses to relapses and expectations of the future need to be explored as the first step in relapse prevention training, so that counterproductive or unrealistic beliefs can be exposed. Clients can then be helped to see that lapses are not signs of failure but opportunities to learn new coping skills, and that maintenance of skills is a lifetime issue. Thus, in relapse prevention, clients are taught to recognize warning signs that symptoms or problems are reemerging, how to deal with such events, and when to seek help again.

Relapse prevention includes the development of self-monitoring skills. Through the self-monitoring process, clients learn what are high-risk or high-stress situations for them and what their capacity is to cope with these situations. In addition, relapse rehearsals can be staged within the session so that risk situations and disabling thoughts, feelings, and behaviors can be identified. Homework tasks geared toward the management of these risks can then be assigned. Clients can be taught to use self-monitoring methods such as the use of a journal or behavioral record in which they record the degree of stress a situation presents, the degree of temptation to relapse, and the coping statements and behaviors they attempted to use. Thus, a client who experienced extreme anxiety at work whenever he encountered a female coworker could record on a scale of 0 (= no problem) to 3 (= severe) the degree of distress he experienced and the degree of his desire to flee, and which coping strategies (e.g., breathing control, refocusing attention outward, thought stopping) he was able to use (Granvold & Wodarski, 1994).

In the final sessions, work continues on helping the client to make the kind of lifestyle changes (e.g., in work, relationships, and leisure activities) that will reduce ambient stresses and personal distress. If significant people in the client's support system have not yet participated in the client's efforts to maintain treatment gains and prevent relapse, they may be willing to join for a final session. In this session, the client, the family or community member, and the clinician review posttreatment needs and referrals to community agencies where needed. Potential obstacles to connecting with services should be discussed, because family and friends can be very helpful in facilitating the connection to community services when they are brought into the plan (Falloon & Fadden, 1993; Ludgate, 1995).

The final task in termination is to evaluate the outcomes of treatment and document them in the retrospective utilization review procedure. If baseline measures were taken in the first session or during the middle sessions, clients will again need to agree to complete another measurement instrument. If no baseline measures were taken, clients will then need to be interviewed specifically about changes in the targeted symptoms or problems. They can be asked to rate the degree to which they believe progress was made toward meeting goals in the treatment plan. These subjective evaluations can then be weighed against prevailing clinical standards—for example, DSM diagnostic criteria—for additional confirmation of the client's progress in treatment (Hepworthy et al., 1997).

Case Illustration: Doreen— Middle and Final Stages of Treatment

The first excerpts below are from the fourth session, when the family was still in crisis and Doreen and her mother were being seen separately. The family at this point was being seen twice a week, so these excerpts are from the second week of treatment. The second set of excerpts is from the ninth session of treatment, when family conflict had subsided and Doreen's school situation had stabilized. The focus had shifted from interpersonal conflicts to the developmental challenges of adolescence. The final set of excerpts is from the 14th session, in which the gains made on positive identity and self-esteem development and family functioning were consolidated. Preparations for maintaining these gains and for termination were focused on in the 14th session.

Session 4

(Doreen had been assigned a homework task of keeping a journal about her observations of her neighborhood.)

WORKER: *Hi, Doreen. How did things go since Tuesday?*

DOREEN: *Well, last night we had a big fight. My mother got a call at her job from the guidance counselor, because I skipped two classes yesterday. I wanted to go watch tryouts for the band. I don't see why I have to go to class if I'm going to have to repeat next year, anyhow. She came home and started screaming at me that she was going to tell Mr. Rivera and my father that I broke the rule about going to school, but I didn't. I just cut two classes.*

WORKER: *You and your mother are going to have to discuss this with Mr. Rivera, so that everyone is clear about what the rules are about school attendance, but you can probably figure out what he is going to say.*

DOREEN: *Yeah, he's going to say that I have to go to all my classes, but I don't think I should have to if I'm going to have to stay back anyway. My mother just screamed at me that I broke the rules and that she didn't want to get any more calls about me on her job. Why is she always trying to tell me what I should do? I wasn't getting into any trouble, I was just watching the tryouts.*

WORKER: *What did you say when your mother got mad?*

DOREEN: *I didn't say anything. I just went up to my room to get my jacket, because I was planning on going over to my friend's house. I couldn't find it right away. By the time I did, I changed my mind. I just stayed in my room, because I knew if I went out on a school night I wouldn't be able to go to my Dad's house on Friday.*

WORKER: *This is really impressive. You were able to get control of your anger so that you can get to do something you have really been looking forward to, and you did it by taking some time to cool down. Do you think you could do the same thing in school when a teacher gets you angry?*

DOREEN: *Well, I can't leave the classroom, so I don't think so.*

WORKER: *Right, you can't, but maybe you could do something like count to 10 before answering back to the teacher (Doreen just shrugs). By the way, I spoke with Mr. Thompson [the vice principal] about your school situation. He said that if you were willing to go to summer school and you passed summer school, you wouldn't have to repeat seventh grade.*

DOREEN: *I don't want to go to summer school!*

WORKER: *I know it is hard to think about going to school in the summer, but you also said you didn't want to get left back. You wanted to stay with your friends. So you are going to have to weigh this out and see which is going to be better for you. Sort of like what you did when you were fighting with your mother and decided to stay home. I'm going to be discussing this with your mother. Should I tell her that you don't want to go to summer school, or that you need time to think about it?*

DOREEN: *I'll think about it.*

WORKER: *Okay, I'll tell her that. I see you brought your journal. What are some of the things you jotted down in it? (Doreen proceeded to provide a vivid description of neighborhood activities, including some humorous portraits of neighbors.) Doreen, that was fascinating. I really got a good picture of your neighborhood. I can see why your mother enjoys sitting on the porch with you. Do you ever get a chance to use this gift of observation at school?*

DOREEN: *(looking surprised and pleased) No. I've never been any good at writing, and anyway, we don't write about this kind of stuff.*

WORKER: *I'll discuss this with Mrs. Jackson [the guidance counselor] and see if she has any ideas for this summer or next year. Maybe there's a program at the community center, like a newsletter put out by the kids, that you could join.*

(For the remainder of the session, we discussed other things Doreen liked to do, especially things that she liked to do with her girlfriends. She admitted that she didn't enjoy her new friends as much as her friends from grade school. We discussed some of the differences between grade school and junior high. Doreen agreed to continue to keep her journal and to use it on her weekend visit with her father. The second half of the interview was with Mrs. S alone.)

(Mrs. S sat down with a groan and said she was really tired.)

WORKER: *Any particular reason that you're tired tonight?*

MRS. S: *No, just a tough day on the job. The supervisor was just hanging over us all this week. She's complaining that we're not entering the numbers fast enough.*

WORKER: *That is a strain, having someone standing over you. Then yesterday you got a call from the school about Doreen and that had to add to the stress.*

MRS. S: *Yeah, I blew up at her when I got home. She thinks that she just has to go to school, and that's wrong. We told her that she has to go to school and she has to behave, obey the rules, and not talk back to her teachers. So she knows that she can't cut classes and get away with it.*

WORKER: *This would be a good thing to discuss with Mr. Rivera to make sure everyone is clear about the rules. But I can see that you're still very angry with Doreen. It seems like this really pushed some buttons for you. Can you figure this out? Was it because you got the call on the job when you were already under stress for not working fast enough, or was it something else?*

MRS. S: *She doesn't seem to care that she's going to be held back. She's going to end up being 16 in the eighth grade and then she'll just drop out. I know it. That's what those kids she's hanging around with now all end up doing.*

WORKER: *It sounds like you're really worried about her future.*

MRS. S: *I know Doreen's not going to go to college, but I wanted her to graduate from high school so she wouldn't have to have a job like mine. Someone standing over you telling you how many keystrokes you have to hit per minute.*

WORKER: *Helping Doreen to finish school is a really important goal. We need to think of all the ways that you could make it happen. When you think back to your teenage years, what do you think would have helped you to stay in school?*

MRS. S: *Not getting pregnant. I would have stayed in school if I hadn't gotten pregnant.*

WORKER: *What would have kept you from getting pregnant?*

MRS. S: *I don't know. I guess yelling didn't stop me. My mother yelled at me a lot, and I still went out and got pregnant. Maybe I needed someone like Mr. Rivera to really lay down the law with me.*

WORKER: *Doreen does seem to respond well to Mr. Rivera's firm rules, but I hear in Doreen's voice another reason why she is trying to keep to the rules. I hear that she doesn't want to leave home and that she really cares about you and Joanne. I know that's hard to believe now when the two of you are fighting so much, but you have 14 good years that can help* *you get through this tough time. I wonder if you saw anything different about the fight you had last night?*

MRS. S: *No. She still wasn't listening to me about going to all her classes and then she just went up to her room and slammed the door.*

WORKER: *But she didn't leave.*

MRS. S: *No, she didn't—and I was sure she would. I got that sick feeling in my stomach when she slammed the door that she would leave and not come home.*

WORKER: *And she has been going to school every day. (Mrs. S nods her head.) All your fears and worries are very legitimate, and we need to do everything we can to keep her safe, but we also need to see this as a series of steps rather than a change overnight. That's the way most people make changes. Does that make sense to you?*

MRS. S: *It makes sense, but I still want her to just stop doing these bad things.*

WORKER: *Of course. This has been very stressful for you. I know you have also been very concerned about Doreen failing this year, so I spoke with Mr. Thompson to see what Doreen's situation is exactly and what if anything could be done for her to pass. He said that the only way she could pass is if she goes to summer school.*

MRS. S: *That's great. I'll give him a call tomorrow and see what I have to do to get her enrolled.*

WORKER: *I talked with Doreen and she's going to need a little time to think this over. Like most kids, she's not crazy about the idea, but she also wants to stay in the same class with her friends, so she'll have to make a decision. Even if she doesn't go to summer school it would be a good idea for her to be involved in some sort of writing program this summer so she has a chance to make use of her wonderful observations and storytelling— you're looking surprised.*

MRS. S: *I never thought about it that way, but of course it's true. She always cracks me up with her descriptions of some of the characters in our neighborhood.*

WORKER: *I suggest that you and Doreen keep the same homework assignment, because it gives you both some fun time together and it gives Doreen a chance to write. She's going to her father's this weekend, isn't she? (Mrs. S says yes.) Good. I've asked her to keep a journal for that visit.*

Session 9

This is the seventh week of treatment. Doreen had begun summer school the previous week. She had also met in summer school kids who belonged to a religious group, who encouraged her to join their after-school activities.

DOREEN: *Hi! (bright and cheerful)*

WORKER: *Hi. How are things going?*

DOREEN: *Things are going okay. I've been really busy. We go out every day to raise money and then when we get back to the apartment, there's cleaning, cooking, and envelopes to fill.*

WORKER: *Are you talking about the Muslim group that you visited last week? (Doreen nods yes.) How much time are you spending with them?*

DOREEN: *I go to their apartment every day, except on the weekend when I go to my father's house. My mother says I shouldn't go there every day, but she likes that they make us do our homework, and they preach against drugs. They also tell us that we should obey our parents and our teachers, so Mom likes that.*

WORKER: *When you say "they," who are you talking about?*

DOREEN: *That's Jade, she's the leader's wife, and her sister Donna. They took over when her husband was sent to jail. They talk to him every day. He tells them what scripture we should be studying and what we should be doing to earn money. Richard also talks to us. He tells us to study hard in school and to listen to what adults tell us to do.*

WORKER: *Have you talked with your parents about this group, the kinds of things you're doing and what you're learning?*

DOREEN: *Yeah, Mom likes what they're teaching us, but she just doesn't want me to go there every day. But they ask me to come over every day, because there's so much work to do.*

WORKER: *Well, it's easy to see how your mother might have mixed feelings about this group. On the one hand, the group seems to be helping you with some things that have been problems between you and your mom: doing your schoolwork and following your mother's rules. On the other hand, they do seem to require a lot of your time. Do you think that maybe your mother is missing you?*

DOREEN: *(smiling) Maybe. She asked me to be home when she gets home from work so we can go out to eat together. I got two B's on quizzes yesterday, so she's pretty happy.*

WORKER: *You look happy, too. It sounds like you are off to a good start in summer school. Tell me about what your day is like in school. What are the things you like about it and what don't you like?*

DOREEN: *The teacher's okay. He's kind of tough, but all the kids listen to him. There are only 15 of us in the class. It's a lot more fun that way, because we get to do more things together. Tanya and I get to study together in class for all the tests.*

WORKER: *The class does sound like a good fit for you. Do you remember I said last week that I would try to get in touch with your teacher? Well, I did get a chance to talk with him briefly. I just let him know that I was available for consultation and told him about the work we had been doing with the journal. I told him how much I enjoyed listening to your descriptions of life around you. He was interested in seeing your journal. You can decide if you want to share it with him.*

DOREEN: *I don't mind if he reads it. This week, I just wrote about my weekend at my father's house, because I don't have time to write in my journal during the week. (She then read from her journal about a family barbecue and a trip to a mall, which was entertaining. It revealed a positive relationship with her stepmother and 8-year-old stepsister and led to a discussion of how much she enjoyed spending the weekend with her father.)*

WORKER: *Doreen, I would like to change the homework assignment a little bit for next week. Your journal has really helped me to get to know you better. I've learned how much you love rap music and seafood and your little sister. What I would like you to do for next week is to write down what you would like to be doing a year from now and then 5 years from now. I'm going to ask your mom to do the same thing; what she would like to see for you in a year and in 5 years. Next week we will also start meeting for half of the hour with your mother and sister so that we can keep things moving in a positive direction. How do you feel about that?*

DOREEN: *That's all right with me. Joanne's been asking me when she would be coming back in with us. I'll tell her to come with us next week. (Mrs. S had become considerably less anxious and fearful about Doreen. She had not reported any conflicts for the last 2 weeks, and Doreen had readily agreed to attend summer school.)*

MRS. S: *(smiling and relaxed-looking) It is really hot today. We're going to go get ice cream when we're done here.*

WORKER: *Sounds like a great idea. I know Doreen loves ice cream (Mrs. S chuckled and nodded her head in agreement). Well, how are things going with you and Doreen?*

MRS. S: *Good. She's following all the rules and there's no trouble with going to school. In fact, I think she enjoys going to school. She got two B's on tests. On the way here, she showed me an essay she got back today. She got an A. I think my mouth must have dropped open. Doreen never got an A on anything before.*

WORKER: *She's got a good teacher and the class is small, which is good for her. It looks like she's one of those kids who was having a hard time making the leap from elementary school to middle school. She seemed to need a little more time staying in one classroom with one teacher. When she starts school in the fall we will need to work with the school to help Doreen make the transition back to changing classrooms. So being in a good school situation is good for her, but I think there are a couple of other reasons why she seems happier and is settling into school so well. First, it is really important to her that you all are getting along better now and that you can have enjoyable times together again.*

MRS. S: *Yeah, she does seem to enjoy being with us again. My mother noticed that, too. We just don't get to see her that much now that she's spending all her time during the week with those Muslims and then on the weekend she's with her father.*

WORKER: *I sense that you're not quite comfortable with her spending that much time with that group.*

MRS. S: *Well, they have them out selling books and things every day. Doreen comes home really tired. I guess I shouldn't be complaining since she's getting her homework done and they do teach the kids good values. They're against drugs. They tell them to listen to their parents and to stay in school. I've talked to some people in the neighborhood who think that they exploit the kids, so I'm a little worried.*

WORKER: *I'm a little worried, too, because there is a cult-like quality to the group. I think if you can keep in close communication with Doreen, we will be able to see if there's anything to worry about. She doesn't appear to be hiding anything about the group, and she is eager to talk about her activities. The impression that I get in talking with her is that she is using this group to help her to sort out who she wants to be and how she wants to live her life. You remember last week we talked about this being one of the challenges that teenagers face and that this seemed to be something that Doreen was having a particularly tough time dealing with.*

MRS. S: *I think she's also not sure who she wants to be her friends. She lost touch with the friends she had at Martin Luther King, and the friends she made this year got her in trouble. Maybe she's just happy to find another group of kids she can hang around with.*

WORKER: *I think you're right. She's searching around and trying on a lot of different ideas. I think what we need to do is to give her as many good options as we can come up with, so she can see that she has more choices than just being a bad or tough kid. I talked with Doreen's teacher about her gift as a storyteller to see if there wasn't some way that could be used in her assignments. I told him that I thought she had the eye and ear of a journalist and maybe those skills could be used in her writing assignments. You're smiling?*

MRS. S: *I was talking to my mother about what you said about Doreen, and we were saying that we always knew that about her, but we just never paid much attention to it. I mentioned it to her father, too, and he just smiled. I'm happy that Doreen has something special of her own.*

WORKER: *Well, with things calming down and stabilizing, I thought this would be a good time to start having family sessions again. I spoke with Doreen, and she is willing to do this, so next week we can split the time between Doreen and the whole family. This will give us a chance to review the changes that have taken place since you began coming here. We also should talk about any additional changes that may be needed and then start to plan for when you won't be coming here anymore.*

MRS. S: *Yeah, I think that would be good. Joanne asks me what's going on with Doreen, so she can get to see for herself.*

Session 14

Sessions 10–13 were held every other week, and 14 and 15 (the final sessions) were once a month in order to give sufficient time to monitor Doreen's return to middle school. By session 12, Doreen had discontinued her involvement with the Muslim group because they demanded too much of her time. The last two sessions were divided into 15-minute segments with Doreen, Mrs. S, and the family.

DOREEN: *(drops into the chair with a groan) I am beat. We had a long band practice today. And I let my girlfriend talk me into practicing with her. She's on the track team.*

WORKER: *Stretch out and tell me how the first month of school is going.*

DOREEN: *It's going pretty good. It wasn't hard getting used to changing classes. I don't know why, but everybody just seems friendlier this year. Kids I hadn't seen since last June were coming up to say hello. Nobody could believe that I went to summer school and passed. When I told them the grades I got, they* really *didn't believe me.*

WORKER: *What about the kids you used to hang out with? How are things going with them?*

DOREEN: *We just say hi. Sometimes they ask me to go places with them after school, but I've been too busy. I've been babysitting for my cousin a lot. His mother doesn't have a babysitter now, so I've been going over there to help out.*

WORKER: *What about your classes?*

DOREEN: *Well, the teachers are not as interesting as Mr. Jones. He was a good teacher, but so far it's okay. I'm doing the best in English, and social studies is good, too.*

WORKER: *It does sound like you are off to another good start. I think you learned some important things in summer school, like keeping up with your work every day and studying with someone for exams. You also did a good job of asking Mr. Jones when you didn't understand the math assignments. Getting help from Joanne with your math homework was also a good idea. The last time we met, we talked a little bit about how to tell when you're starting to run into difficulty in a class and what you could do about it. I wondered if you had any other ideas about this, based on your experiences the last school year?*

DOREEN: *Last year, I just didn't care. I didn't do any work.*

WORKER: *Were there any subjects that you were having trouble understanding and maybe that was why you just stopped doing the work?*

DOREEN: *No, I just wanted to hang out with those kids. They cut classes a lot and they never did any work, so I didn't do any work. But this year is going to be different. Mr. Thompson stopped me in the hall last week to congratulate me on doing a good job in summer school. He said he hoped I would keep up the good work this year, and I just smiled and smiled.*

WORKER: *That's great. I'm glad he took the time to tell you, because you really did do a great job. I spoke with Mrs. Harris, the guidance counselor, to let her know where things were with you and to see if there were things the school could do to support all your efforts. She said that she would be happy to meet with you from time to time to discuss how things are going and to help out if problems arise. She also suggested a couple of after-school activities that she thought you might like. She thought you might be interested in helping with the school newsletter. All you need to do is stop by and make an appointment with Mr. Thompson's secretary.*

DOREEN: *Okay, but it will have to be after my cousin finds a babysitter.*

WORKER: *I'm going to be meeting with your mother next, and after that we will all meet together to review again what you all have accomplished here in terms of solving your fights and what you can do in the future when you have disagreements.*

(Mrs. S had come to view Doreen's problems in a different light. She came to see that maybe there was some benefit to Doreen's rebelliousness, and she wondered whether Joanne, not having gone through this, was having a harder time growing up than Doreen. Mrs. S noted that perhaps Joanne was too dependent on her and her mother. She had transferred to a local college and was living at home.)

MRS. S: *Is Joanne supposed to come in now?*

WORKER: *Not yet. I wanted to meet with you briefly, so that you and I could discuss how you feel about where things stand now in view of the fact that the next time we meet will be our last meeting. Even though we've talked a lot about how you see things progressing and how you feel about managing potential problem situations with Doreen in the future, sometimes people feel differently when it is actually time to stop.*

MRS. S: *I still think we're ready to stop. At least, Doreen and I are ready. I'm not so sure about Joanne. She's still calling me every day at work. My mother and I were talking about Joanne moving in with her. Maybe that would help her start to stand on her own two feet.*

WORKER: *Has she decided if she wants to see a counselor at her college? I would be happy to speak with the counselor if Joanne decides to see someone.*

MRS. S: *She's starting to consider the possibility of speaking to someone. At first, she wasn't too interested. She didn't see the need, but when I told her that you said that a lot of kids her age go to see college counselors to talk about what they want to do with their lives, she was more interested. I told her that you had worked as a college counselor and had talked with a lot of other kids like her.*

WORKER: *Yes, each stage of development has its challenges. We've been dealing with the challenges of being a teenager, but there are some really big challenges for young adults, too: figuring out what kind of work you want to do and who you want to be with and where you want to live.*

MRS. S: *That's true. I think it would be really good for her to talk to someone. It helped Doreen so much.*

WORKER: *And having you as a steady base of support for her while she figured out which road she was going to take was even more important. We discovered that Doreen really needs you, but in a different way than before, as you can see with Joanne. So do you feel ready to take this journey with all its twists and turns?*

MRS. S: *(smiling) I think so. After what we've been through, I think I can handle the usual twists and turns.*

WORKER: *Do you think you have enough sources of support now if problems do arise? You were planning to talk about this with Doreen's father and your mother and sister.*

MRS. S: *I talked with Ray and my mother about using them if Doreen and I ever get into a bad fight. I don't think we will, though, because we both know to walk away and cool down for a while.*

WORKER: *I'm glad they will serve as backups. I spoke with the guidance counselor at Doreen's school, and she agreed to serve as a backup at school. I told Doreen that she could stop by to see the counselor, who said that she would check in with Doreen if she didn't hear from her in a couple of weeks. This is just to let Doreen know that there's someone available to help her if she runs into difficulty with any of her classes or her teachers. The counselor knows that in the future, if there are behavioral problems again, she can refer Doreen back to this clinic.*

MRS. S: *Doreen seems to have a better attitude about school. I think she knows now that she can do it if she just tries.*

WORKER: *She is off to a good start. There seem to be enough people in the school now who know her and are interested in her, so it does seem like it's a better fit than last year. Well, why don't we invite the girls in now and give everyone a chance to check in with each other?*

The family session was marked by joviality and affectionate teasing. We reviewed a few conflict resolution skills, but most of the time was spent reflecting upon their ability as a family to survive this crisis. They appeared to have regained their faith in themselves as a family unit, which was very important to them. Following the final session, a follow-up telephone call 6 weeks later found the family still functioning at their discharge level.

The treatment for Doreen and her family was a phased approach to treatment that began with a crisis intervention approach, moved into an exploration of adolescent developmental issues, particularly identity formation, and ended with a constructivist, relapse prevention approach. The treatment was guided by a case formulation that centered on the family's difficulty in handling adolescent developmental challenges that appeared in part related to Mrs. S's unfinished business from her own adolescence. The focus in treatment was upon building on and reinforcing individual and family strengths, with the objectives of quickly restoring Mrs. S's sense of efficacy as a parent, restoring family bonds, and assisting the development of a positive identity for Doreen.

In addition to utilizing existing strengths and mobilizing coping skills, the brief interventions that were used in the middle and final sessions were (1) assigning homework tasks to reduce family conflict, restore family bonds, and promote positive identity formation in Doreen; (2) using time and modalities flexibly within the session and across the course of the treatment in accordance with individual and family needs; (3) providing the mother with support for her existing parenting skills and education about parenting an adolescent; (4) consulting with and coordinating interventions with school and Family Court; and (5) assisting Mrs. S to develop a different narrative of her adolescence, and assisting the family in constructing a healing narrative of their recent discord.

Summary

The key intervention strategies that enable treatment to be brief were presented in this chapter. Among these was the strategy of early intervention as a means of solidifying the helping alliance and increasing the clients' motivation to continue to work in treatment by inspiring hope that they can be helped. Various early intervention strategies, such as reframing, the introduction of new ways of thinking and doing, and opportunities to learn new skills and practice them through homework assignments, were described. The typical problems of the middle phase of treatment—for example, maintaining a focus and dealing with resistance to change—and the tasks of termination were also examined.

Assessment–Intervention Exercise: Mark

Use the following vignette to answer the questions in this exercise.

Mark M is a 10-year-old boy and is Mrs. C's eldest son. He lives with his
mother and stepfather and has an 8-year-old sister and a 4-year-old half-
brother. His mother is employed as an office manager, and his stepfather
works as a mechanic. His parents were divorced when he was 5 years old.
His father, a Vietnam veteran, committed suicide 2 years ago after a long
period of alcoholism and severe PTSD.

Mark was referred to the mental health services at the family's HMO by
the children's psychiatric hospital where he has been hospitalized for one
year following the onset of a major depression with suicidal ideation. Mark
had been in treatment for depression on an outpatient basis for 6 months
prior to his hospitalization. His mother has been diagnosed with bipolar
disorder. With careful monitoring, her illness has been stabilized.

Mrs. C stated that she was coming to the clinic on the hospital's
recommendation that she and Mark get established in therapy prior to his
release. Mrs. C was initially uncertain about the purpose of the referral,
except that Mark's discharge was dependent on his connection with an
outpatient therapist. With guidance, she was able to articulate specific goals
and objectives based on past difficulties and current concerns. She was
thoughtful and intelligent and able to analyze the family situation with
understanding and empathy for the competing concerns of each of her
children. Mrs. C was mainly concerned about Mark and the family's
adjustment to his return home. She had many questions about how to
facilitate this process. In spite of her worries, she expressed positive feelings
toward Mark, saying that he had always been a good kid and she had greatly
missed him.

Mark was scheduled to enter a special education program for children
with emotional and behavior disorders. Mrs. C and her husband had visited
the school to learn about the program and to provide the school with
information about Mark. Mark had been an A student in a regular school
program before his hospitalization and in the hospital. He was able to
identify worries and concerns and to share these with his mother. He is not
currently on medication.

1. What family strengths and resources might be identified and utilized during this transition period?
2. How would you engage this family and motivate them to continue in
   treatment after Mark is released from the hospital?
3. Speculate on what might be the central concerns for Mark and his family
   and, therefore, what would be meaningful and motivating goals for them.

Assessment–Intervention Exercise: Mark (continued)

4. *Select the level of intervention and practice modality (or modalities). Develop a treatment plan in which there are clear linkages between the definition of the problem to be worked on, the goals and objectives to be accomplished, and the methods of intervention.*
5. *Describe how you would use time flexibly and creatively to make maximum use of a 15-session limit.*

Answers to this exercise are discussed in the Appendix.

Recommended Reading

Berg, I. K. (1994). *Family based services: A solution-focused approach.* New York: W. W. Norton.

Budman, S. H., Hoyt, M. F., & Friedman, S. (1992). First words on first sessions. In S. H. Budman, M. F. Hoyt, & S. Friedman (Eds.), *The first session in brief therapy* (pp. 3–8). New York: Guilford Press.

Granvold, D. K., & Wodarski, J. S. (1994). Cognitive and behavioral treatment: Clinical issues, transfer of training, and relapse prevention. In D. K. Granvold (Ed.), *Cognitive and behavioral treatment: Methods and applications* (pp. 353–375). Belmont, CA: Brooks/Cole.

Ludgate, J. W. (1995). *Maximizing psychotherapeutic gains and preventing relapse in emotionally distressed clients.* Sarasota, FL: Professional Resource Press.

CHAPTER 6

BRIEF TREATMENT WITH CHILDREN AND FAMILIES: FAMILY SERVICE AGENCIES

Introduction

Questions about how to do brief treatment with children and families are among those most frequently asked in brief treatment workshops. This is perhaps reflective of the challenges and tensions that are involved in working with vulnerable populations, particularly when that work is time limited. These clinicians express a great deal of uncertainty about their ability to select the limited, discrete goals required in brief treatment, because families and children often present with such varied and complicated problems and needs. They also express concern that they will not have enough time to address the environmental risks that are negatively affecting a child's development or a family's functioning, when evaluation of environmental risks is considered to be an essential component of effective brief treatment.

This chapter is designed to address clinicians' concerns by presenting a way of conceptualizing child development and family functioning that is conducive to doing brief treatment with families. Key treatment strategies that help to abbreviate work with families will be described and illustrated. In addition, this chapter presents the research evidence that supports the effectiveness of brief treatment with children and families and the practice paradigm shifts that are taking place in children and family services. The previous chapter illustrated several of these concepts and treatment strategies in the description of the course of treatment with an adolescent client, Doreen. Brief treatment principles and strategies were also embedded in the questions for the assessment and intervention exercise (Mark) at the end of Chapter 5. This chapter begins with the answers to the assessment and intervention exercise as an introduction to those principles and strategies.

> Mark M is a 10-year-old boy and is Mrs. C's eldest son. He lives with his mother and stepfather and has an 8-year-old sister and a 4-year-old half-brother. His mother is employed as an office manager and his stepfather works as a mechanic. His parents were divorced when he was 5 years old.

His father, a Vietnam veteran, committed suicide 2 years ago after a long period of alcoholism and severe PTSD.

Mark was referred to the mental health services at the family's HMO by the children's psychiatric hospital where he has been hospitalized for one year following the onset of a major depression with suicidal ideation. Mark had been in treatment for depression on an outpatient basis for 6 months prior to his hospitalization. His mother has been diagnosed with bipolar disorder. With careful monitoring, her illness has been stabilized.

Mrs. C stated that she was coming to the clinic on the hospital's recommendation that she and Mark get established in therapy prior to his release. Mrs. C was initially uncertain about the purpose of the referral, except that Mark's discharge was dependent on his connection with an out-patient therapist. With guidance, she was able to articulate specific goals and objectives based on past difficulties and current concerns. She was thoughtful and intelligent and able to analyze the family situation with understanding and empathy for the competing concerns of each of the children. Mrs. C was mainly concerned about Mark and the family's adjustment to his return home. She had many questions about how to facilitate this process. In spite of her worries, she expressed positive feelings toward Mark, saying that he had always been a good kid and she had greatly missed him.

Mark was scheduled to enter a special education program for children with emotional and behavior disorders. Mrs. C and her husband had visited the school to learn about the program and to provide the school with information about Mark. Mark had been an A student in a regular school program before his hospitalization and in the hospital. He was able to identify worries and concerns and to share these with his mother. He is not currently on medication.

1. What family strengths and resources might be identified and utilized during this transition period?

   Mrs. C recognizes when she needs help and seeks out help and resources for herself and her family. This receptiveness was important in terms of setting up the support network essential for Mark's transition back into his family and community. She is empathic, caring, and able to differentiate and respond to her children's needs. These are important parenting skills that were drawn on and supported during the difficult initial period when tensions, rivalries, and conflicts among the children were common. The fact that Mr. C visited the school indicated a degree of investment in Mark, which became the basis of a significant intervention in the goal of ensuring Mark's positive adjustment home. Mark's intelligence, verbal skills, and capacity to trust adults were important resources in dealing with the transition from hospital to home, bereavement issues, and adjustment to a new school.

2. How would you engage this family and motivate them to continue in treatment after Mark is released from the hospital?

While outpatient treatment was a condition of discharge from the hospital, Mrs. C (and subsequently Mr. C) quickly became engaged in treatment when the intake session moved away from the referral information to focus on her knowledge of Mark and the family situation. The exploration of her worries about Mark and his return home as well as her wishes for him and the family led to a series of well-constructed goals and objectives.

3. Speculate on what might be the central concerns for Mark and his family and, therefore, what would be meaningful and motivating goals for them.

The central concern for everybody was whether they could become a family again. Would they know how to live with each other again? For Mark the concern was whether he would be left out now. For Susan, his sister, the concern was about Mark taking all of her parents' attention, as he had before his hospitalization. Loss was a theme that resonated for all family members in individual and family therapy sessions. The other major concern for the parents was their ability to keep Mark safe; they were worried that the depression and suicidal thoughts might return when he came home.

4. Select the level of intervention and practice modality or modalities. Develop a treatment plan in which there are clear linkages between the definition of the problem to be worked on, the goals and objectives to be accomplished, and the methods of intervention.

Given the relative solidity and stability of the family structure, the emotional availability of the parents, and their ability to utilize community resources, Level II interventions that focused on the restructuring of family alignments to allow for reintegrating Mark back into the family and on the working-through of loss issues were selected. The first goal was to structure family time so that the time spent with the children was relatively balanced among them. One objective toward this end was for Mark to have more individual time with his stepfather (weekly fishing trips were arranged). The second goal was for the children to develop age-appropriate conflict resolution skills and for the parents to establish a means for resolving conflicts among the children. One objective was for the parents to pay attention to times when the children were getting along. The third major goal was to reduce the likelihood of relapse of depression. One objective was for the parents to learn about the nature and management of depression. Another objective was to participate in a support group of parents of depressed children. The final goal was to assist Mark in rejoining peers and the community in general. One objective was for the parents and the therapist to maintain weekly contact with the school to monitor peer relationships and mood states. Another objective was to arrange for after-school activities in neighborhood youth clubs and with the Boy Scouts.

5. Describe how you would use time flexibly and creatively to make maximum use of a 15-session limit.

Three sessions were used before discharge to prepare for the return home. The first week, two sessions were scheduled. Thereafter, there were weekly sessions that were gradually phased out. Varying combinations of individual play therapy, sibling play therapy, parental guidance, and family therapy sessions were used.

Several brief treatment principles and intervention strategies are illustrated by the assessment and intervention with Mark described above. Chief among these are the principles of competency-based practice; collaboration; a here-and-now, problem-solving approach; and flexible, multisystem interventions. The discussion that follows will describe the evolution of these concepts in brief treatment and describe how they are put into practice.

Changing Paradigms in Child and Family Services — Resiliency and Brief Treatment

The behavioral theories and practice models that until recently were dominant in the field of clinical social work did not facilitate time-limited work with children and families. This is because these theories tended to focus on pathology and the presumed origins of pathological functioning rather than on the factors that promote resiliency and competency. Thus, child emotional and behavioral problems were generally ascribed to inadequate or pathological parents (Johnson, Cournoyer, & Bond, 1995). Such a conceptual framework makes it difficult for clinicians to recognize parental strengths and to establish collaborative relationships with parents, both of which are essential to brief family treatment. The reintroduction of the strengths perspective in social work and the advent of competency-based therapies and of constructivist therapies that emphasize multiple realities and nonhierarchical relationships have provided a theoretical foundation more conducive to time-limited work with children and families.

At the same time, research evidence that brief treatment can be as effective as long-term work with children and families has been accumulating. Smyrnios and Kirkby (1993), for example, found that when they compared three groups of children and their parents who had been randomly assigned to time-unlimited treatment, time-limited treatment (12 sessions), or a minimal-contact control group (two assessment sessions and one for feedback), there were few differences among the three groups on the posttreatment tests. That is, all groups showed significant improvement from pretest to posttest and, on a 4-year follow-up, all continued to show significant improvement. Among the conclusions that Smyrnios and Kirkby reached about the study results were that (1) consistent with other studies, long-term therapy is not more effective therapy; (2) families gain a benefit from the minimal contact of assessment and feedback equivalent to that of long-term treatment, and this should be the preferred practice over placing them on waiting lists for long-term treatment; and (3) the results are consistent with the view that "some childhood disorders are transient, related to specific phases of development, and often improve without treatment" (Smyrnios & Kirkby, 1993, p. 1025). Weisz and Weiss's (1989) study of the effectiveness of very brief treatment evaluated the outcomes of children who had been seen in a single session with their parents. They found that at 6-month and 12-month follow-ups, teachers and parents continued to rate the children as significantly improved in the problem areas for which the children and families had sought treatment.

The normal course of child development can also be viewed as favoring brief treatment with children and their families. Not only are some childhood disorders transient, but children's normative push toward mastery and competence can provide the impetus and energy for making rapid changes in behavior. White asserted in 1963 that there is an innate motivation to interact effectively with the environment that is demonstrated in the energy children exert in mastering their environment. His observations on mastery and sense of efficacy are now being incorporated into competency-based practice models. Waters and Lawrence (1993), for example, have developed a family therapy model that draws on this inherent motivation to master and fit in with one's environment. In this practice model, the central task for the clinician is to find a way to channel this energy from maladaptive to adaptive interactions with the environment. One way to accomplish this, they suggest, is to shift the focus from problematic behaviors to the healthy strivings that often underlie dysfunctional patterns of behavior. The basic healthy strivings are considered to be the desire for mastery and the desire to belong or fit in with one's social environment. Healthy strivings can become distorted when a child lacks the environmental support, knowledge, or skills to realize them in an adaptive way. Treatment then consists of providing the support, knowledge, and skills that enable clients to attain their healthy goals.

There has been a similar shift to a competency focus in the research on stress and coping in childhood. In the past, clinical theory and research focused on children and adults who were not able to cope with childhood adversity and who as a consequence became symptomatic or had problems functioning adequately. Given the fact that the majority of individuals exposed to childhood adversities such as poverty, community and domestic violence, parental psychopathology, loss of a parent, physical and sexual abuse, and so on, do not succumb to these adversities, it was logical that there would be a shift in focus to the majority experience of adaptation and the phenomenon of resiliency (Rutter, 1987; Garmezy, 1985; Werner & Smith, 1992). Researchers have attempted to learn the characteristics of children that are associated with resiliency and the protective factors that promote successful coping when children face adverse environments or when neurobiological deficits, such as learning disabilities and attention-deficit disorder, place the child at risk for academic and social failure. The findings from these studies have yielded insights into how family and community resources can be mobilized to mitigate the negative consequences of stress and how clinicians can help children and families develop successful coping strategies (Katz, 1997; Aldwin, 1994).

Among the other insights garnered from these studies about coping and stress is that stress not only has negative effects but can also have positive developmental and transformational effects. Stress experiences can provide an inoculation or steeling effect for the management of subsequent adverse events, whereas the individual lacking experience coping with stress may become overwhelmed in the face of adversity. If individuals under stress are able to maintain competent functioning, find a way to control the negative consequences to themselves, and hold on to a positive image of self in spite of the stressful event, then that can be a positive turning point for them. It can lead to an increase in both self-esteem and sense of efficacy (Rutter, 1987).

Stress can also be a spur to psychosocial development by calling forth such transformational coping strategies as the capacity to reframe, change one's perspective or values, or use creativity and humor to deal with the situation. Studies of individuals with artistic or scientific genius have found that a significant proportion of them suffered stressful events in childhood. As reported in Aldwin (1994, p. 257), "Goertzel and Goertzel's (1962) study of over 400 famous men and women in the 20th century . . . found that over 75% of these exemplars were highly stressed in childhood by physical handicaps or defects, difficult parenting, broken homes, or poverty." Studies on resiliency, then, can help clinicians working with children growing up in adverse environments, because they offer a more optimistic view of development of children and their capacity to withstand stresses.

Several factors have been identified as potential buffers against stress for children who have been exposed to severe or chronic stresses. While these protective factors will be discussed as separate dimensions, they must be understood as operating within a person-in-an-environment, transactional process. That is, these factors are not inherently protective across the life cycle, but are potentiated or diminished according to the nature of the interactions between the stressful event or events, the personal protective and risk factors, and the environmental resources or deficits at any given point in time (Aldwin, 1994).

Several personal characteristics were found to be present in children who succeeded in spite of a number of risk factors in their lives. The characteristics of these resilient children included intellectual, artistic, or athletic gifts; a sense of pride in their accomplishments; active, social, sunny temperaments that attracted others to them; and the inclination to seek out affection from siblings and extended family members or to engage other supportive adults when their parents were unavailable or unable to provide nurturance and support (Katz, 1997). Resilient children also tended to have present in their lives certain environmental protective factors. Foremost among these factors was the presence of a single, caring adult in the child's life, even if that presence was fairly circumscribed (Werner & Smith, 1992). Also noted as being helpful for developing resiliency and competency in children were opportunities outside the home where the child's abilities and gifts are recognized and rewarded. Adults who survived adverse childhood experiences have frequently identified success in school and school as a refuge from difficult home situations as important factors in their success. Involvement in extracurricular and church activities can also provide opportunities for recognition and success, particularly for children with learning disabilities or attention-deficit disorders who are not meeting with success in school (Katz, 1997).

Resilient children are able to make use of whatever social support system exists for them because they possess certain coping strategies. First, they seem to recognize the need to take emotional distance from parental mistreatment. They tend to locate the family problems in their parents and not in themselves and look elsewhere to receive nurturance or support. Resilient children are also able to express emotions in ways that garner adult support or to use humor and altruism as defenses against overwhelming emotions, another socially attractive characteristic. Other coping strategies found among resilient and competent children and adults who survived difficult childhoods include the ability to (1) identify personal strengths and build on them; (2) reframe the view of self from helpless or damaged to strong and effective; (3) reframe stressful or traumatic events as opportunities to gain strengths or coping skills; (4) identify and tolerate painful or overwhelming feelings; (5) find creative solutions to difficult problems or situations; and (6) use good problem-solving skills such as perseverance and partializing (dividing problems into manageable parts) for managing stressful situations. No child shows all of these dimensions of resiliency, and in fact it is characteristic of children who grow up in high-risk environments that they show a "checkerboard of competence and vulnerabilities that may change over time" (Aldwin, 1994, p. 256).

Longitudinal studies of children who became functional adults following childhood episodes of emotional or behavioral disturbance reveal another important finding: There are a number of opportunities throughout the life cycle that can become positive turning points. For example, for some individuals who had troubled and troubling childhoods, entry into school, enlisting in the army, meeting with success in a job, or finding a supportive relationship in adulthood was a transforming experience. That is, changes in behavior, outlook, and self-esteem occurred, and thus the life trajectory for such individuals was significantly altered (Katz, 1997). While such ordinary life experiences may make little difference in the lives of individuals from ordinary backgrounds, they can become beneficial turning points for individuals from disadvantaged backgrounds. Memoirs are replete with stories of turning points. Rosemary Bray, a journalist, writes of this in *Unafraid of the Dark*. She grew up in a housing project in Chicago, with her family on welfare, and an alcoholic, abusive father, but she survived to successfully attend an Ivy League college. The turning point for her came when she won a scholarship to a private school, where she found a teacher who cherished her as a student. Thus, while an adverse childhood environment can have long-term negative consequences, it is still possible for children to become competent, resilient adults if the right opportunities are made available to them.

Implications of Resiliency Studies for Brief Treatment

The paradigm shifts that have taken place with regard to theory and research studies on child development, stress, and coping have implications for practice in several areas that are important to effective brief treatment with children and families: values, the helping relationship, and multisystem interventions. A change from a problem-saturated, deficit view of children and families to one that recognizes the motivational force of strivings for mastery and belonging that are present in all families and children—even troubled ones—will have an impact on how the clinician approaches treatment. A greater appreciation for the child's and parents' normative capacity for change and growth and of the power of normative developmental processes will likely affect the worker's expectations of treatment. That is, with an understanding of development as being on their side, clinicians are more likely to expect change to occur and in a shorter period of time.

The establishment of a strong working alliance with families is essential in brief treatment, but such alliances are always challenging to form whether the work is long term or short term. In part this is due to the fact that, at presentation for help, families are likely to be feeling demoralized by their inability to resolve their problems and feeling inadequate in their roles as child and parent. It is likely to be a low point in terms of self-blame, guilt, and low self-confidence (Webster-Stratton & Herbert, 1994). Therefore, an assessment that focuses equally on strengths, resources, and coping strategies of families as well as their problems can diminish the state of demoralization and increase the family's optimism that they can be helped by this outsider. In addition, families are likely to experience an immediate sense of hope if, early on in the treatment, a positive developmental perspective on a child's problems is offered, and the problems are restated as healthy strivings (Waters & Lawrence, 1993).

The research on resilient children identified several personal and environmental protective factors that promote competency and resiliency. Insights from these studies can be used to inform intervention planning for all children and families seeking help, but will be particularly useful in working with multistressed families. Looking first at the domain of personal protective factors, it may not be possible to alter significantly a child's difficult temperament (e.g., a child with a high level of activity, reactivity, and distractibility, and prone to temper tantrums and emotional outbursts) in the direction of one that readily elicits positive responses from adults and other children. However, intervening to improve the goodness of fit between a child with a difficult temperament or a neurobiological disorder and his or her home, school, and community environments can improve the child's chances of being successful in mastering developmental tasks and gaining a sense of belonging.

Identifying alternative strengths and talents, and helping parents and teachers to recognize and support these unrecognized gifts, is one way to improve the goodness of fit for the child whose difficult behaviors may have led others to become rejecting and dismissive toward him or her. It takes work to change negative perceptions and to incorporate alternative talents into school programs where the child is expected to conform to the school's expectations of adequate performance. After-school programs or community centers may be able to provide opportunities for success.

> Justin, a 10-year-old boy with learning disabilities, described himself as being "good at nothing," by which he meant he saw himself as a failure at school and at athletics. A review of his interests revealed a fascination with and skill in using computers. When his teacher was approached about using this skill in the classroom (this was at a time when computers in elementary school were rare), she was opposed, because "Justin will never learn to write properly if he uses a computer. His handwriting is atrocious." Working with Justin's father, who was also learning disabled and wanted his son to have a better educational experience than he had had as a child, we located a Saturday morning computer class. Justin's low self-esteem improved significantly as he began to receive recognition and respect from his classmates and to receive positive feedback from his computer teacher. At a 6-month follow-up to the 12-session contact, school continued to be a struggle for Justin, but he maintained a more positive view of himself and his future.

In addition to seeking to optimize the child and environment fit, therapy can be directed toward developing the problem-solving, feelings management skills that appear to promote resiliency in children. This skill development can be done in individual, family, or group therapy. Through the use of tasks, educational games, targeted exercises, and play therapy, children have the opportunity to learn the following skills: (1) asking for and accepting help; (2) knowing, tolerating, and expressing feelings productively; (3) managing stress through relaxation, play, and stress-reducing thinking, and developing frustration tolerance and anger management; (4) generating solutions and persevering in problem solving; (5) rejecting dysfunctional thoughts and substituting self-affirming thoughts; and (6) planning for and moving toward goals. Skill development requires an action-oriented, goal-directed therapy and the flexible use of multiple skill-promoting techniques. These techniques include cognitive restructuring of self-defeating thoughts; behavior modification through the use of modeling, instruction, role-playing, and feedback; homework assignments that provide practice opportunities and self-monitoring of progress; and positive reinforcements (Strayhorn, 1988; Forman, 1993).

Group and family psychoeducational programs are particularly effective modalities for helping children to develop resiliency because of the opportunities for support and for practicing new skills. The Penn Prevention Program is an example of an effective group treatment program that helps children at risk for depression to develop long-term resiliency. It is a 12-week, in-school, coping skills course aimed at teaching optimism, a positive attributional style, and interpersonal problem-solving skills for counteracting the negative effects of stressful life situations. Through a variety of classroom activities and exercises, the children learn how to recognize automatic thoughts that are self-blaming, catastrophizing, or overgeneralizing. They learn to question these thoughts and to recognize their ability to control and change these thoughts. The children are then presented with social problems that they discuss and solve as a group (Seligman, 1995).

Psychoeducational work with parents and families is an important adjunct to work with children on coping skills. Psychoeducational groups help families to support the development of these skills in their children by giving them the necessary support and information for dealing with their children's difficulties. Parents are given information about normative child development and about the special needs of their child. They also receive instruction in alternative methods for managing problem behaviors and instruction in how to teach and reinforce their child's acquisition of coping skills. A central goal of this approach is to help parents quickly gain or regain a sense of efficacy as parents by giving them the knowledge, skills, and sense of control to feel they are acting competently in problem situations. The emphasis is as much on mastery of the process of problem solving as on the specific skill development, so that parents will know on their own how to generate solutions, evaluate and select the best options for them, and persevere until the new coping skill is acquired by their child.

It is clear from the studies on resiliency that a multisystemic approach to practice will need to be the rule in working with vulnerable children, since a multisystem chain of protective influences offers children the best chance of succeeding when there are many risk factors in their lives (Fraser & Galinsky, 1997). That is, improving social supports in the child's home, school, and community in conjunction with improving personal competencies may reduce the risk of pathological development, since the presence of good social support has been found to have been a significant protective factor in the lives of resilient children. Specifically, this means that there is at least one supportive, caring person who validates the child's existence and serves as a buffer against the multiple stresses in the child's life. As part of the assessment process, potential sources of support need to be identified. This requires that the clinician look beyond the nuclear family for other sources of support rather than focusing exclusively, as in traditional therapeutic approaches, on making dysfunctional or inadequate parents more adequate. Again, the ecomap is a very useful tool toward this end. In the case illustration of competency-based practice that follows at the end of this chapter, the ecomap revealed that a potential source of support for a conduct-disordered child and his mother was the mother's Narcotics Anonymous support group. Members of this group had demonstrated both an interest in and a tolerance for the boy's behavior that other adults in the family's community did not have. Therefore, they were made part of the behavior modification program, especially the positive reinforcement component.

Schools are often overlooked as potential sources of support and self-esteem enhancement because contact with schools generally only occurs when a child is in difficulty there. Furthermore, by the time a child is referred, he or she may already be perceived negatively by school personnel, and at that point the school may be more of an environmental risk factor than a protective one. However, given how much time children spend in school, it is important to do a careful survey of all adult contacts in the child's school to identify actual or potential sources of support. Such potential sources of support are easily overlooked when there is an intense focus on the child's academic or behavior problems. In the same case illustration, the boy's teacher turned out to be a significant support for him in spite of the amount of disruptive behavior he exhibited in the classroom. His teacher could see both his intellectual potential and his hidden desire to please, and she willingly participated in a behavior modification plan for school that was coordinated with the one being used at home.

As Katz (1997, p. 96) notes, neighborhood schools are a great resource for

> protecting, nourishing, and stimulating children raised under conditions of severe adversity. . . . They can stimulate and nourish talents which might otherwise go unnoticed; remediate specific areas of vulnerability; enhance social and interpersonal abilities necessary for friendships and other relationships to develop; permanently alter the developmental trajectories of children who would otherwise develop serious emotional and behavioral difficulties; and they can instill a sense of hope and future in children and families who would otherwise give up.

The current push to place mental health services in the schools is in part a recognition of Katz's thesis about the potential reparative role of schools in children's lives. School-based mental health programs seek to develop collaborative relationships with teachers and other school personnel, with the objective of reinforcing the pivotal roles of those people in the lives of their students. School personnel need to know that there is a correlation between academic success and positive relationships with them (Richman & Bowen, 1997), while school-based clinicians need to appreciate the kinds of stresses and obstacles that interfere with success of school personnel in this critical role. Thus clinicians will need to provide support for burdened teachers and staff. This support might begin by acknowledging the difficulties that the child's problem behaviors are creating for them in the classroom, and making an effort to problem-solve jointly about ways to be more effective in bringing about desired changes in behavior.

With this kind of support, school personnel may be ready to develop another view of a child exhibiting behavioral and academic problems. To support this, the clinician encourages the school personnel to search for times when the child or adolescent exhibits positive academic or social behaviors that can be used to build the child's self-esteem. Jointly they also search for areas of strength (multiple forms of intelligence) that fall outside of the conventional concepts of ability and that could be utilized in school. An alteration in how children view themselves and in how others view them can be the first step leading to a more positive interaction between teacher and student and a greater investment on the teacher's part in the child's progress.

After-school programs and community organizations can also serve important stress-buffering, protective functions for children, particularly in poor, high-risk neighborhoods where outdoor play may be curtailed because of violence in the neighborhood or because working parents want their children to stay at home when they are at work. Katz (1997) describes these programs as urban sanctuaries because they offer children or adolescents safety and opportunities to learn real skills and lessons in taking responsibility. They may also be able to develop competencies that may be overlooked or not valued in regular academic programs, while receiving the support and attention of another adult who values these skills. Referral to these programs should be considered a preferred brief treatment intervention for children growing up in adverse environments.

Mentoring programs are also invaluable in promoting resiliency in children. Such programs not only introduce children and adolescents to the workplace and to career ideas, but they also provide children with role models and a stable, caring relationship that can help them develop an alternative view of themselves. Adolescents who have been mentored can in turn benefit by becoming mentors to younger children for, as the resiliency research indicated, competency is enhanced by involvement in activities that help others. In addition to tutoring, teenagers can be encouraged to lead recreational activities for younger children or participate in community renovation projects (Richman & Bowen, 1997). Clearly, intervention at the community level is an important part of the treatment process with children and adolescents in general, but this is particularly true for brief treatment because involvement in community activities can facilitate and enhance the rapid development of coping skills. Therefore, assessment and intervention at the community level should also be an important part of any brief treatment plan when working with children and adolescents. The ecomap is also useful here for evaluating needs and charting progress in building in supports for the child and his or her family.

The Collaborative Relationship

In addition to the shift to a competency focus in child and family services, the other paradigm shift that has occurred is in the conceptualization of the role of parents in the treatment process. There has been movement in family and children's services away from viewing parents only as informants, or as patients whose dysfunction created their child's difficulties, toward viewing parents as knowledgeable caregivers with whom one needs to establish a collaborative partnership (Collins & Collins, 1990). There has also been a shift in the treatment of children from an exclusive focus on remediation of parental deficits to an inclusion of empowerment strategies in the treatment process.

The change in parental roles in treatment began when parent consumer groups in the early 1980s began expressing dissatisfaction with the attitudes of mental health professionals toward them and with the treatment their children were receiving. Among the complaints and concerns that parents expressed were (1) dissatisfaction with the amount of information shared with them about their children's difficulties and about treatment options; (2) dissatisfaction that their own parental expertise about their children was not valued and that they were not included in treatment planning; (3) inadequacy of advice, guidance, or skills provided to them for managing their children's problematic behaviors; (4) an attitude on the part of mental health professionals that parents were to be blamed for the children's problems while neurobiological reasons for the problems were not considered; and (5) dissatisfaction with treatment, which the parents perceived as being ineffective and fragmented (Johnson et al., 1995).

In 1984, the first ten state Children and Adolescent Service System Programs were funded to provide community-based, coordinated services. These services were a response to the reports in the children's mental health literature that detailed the problems in alliance formation between clinicians and parents and in high rates of attrition in children's mental health services. The state programs stipulated that families needed to be involved in all aspects of the planning and delivery of services. Programs were also mandated to be family centered and to use a collaborative approach with parents in order to eliminate bias against families in child mental health services (Johnson, Cournoyer, & Fisher, 1994).

Several changes in practice principles and intervention strategies are indicated by these philosophical and policy changes. First among these is the need for a broad-based, holistic conceptualization of children's behavioral and emotional problems. Assessment and intervention planning need to include the dimensions of temperament, neurobiological disturbance, and situational stresses along with etiologic factors that center on parental pathology or family dysfunction. It is also important in the assessment of the child and family to make an attempt to discriminate between trait and state. That is, it is important to consider the possibility that family dysfunction or problematic interactions between parent and child are the consequences of the stresses of living with biologically determined, difficult, highly demanding characteristics of the child. From this perspective, equal time should be spent assessing the effect of the child's problems on the relationships between parents, between parents and other children, between the family and the extended family, and between the family and school and community agencies. Thus, in this approach, one of the first questions in the assessment interview would be, "Tell me what life is like at home with your child" (Webster-Stratton & Herbert, 1994, p. 111).

In the initial interview, the clinician immediately acknowledges and draws on the parents' expert knowledge of their child. In the past, information gathered from parents was seen mainly as data for formulating hypotheses about family dynamics or parental deficits—for example, were the parents rejecting, disengaged, enmeshed, over-controlling, displacing marital conflicts onto the child, and so on (Johnson et al., 1994). In collaborative models, information gathered from parents during the assessment process is used to guide the selection of goals and treatment methods. In the initial interview, parental concerns, hopes, and expectations of treatment are respected and incorporated into the treatment plan. The brief therapist's role is to move the discussion from one of a search for reasons or explanations for the child's problem behaviors to one focused on the descriptive details of problematic interactions. Thus the collaborative approach to treatment moves the case conceptualization away from blaming either the child for being bad, or the parents for being inadequate, to an understanding of how a child's special needs and family stresses have led to conflict and family disequilibrium (Webster-Stratton & Herbert, 1993).

Another change in the parent-professional relationship has been the move toward viewing parents as consumers of mental health services who have a right to information about the potential benefits, risks, and costs of all treatment options, as well as the limits of what is known about the causes and effective treatments for childhood behavioral and emotional problems. Reports from parents indicated that they found professionals helpful when the professionals offered clear guidance about how to help the child as well as help in making decisions about treatment options. Parents appreciated getting help in finding needed services, and they appreciated clinicians who attempted to be responsive to their questions. Parents also reported wanting professionals to recognize that the parents care about their children and are doing the best they can rather than viewing them as resistant and uncaring (Johnson et al., 1995).

Empowering parents to feel effective in their role as parents has become a central goal in the collaborative model of practice with children and families. Research is being conducted in child and family services to determine the factors that contribute to the formation of a collaborative helping relationship and to the empowerment of parents. Webster-Stratton and Herbert (1994), on the basis of their research on an intervention program developed at the Parenting Clinic at the University of Washington, have identified several strategies for empowering parents. These include encouraging parents to develop their own strategies for managing their children's behavior, based on past experiences and knowledge, and challenging feelings of helplessness or powerlessness that stem from past experiences of failure. The latter is achieved through cognitive restructuring—that is, having parents learn to substitute calming and coping thoughts for defeatist ones. Parents are also taught how to problem-solve, so that they will know how to deal with problems they encounter after therapy ends. Therefore, parents are encouraged to brainstorm about solutions to problem behaviors and then to select the strategy that makes sense to them and that they can follow through on. To help parents persevere in working on problems, a group format for learning problem-solving skills is suggested. In addition, parents are taught how to seek support and respite care from family members and from the community through involvement in self-help groups.

Brief Treatment with Families and Children

The competency-based, collaborative approach outlined above is a particularly useful one when working with involuntary or reluctant families and children, a significant proportion of the clinic population. The likelihood is high that when families are mandated to receive services, they will be angry, resentful, or evasive. From the perspective of these families, the social worker represents the authority structure threatening the survival of the family "by pointing out what they are doing wrong, telling them what to do" and demanding that the family "change its views, values, and lifestyle" (Berg, 1994, p. 58). In addition, multi-stressed families often have had previous contacts with social service or mental health systems that may not have been helpful or in which they felt coerced. Such families will need the opportunity to discuss their negative expectations (e.g., that meeting with a social worker will not be helpful) and negative feelings, particularly their fears about what will be asked of them. Therefore, it is important to quickly reduce a family's feelings of powerlessness and reduce their concerns about being negatively judged.

Interviewing a family about their strengths and dreams as well as about their personal experience in living with a problem can diminish some of their concerns about being negatively judged or not being understood. For these families, it will be especially important that the identified problems and goals of treatment reflect their perspectives on the problem as well as those of the referring source. Helping families to recognize the underlying healthy strivings behind problematic behaviors and family conflicts is another way to engage reluctant families, because hopelessness and self-blame often lie behind a family's reluctance to accept help, as in the following vignette (Waters & Lawrence, 1993).

> After repeated requests by the school and under threat of expulsion for his aggressive behavior, Mrs. W brought her 12-year-old son, Bobby, for

evaluation. Struggling to hold onto a squirming toddler and attend to her 5-year-old, Mrs. W launched into an extended tirade about the school singling Bobby out and not giving him any help with his reading problem, and how he was never a problem at home. When the therapist remarked that it was clear that she felt very protective toward Bobby and wanted the best for him, Mrs. W started to cry and said that she had to be because she had had to protect him from his father, who had been violent and abusive toward her and Bobby. She then talked about the pressures she felt as a single parent. The focus initially, then, was on reducing the stresses she felt as a single parent, beginning with the goals of finding a child care alternative to Bobby having to baby-sit every day after school and providing Bobby with more opportunities for sports and group activities.

After an agreement has been reached with the parents or family on the problem definition, the brief therapist guides the family in setting precise goals for the resolution of the problem or problems they have selected to work on and then helps the family to maintain a focus on these goals. These activities are especially important in working with multistressed families, where there are many compelling problems and where families may lead crisis-ridden lives. The process of setting simple, achievable, well-defined goals with these families can be educational and therapeutic, because the parents in these families may not have had the opportunity to learn how to sort out, select, and break tasks down into manageable pieces, that is, how to problem-solve. Getting a clear idea about what needs to be done, a vision of what things will look like when they improve, and an idea of how they will get to that point can reduce the demoralization that is present when a family situation seems chaotic and unmanageable (Waters & Lawrence, 1993).

The goals in brief treatment with families should be defined in behavioral terms, particularly for managed care purposes, because when there are external indicators of therapeutic progress it is easier for the family and the managed care organization to recognize changes. Goals in brief family work are also best described in interactional terms rather than in terms suggesting the remediation of one member's symptomatic or problem behavior. Setting interactional goals helps to move the therapy process into a direction where changes can occur, whereas parents frequently enter therapy expecting that the therapist will "fix the child through child therapy" or "alter the child's temperament with medication" or that they will be blamed for the problems that the child is experiencing (Webster-Stratton & Herbert, 1994, p. 112). Thus, in a case where the mother began the evaluation of her 10-year-old daughter's angry, oppositional behavior by asking for medication for her daughter, goals that focused on specific daily problematic interactions reduced the oppositional behavior. In a step-by-step manner, aspects of behavior were altered and interactions restructured while opportunities for more positive interactions were increased.

The emphasis on behavioral, interactional goals is complemented in brief family therapy by a focus in treatment on helping the child and family to cope with and in some cases to live within their current reality rather than working through feelings about past situations (Kreilkamp, 1988). Taking a family history is part of the assessment process, but the information from the history or the genogram is used cautiously and selectively, only to the extent that the information advances understanding of how to resolve the family's current difficulties or how to increase client motivation. Apart from the fact that there are not enough sessions in time-limited work to allow two or three for assessment purposes alone, elaborate history taking can have the effect of expanding the database so that it becomes difficult for the clinician to delineate realistic, achievable goals. In the process of exploring the origins of problems, the impact of current psychosocial stressors on the family's functioning can be underestimated (Berg, 1994). This could result in a discrepancy between what the clinician feels the family should accomplish and what the family is motivated to work on, given the research evidence that most clients want help with concrete problems in functioning and relating. The counterbalance for becoming enmeshed in the past or in pathology-saturated views of the family is to spend an equal amount of time in the assessment process gathering information about the family's day-to-day experience of their problems, their thoughts and feelings in reaction to the problems and stresses in their lives, their attempts at resolution, and their successful coping efforts.

Rapid assessment instruments can be quite useful in complex family situations in refining or narrowing the scope of attention and for gaining specificity in terms of identifying the most problematic interactions. Fischer and Corcoran (1994) list in their sourcebook *Measures for Clinical Practice: Vol. 1, Couples, Families and Children* several instruments for measuring general family functioning. For example, there are several instruments in this sourcebook for assessing the quality of family relationships, such as the Index of Family Relations (Hudson, 1992), and for measuring family coping capacities in stressful situations, such as the Family Crisis Oriented Personal Evaluation Scale (McCubbin & Thompson, 1991). In addition, there are numerous instruments for assessing couple relationships—for example, the Conflict Tactics Scale (Straus & Gelles, 1990)—that help pinpoint the core relationship difficulties.

If it appears that a disorder such as depression or substance abuse is affecting the parent's ability to parent or to work toward treatment goals for the family, then an individual mental status exam and individual rapid assessment instruments such as the Beck Depression Inventory will need to be included in the assessment process. Too often in the past there was a tendency to prioritize system interventions over individual interventions when a family member was suffering from a mood disorder or other Axis I disorders, on the theoretical assumption that changing problematic interactions or restructuring the family would lead to a diminution of the individual's symptomatology. Painful and problematic family relationships can be a consequence rather than the cause of mental illness of one or more family members. Consequently, the individual disorder needs to be aggressively treated as well as any dysfunctional family interactions (Shuchter, Downs, & Zisook, 1996).

The final dimension that must be explored in a family assessment from a time-limited perspective is that of the quality of the family's social environment. The evaluation should involve determining whether the family's support system provides buffering against stresses such as poverty, racism, and parental illness. There may be people they can turn to for protection, advice, guidance, or emotional and material assistance in times of need (Whittaker, 1986). An evaluation of the family's competency in utilizing social supports and the quality of the transactions between the family and their support system is an important part of this assessment. The ecomap can be used for reviewing how helpful or how stressful the client's relationships are with members of the social support network and where the missing links are in the network.

The assessment of the social environment should also include an evaluation of the relevance of ethnicity and culture factors in the family's experience of stresses, problems, and social supports as well as in their view of the help being offered to them. Tseng and Hsu (1991) emphasize the need to understand that all aspects of the family structure and functioning can be different from what is considered normal in Western countries and that there are likely to be cultural blind spots that can lead to an incorrect diagnosis of the family. They also encourage therapists to have enough knowledge of the family's cultural background that they can be respectful of the family's hierarchical authority structure, patterns of communication (e.g., etiquette about who speaks when and to whom), and restrictions about exposing private matters or expressing feelings. Tseng and Hsu have a fairly elaborate assessment protocol that includes assessment of the marriage form, descent system, rules of marital choice, mate selection, postmarital residence, family authority, loyalty bonds, and cultural values, beliefs, and attitudes about child-rearing, gender roles, and so on. However, given the time constraints of brief therapy, a model such as the culturagram (Congress, 1994) is a more realistic method of cultural assessment. This approach explores the central stresses of migration and dilemmas of acculturation, although here again not every dimension will need to be explored in depth.

> This family-assessment tool [the culturagram] assesses (1) reasons for immigration; (2) length of time in community; (3) legal status; (4) age at time of immigration; (5) language spoken at home and in the community; (6) health beliefs; (7) celebrated holidays and special events; (8) impact of crisis events; (9) values regarding family, education, and work; and (10) contact with cultural institutions. (Congress, 1994, p. 513)

Out of the assessment process there should emerge a picture of how stressed the family is, what risk factors are present that can compromise family functioning, and what internal and external resources are available to them for aiding in the resolution of problems. As in work with individuals, the assessment should direct the worker to select the appropriate level of intervention (a family version of the Levels of Intervention model will be presented below). For example, families in crisis because a family member is having a serious behavioral or psychological disorder or families coping with multiple stresses will need supportive, structured, immediate problem-solving interventions related to safety issues, and a high level of therapist activity. On the other hand, a family experiencing difficulties in making a transition from one developmental stage to the next—for example, parent-adolescent conflicts over intimacy and autonomy—but who are not in crisis and are able to meet basic needs will not need as much concrete help or guidance. Instead, in that situation techniques that deal with relational and communication problems are indicated (Kilpatrick & Holland, 1995).

Engagement and Assessment Issues with Children and Adolescents

There are several issues in working with children and adolescents that will need to be addressed early in the treatment process in order to successfully engage them in treatment. By the time a family seeks help for a child, there are often disabling patterns of resentment, mutual recrimination, and anger that have come to characterize family interactions. These negative family dynamics are related in part to the assumption in this culture that parents are responsible for their child's difficulties; therefore, the parents feel blamed and blame themselves. The parents' intense feelings of shame, guilt, and inadequacy and their anger and resentment toward the child for these feelings of inadequacy can result in the child or adolescent entering treatment with an expectation of further condemnation or rejection by an adult. Consequently, there may be a reluctance to get involved with another adult. The child or adolescent often engages in a range of self-protective behaviors that may appear to be resistance, avoidance, passive-aggressiveness, or noncompliance (Berg, 1994). In addition, once children are labeled as having emotional or behavioral problems, they may come to be seen and see themselves as only sick or bad (Poertner & Ronnau, 1993). Finally, children and adolescents are typically involuntary clients, so that in addition to fears, anxiety, and negative expectations there may be anger and resentment about not having a choice about being in treatment (Rooney, 1988).

It is easy when assessing children to become focused on their problems or symptoms and to overlook areas of competency or the potential for developing competency. Children or adolescents often enter treatment at a point of crisis, with parents or a referral source pressing for a quick resolution of the presenting problems. However, as Selekman (1993) demonstrated in his work with difficult adolescents, adopting the strengths perspective fosters the development of rapport. He begins the assessment process by "inviting each family member . . . to share . . . what they do best, their personal strengths, talents, and hobbies." He also recommends building rapport by "using a lot of humor, normalizing and positively relabeling family behaviors . . . and improvising on central family themes" (Selekman, 1993, p. 46). This approach is particularly effective with adolescents because of their natural interest in sorting out who they are and what they can do and because it diminishes the fears of being crazy or defective that strongly contribute to resistance in adolescents. The case illustration of Doreen in Chapter 5 demonstrates how effective these techniques can be with an adolescent client who presents as sullen, hostile, and nonresponsive.

Other solution-focused interviewing techniques, such as the "miracle" question (a question that asks the client to imagine that a miracle has occurred and his or her problem is solved and to imagine what they would notice as different that would tell them that the problem is solved) or questions that direct attention to times when the problem does not occur, can help provide children with the motivation to work toward changing behaviors, because such techniques encourage them to envision a future in which the presenting problem(s) will no longer dominate their view of themselves nor negatively influence their interactions with family members and significant other people in their lives (Berg, 1994). Once rapport has been established and the assessment process has been explained, then the usual structured methods of obtaining data about the presenting problems and the child's functioning can be pursued.

When a child or adolescent is experiencing emotional or behavioral difficulties, an individual assessment is necessary in addition to an evaluation of the child within his or her family context—and ideally this will be done within his or her school or community context—when the child is experiencing problems in those areas. However, this type of multisystem assessment can be a challenge to complete within the first or second session. It is a good idea to set aside an additional 15 to 30 minutes for first sessions, since families in crisis need additional time in order to stabilize and reduce the high level of distress. Time during the first session will need to be employed flexibly. The clinician will need to divide up the 60 or 90 minutes so that the parents can be interviewed separately, the child or adolescent separately, and the family as a whole, while being prepared to allot more time for those members of the family in the greatest distress. One can optimize the evaluation time by obtaining information through questionnaires prior to the interview or by having the family come a half hour early to fill them out. These questionnaires can then be used as a basis for gathering additional information, even if the parents were not able to complete them. They are especially helpful in gathering information on the child's developmental history and on significant events in the family's history.

In addition, the parents can complete rapid assessment questionnaires while the child is being interviewed. Fischer and Corcoran (1994) include several such questionnaires in their sourcebook, including the Behavior Rating Index for Children (Stiffman, Orme, Evans, Feldman, & Keeney, 1984) and the Eyberg Child Behavior Inventory (Burns & Patterson, 1990). These two instruments can help to delineate quickly the areas of difficulty (e.g., problems getting dressed, noncompliance with rules, temper tantrums, fighting with siblings, aggressive behaviors, etc). To assess social and emotional problems, there are instruments such as the Child Behavior Checklist (Achenbach, 1991), which provides a profile of the child or adolescent in terms of internalizing behaviors (depression, anxiety, somaticizing, and social inhibitions) and externalizing behaviors (delinquent behaviors, attention problems, and aggressiveness). There are also diagnosis-specific instruments such as the Depression Self-Rating Scale for Children (Birelson, Hudson, Buchannon, & Wolff, 1987) that can aid in the determination of the existence of a clinical disorder.

The assessment for a child in brief treatment will generally combine an evaluative play session and direct interviewing of the child. Play therapy can facilitate the engagement of children in the therapy process and aid in the gathering of accurate information about how they are experiencing their problems or symptoms (Webb, 1996). Even if the children's problems are neurobiological in origin or are reactive to family stresses, their feelings and interpretations of what is happening in their lives can be critical for how responsive they will be to interventions. In addition, problematic behaviors usually have multiple causes, therefore, the child's thoughts and feelings may be contributing to and maintaining these behaviors. For example, anxiety and depression can be complicating features of attention-deficit/hyperactivity disorder. Therefore, treatment of the mood disturbances is also necessary to reduce hyperactivity and increase the child's attention span. The use of unstructured and semistructured play activities—for example, the opportunity to draw anything they like, followed by a request to draw a picture of the family—can reveal thoughts and feelings that they are unable to verbalize because of alexithymia or are fearful and ashamed about revealing. Puppets, dollhouses, and play dough are also useful projective devices for accessing children's thoughts and feelings (Webb, 1996).

Adolescents will generally be interviewed directly, although younger adolescents and preadolescents may be more comfortable talking while playing cards or a board game. In general, the assessment process is uncomfortable for adolescents, and they are often resistant to engaging with the therapist and with providing information about the situation for which they have been referred. It is generally more productive to begin with a statement of fact of what the referral is about and then to move to an inquiry about the teenager and his interests and activities, looking for areas of strength and highlighting these for the teenager and later for the whole family. If the adolescent is responsive to this approach—and many are, because it does not replicate the disapproval or concern they are receiving from other adults—it may then be possible to explore his or her experiences and viewpoints about the areas of difficulty or conflict with parents, school, and so on (Johnson, 1995). It is also useful to deal with the adolescent as one would with any involuntary or mandated client, which is to elicit the negative feelings and expectations about the therapy process and about what it means to them to have to come for treatment. If the adolescent has been able to talk about his or her concerns or perspective on problems, then it may be possible to end the first individual assessment session with goals for treatment that have been identified by the adolescent. However, it may take a session or two more to reach this point.

For both the child and the adolescent there will need to be an assessment of the quality of their social environments. Information from the school and other social service or mental health agencies needs to be obtained quickly so that an effective intervention plan can be developed. To this end it is important to expedite the sending of release-of-information forms to schools or social service and mental health agencies (e.g., by fax) and to ensure that the releases enable the therapist to get information orally while waiting for the written report. Home visits and school visits are excellent ways of getting more accurate information because they enable the clinician to observe the child in a more natural setting and to observe the quality of interaction with peers, teachers, relatives, neighbors, and so on, and a chance to observe cultural patterned interactions. These recommendations are made with a recognition of how difficult it is for workers to find the time to make home visits and to do a complete multisystem scan and how difficult it is to get administrative support for these procedures. However, given the fact that environmental interventions on behalf of children are essential for rapid problem resolution and relapse prevention, taking the time to assess the child's environment may in the end be the most efficient and effective use of time. The same is true for taking the time to develop collaborative relationships with key individuals in health, social service, mental health, residential treatment, welfare, and educational organizations, because in the end these relationships facilitate the development of a care plan and expedite service delivery, which is essential to effective time-limited work.

Workers can advocate for collateral contacts on the basis of the need for accurate assessment and on the basis of efficacy and efficiency. Treatment plans presented under managed care for review are expected to show a direct connection between the child's impairments in functioning or targeted symptoms and the planned interventions. To be able to provide that degree of specificity in targeting symptoms for treatment when the problem is in the school or in the home, the case can be made that observation and collateral contacts are necessary. The case for collateral contacts in order to stabilize or modify a child's environment can also be made on a cost efficiency basis; that is, intervening with school or community agencies is far less expensive than having to move the child to a more restricted and costly setting out of the community.

Treatment Plan: Selecting Modality and Practice Interventions

The selection of a modality (individual, family, couple) is dependent upon a number of factors, and these factors may change over the course of the treatment, resulting in the use of different modalities or combinations of modalities at different points in the treatment. Among the most important factors influencing the initial selection of modality and treatment methods is each family member's degree of readiness for making changes. This can be determined by using either the Prochaska-DiClemente model (Prochaska, DiClemente, & Norcross, 1992) of precontemplation, contemplation, and action stages of motivation or de Shazer's (1985) model of therapist-family relationship patterns (visitors, complainants, and customers).

Treatment is most profitably begun with members who are actually customers—that is, those who are contemplating or are ready to take action. An attempt should be made in the first session to move family members who are visitors to become customers by soliciting their views on the problem situation and its resolution and by providing an early gain in treatment. Members in the precontemplation stage may be persuaded to participate later in the treatment when they observe the family's needs being met. The de Shazer and Prochaska-DiClemente approaches can be used throughout the treatment process to calibrate the treatment—for example, giving data collection assignments to family members in the contemplation stage, but giving homework for behavior changes to members in the action stage (Johnson, 1995).

Selection of modality will also be dependent upon the needs of the family members, particularly the identified patient, and will vary in accordance with which part of the family system is most influential in changing the presenting problems. Thus, it is possible that the child or adolescent who is the identified patient may need to be protected from the anger and hostility of the other family members and therefore be seen separately until the crisis state is resolved and the negative feelings subside to a point where it would not be toxic to see the family as a whole (see the case of Doreen in Chapter 5). Similarly, if parents' marital difficulties are having a significantly negative impact on the children, or if the child's problems (e.g., depression, sleep disturbance, soiling) are closely tied to the marital problems, then couple therapy and individual therapy may be the modalities of choice. Here again, over the course of the treatment, there may be enough change in the subsystems of the family system to consider other treatment approaches.

As with the Levels of Intervention model for adult clients, selection of an intervention plan for a child or family requires the differential evaluation of such factors as the severity of the presenting problems, degree of impairment in functioning, degree of risk for harming self or others, number of stresses currently impinging upon family functioning, presence of substance abuse or

Levels of Intervention Model

Level I

A. Problems involving safety, self-care, severe symptoms, stability, and substance abuse issues. Families at this level have difficulty meeting basic needs of food, clothing, or shelter, or minimum level of nurturance, health care, etc.

B. Interventions: crisis intervention, case management (advocacy, mediation, and referral), psychoeducation, problem-solving models (e.g., cognitive-behavioral), addictions treatment, family preservation techniques, guidance, maximizing personal strengths and support network.

Level II

A. Problems with conflicted, confused, or misidentified thoughts or feelings; interpersonal conflicts; work and/or parenting functioning. Families are sufficiently organized to provide minimal structure, limits, and safety, but maintaining authority and boundaries or setting limits are problems.

B. Interventions: exploratory (insight) and expressive therapies; interpersonal and coping skills development; bereavement work; cognitive restructuring; solution-focused, structural, and family systems interventions.

Level III

A. Problems of selfhood: self-esteem, identity, and self-evaluation. Client has made the movement from a focus on past and worry about future to present, or there is an emphasis in treatment on consolidation and maintenance of therapy gains. Desire for greater intimacy, connection, and self-actualization.

B. Interventions: narrative constructivist and object relations (individual and family) approaches. Reconstruction of a personal narrative that moves the individual or family from a passive to an active role and from negative self-evaluation to an appreciation of his or her or family strengths.

(Derived from Beutler & Clarkin, 1990, and Kilpatrick & Holland, 1995) major psychiatric disturbance, personal and family coping skills, personal strengths, and the quality of the social support network and community resources. The balance between personal and environmental risk and protective factors and resulting level of functioning will determine the level of intervention that will best meet the needs of the family.

Kilpatrick and Holland (1995) proposed a differential assessment and intervention model for working with families that is similar to the construction of the Levels of Intervention model. Their model differentiates four levels of need and functioning. Level I families have basic survival and well-being needs that are not being met, with associated impairments in many areas of functioning. Level II families have a need for more functional structure and organization to ensure that limits are set in the interest of family safety and stability. Level III families have adequate coping mechanisms but difficulty in maintaining boundaries. With Level IV families, "such issues as inner conflicts, intimacy, self-realization, insight, and spiritual yearnings become the primary focus" (Kilpatrick & Holland, 1995, p. 10). Suggested differential intervention techniques include, for Level I, family preservation and case management techniques; for Level II, cognitive-behavioral and structural family techniques; for Level III, family systems and solution-focused interventions; and for Level IV, narrative and object relations interventions.

The Kilpatrick-Holland model for working with families is congruent with the Levels of Intervention model proposed here in terms of the types of problems identified at the different levels of functioning and the types of intervention strategies selected for each level. The points of difference are in the breadth of the categories at each level and in the stability of the intervention approaches. Thus, the families at Level I of functioning in the Kilpatrick-Holland model are described as multiproblem families, where there is likely to be parental psychopathology or substance abuse, poverty, illness, chronic discord, and charges of abuse and neglect, and where children are at risk for being placed out of the home (Grigsby, 1995). By contrast, the Level I category of families in the Levels of Intervention model would include, in addition to the above-described multistressed families, those that were previously functioning adequately but are currently in situational crisis and families that have finally succumbed to crisis after an accumulation of stresses.

Grigsby (1995) describes Level II families as those so lacking in organization and in executive capacity that a child's behavior can become so out of bounds and stressful to the family that they may consider placement of the child out of the home. Interventions that would be helpful to these family members, who are stuck in painful and counterproductive patterns of interaction and who are unable to problem-solve as a consequence of being caught up in conflict, are interventions that stress coping, conflict resolution, and communication skills. Therefore, these types of family problems are placed in Level I of the Levels of Intervention model because of the need for cognitive-behavioral and structural family therapy interventions to remediate the excesses of behavior and deficiencies of organization and structure.

Level II interventions in the Levels of Intervention model are primarily expressive, exploratory, and experiential, making this category more akin to the Level III interventions in the Kilpatrick-Holland model (solution-focused family systems interventions). Families at this level are not or no longer in crisis; are stable enough to provide adequate nurturance, protection, and attention to their children's needs; and have basic communication and conflict resolution skills; but they are struggling with emotions, conflicts, and faulty attributions that are the sequelae of past and current struggles in coping with stresses (e.g., adapting to the challenges of a child with ADHD).[1] Examples of these types of family issues are unresolved losses, difficulty in grieving a current loss, anxiety and depressive reactions in family members, reactive academic and behavioral problems, and reactive marital and family conflicts. Level II interventions are geared toward identifying unidentified or misidentified feelings and thoughts, but with the purpose of having family members take different actions than the repetitive, nonproductive patterns of interaction in which they have been stuck. Some of the methods useful with families at this level of intervention are behavior enactment methods—for example, role play, behavioral rehearsal, gestalt experiential techniques, visualization and guided imagery, regrieving exercises, and homework assignments that challenge and reconfigure thoughts and feelings.

Level III interventions (Level IV in the Kilpatrick-Holland model) are directed toward meaning reconstruction, "the creation of positive new interpretations" (Weick, 1997, p. 366) of negative or challenging life experiences, so that families can draw on their strengths and have a sense of competency and resiliency when future stresses arise. Self-work within the context of the self in relation to other family members is a part of the Level III intervention approach, with the aim of helping family members to be able to appreciate their differences and their points of connection. This work is intended for families who are no longer beset by repetitive patterns of mutually unrewarding interactions but who remain vulnerable to dysfunction under stress because they are still bound to views of themselves and each other that reflect their past reality rather than their current reality. Therefore, constructivist approaches allow the family members to revisit "historical, developmental (e.g., attachment) and self-organizational themes" (Granvold, 1996, p. 348) in order to direct their attention more to the future and toward competent actions in the future. Level III interventions are particularly useful when working with families

---

[1] Acronyms introduced in this chapter: ADHD, attention-deficit/hyperactivity disorder; NA, Narcotics Anonymous.

struggling with the demands of acculturation and assimilation or with ongoing adaptation to special-needs children, and they are usefully employed at termination, when it becomes important for families to leave treatment with a recognition of their work and accomplishments in therapy.

Individual Intervention with Children and Adolescents

The process for arriving at an individual treatment plan outlined for adults is the same for a child or adolescent. That is, treatment proceeds from rapid assessment to case conceptualization to problem definition, treatment focus, goal definition, and methods of intervention (Pekarik, 1996). As with adult clients, the selection of appropriate intervention strategies for children and adolescents is based on client needs and motivation level and preferred clinical practices. Treatment planners for work with children are useful tools for arriving at a targeted, individualized plan for a child client. Examples of these planners are Jongsma, A. E., Peterson, L. M., & McGinnis, W. P. (1996), *The Child and Adolescent Psychotherapy Treatment Planner;* and Johnson, S. L. (1997), *Therapist's Guide to Clinical Intervention: The 1-2-3s of Treatment Planning.*

The Levels of Intervention model can also be used as a guide for selecting appropriate intervention strategies, as can best-practices guides based on research and clinical practice—for example, P. E. Nathan and J. M. Gorman (1998), *A guide to treatments that work.* While there has been a dearth of studies on effective therapy for children and adolescents, the emerging research tends to support Eysenck's (1988) contention that cognitive-behavioral, problem-solving, skills-training methods are the most effective approaches for children presenting with problems of behavioral excesses or deficits (e.g., conduct disorder, attention-deficit/hyperactivity disorder, and social phobia). The effectiveness of psychodynamic, expressive insight-oriented therapy, play therapy, and relationship-based therapy has not been demonstrated for behavioral problems or severe symptoms, but clinical experience and limited clinical research suggest that the expressive approaches are helpful with children suffering from excesses or repression of emotions, as in trauma-associated mood disorders or bereavement situations (Kazdin, 1998). Thus, the Levels of Intervention model, with its continuum of treatment based on the severity of problems and degree of dysfunction the child is experiencing, has some empirical support in the child and adolescent research literature.

Individual therapy with children will generally involve some form of play therapy because children do not talk as easily in therapy as adults and because their concerns and needs are more readily expressed through the play medium (Kreilkamp, 1988). However, in time-limited therapy, the goal of play therapy is mastery, not insight. The goal is not for the child to be able to identify or understand feelings or conflicts, as was typically the case in long-term, unstructured play therapy, but instead for the child to learn to manage and express those feelings in constructive ways and to learn the interpersonal problem-solving and communication skills that will enable the child to get his or her needs met for affection, attention, mastery, and validation (Lock, 1997). Thus, there is a significant educational, social-learning component to short-term play therapy in addition to the expressive component. This emphasis on mastery is also a useful way to keep the therapy focused, as learning problem-solving strategies can be tied to resolving specific problems or toward meeting valued goals, such as making a new friend, successfully attending a class field trip, and so on, as will be illustrated in the case example at the end of the chapter.

Brief treatment with adolescents can also be structured around the development of problem-solving skills, although a more indirect or delayed approach is often required in working with adolescents before they are ready to recognize and work on problems. This reluctance to recognize and discuss problems is a function of normative heightened self-consciousness and concern about being negatively perceived. It may also reflect adolescent struggles to gain autonomy from adult control, since they may see the clinician as someone else trying to tell them what to do if the clinician insists on setting the agenda. Thus, it may be necessary to start with "less threatening topics, such as interests, friends, positive and negative aspects of school, and the family constellation" until the underlying fears and anxieties have diminished (Rubenstein, 1991, p. 224). A developmental focus—for example, a focus on positive identity formation or one that focuses on building on the adolescent's existing strengths— is also a good entry point to treatment or even the sole focus for the treatment. Discussion of talents, abilities, and interests or of healthy strivings can serve as a bridge to more threatening issues such as problems with peers, parents, substance abuse, self-image, and so on, as obstacles to developing these abilities invariably arise. The efficacy of this principle of working with the strengths of adolescents was demonstrated in the treatment of Doreen. The initial emphasis on identifying her skills and interest and developing her storytelling ability in homework assignments appeared to result in an increase in self-esteem, impulse control, and judgment. These improvements in ego functions then enabled her to look more closely at the consequences of risk-taking behaviors for her and to express sad and positive feelings and not just feelings of anger.

The narrative therapy technique of externalization is a very useful method for assisting children and adolescents and their families in working toward change when the child and family have become locked into behavioral patterns due in part to their having come to see the child's problems as his/her total identity or the identity of the family. For example, externalization has proven to be a useful change-inducing technique with such seemingly entrenched problems as encopresis and severe adolescent-parent conflicts. Becoming identified with the problem is the logical consequence of a construction of childhood behavioral and emotional disorders as having their origins in family or parental pathology. To aid children and families in recollecting their strengths, resources, and coping identities, the technique of externalizing a problem is used. Through a series of questions and reframes, the child and family are guided toward seeing the problem as the problem, rather than the child as the problem. The family is encouraged to personify the problem in order to place it outside the child, to look at how the problem has come to dominate their lives, to find exceptions to occurrence of the problem and examine how that occurred, to associate times of exception with the child, to connect the exception to past coping successes, and to imagine a future not dominated by this problem (White & Epston, 1990).

As with younger children, the overarching goals of individual work with adolescents are improvement in coping abilities and a growth in a sense of mastery within their environments. Thus, once goals that the adolescent is motivated to work toward have been identified, the focus of the work shifts to the development of problem-solving skills, including skills in more effective management of emotions and interpersonal relationships. Again the primary intervention strategies will be primarily psychoeducational and cognitive-behavioral for clients in crisis who have safety or substance abuse problems. After the adolescent stabilizes and is less at risk, a combination of problem-solving strategies and opportunities to express worries, fears, concerns, and feelings can be employed. Since obstacles to realizing personal goals often involve problematic relationships with family, school, peers, or all of these, interventions with the family or with other members of the adolescent's ecosystem should be recommended to the teenager once rapport and trust have been established, unless the relationship is too hostile or too destructive. Family therapy can be postponed until the hostility diminishes. Family therapeutic approaches can be incorporated into the individual treatment of the adolescent until and if the family is able to work together (Selekman, 1993). Creativity and flexibility in scheduling are required to work in a multisystem way in time-limited work. Thus, in a 1-hour session, the hour might be divided into 20 minutes of individual work with the teenager, 20 minutes with the parents, and 20 minutes with the whole family. Individual and family work might be alternated during the course of treatment. The work with Doreen illustrated the importance of remaining responsive to the needs of the family in terms of who would be seen and in what modality of treatment. When the family was in crisis and the hostility and tensions were high, individual sessions were used. As the family prepared to terminate, more time was spent in family therapy to ensure that the gains Doreen made in her individual therapy would be maintained after treatment ended.

O'Connor and Ammen (1997) note that any improvement in the child or adolescent's functioning has to be understood and effected within the context of the child or adolescent's ecosystem. Individual therapy offers the child or adolescent the opportunity to identify and highlight his or her "strengths, talents and capabilities in ways that allow important people in the child's life to recognize and value them," but for the child to overcome adversities, the adults in his or her life must be willing to supply the "help and understanding" and accommodation that will allow the child to develop a sense of mastery (Katz, 1997, p. 136). Thus, brief individual therapy with children and adolescents requires collaboration with all relevant participants in the ecosystem and coordination of services among the professional helpers. Clinicians may feel that, given the time constraints of brief therapy, a multisystem approach is unrealistic, but in reality work with the school, health care system, juvenile justice system, or social support network can actually shorten treatment time, help to consolidate therapy gains, and prevent relapses, because children tend to be very responsive to changes in their environments.

Brief Child Therapy

James G, a 6-year-old boy, was referred by his HMO primary care physician for evaluation of academic and behavioral problems. Mrs. G had consulted the doctor on the advice of James's teacher, who was concerned that James would not be ready to move to the first grade from the intermediate class he had been placed in because of behavior problems. Although he appeared capable of good academic performance, his performance was compromised by low frustration tolerance, poor concentration, inability to complete work, inability to follow rules, a high activity level, and verbal and physical aggressiveness toward other children. Other children shunned him in school and at home. James was repeatedly excluded from extracurricular activities in school, such as field trips, and he had been asked to leave several preschool, after-school, and summer programs and Sunday school.

James was evaluated by the child study team when he was in kindergarten. He was found to be of average intelligence and had received a tentative diagnosis of attention-deficit/hyperactivity disorder. He was not placed on medication, but it was recommended that he be placed in the intermediate class, between kindergarten and first grade, a more structured environment with a lower student-teacher ratio. Mrs. G reported that James had always been an active but manageable child until he entered preschool at age three, when he began exhibiting aggressive, defiant behavior. This was also a period of turmoil in the home as both Mr. and Mrs. G were abusing cocaine. When James was 4, his father was incarcerated for selling drugs, and when he was 5, James was hit by a car, resulting in serious injury to one leg that now requires a brace.

James is the younger of Mrs. G's two children. She has an older son, who is 17 and currently not in school. Mrs. G, age 34, has been steadily employed as a secretary for the past 10 years, except for a period of 6 months when she entered a drug rehabilitation program. She has been in recovery for a year and is strongly committed to her recovery and her attendance at NA. She receives considerable support from other members of NA. In fact, a male friend from the group accompanied them to the intake session to watch James. Her mother and siblings are also supportive, but they had difficulty dealing with James and, therefore, Mrs. G could only count on child care when she was attending a NA meeting.

James and his mother were first seen together for a family evaluation. James was seen alone, and then his mother was interviewed for a developmental history and treatment planning. James's out-of-bounds behavior was evident immediately in the joint interview. He came in without difficulty, sat down, and started to work on his homework. However, he became frustrated when he was not able to do a homework assignment on his first attempt. He snapped the pencil, threw it away, and cursed. Mrs. G appeared embarrassed, exasperated, and uncertain about how to respond except to admonish him for this behavior. However, she remained calm and gentle with him during this episode. In discussing the reason for the referral, Mrs. G talked about James's teacher (Ms. T) being concerned about James not being ready for first grade, even though he was bright and capable of doing first-grade work. Mrs. G said she agreed with the teacher that James is bright and that she was as puzzled as Ms. T about why he was having so much difficulty in school since he wasn't a problem at home. However, Mrs. G respected his teacher's judgment that James should be evaluated because Ms. T had tried hard to help him, without success. James volunteered that he was mad at his teacher because he had not been allowed to go on a school trip that day. When asked about some of the things he and his mother enjoyed doing together, James talked about going to the park and going out to eat, while Mrs. G mentioned their nightly bedtime story and playing board games together.

First Session: Evaluation (James G)

James was comfortable with his mother leaving the room for a separate evaluation. The room had been prepared for him by removing all the toys and games but paper, markers, play dough, and a toy hospital.

WORKER: *James, would you like to draw? (He didn't answer, but opened the play dough can instead. He didn't try to make anything, but mostly pounded and pushed the dough in an aggressive manner.) It looks like you are still mad? (no answer) Are you still mad about the field trip?*
JAMES: *Ms. T promised that I could go, but then she said I had to get off the bus and stay in the office. (Worker: Why?) Eric was starting trouble with me again. He sat in my seat, so I pushed him out.*
WORKER: *So, you had to stay behind because you pushed Eric? (James nods his head, more in sadness than in anger.) I can see that made you sad missing out on the trip.*

JAMES: *Eric keeps bothering me. I'm going to have to hurt him.*
WORKER: *You really wanted to go on the trip today. Maybe one of the things you and I could talk about is what to do when someone like Eric is bothering you, so you don't keep losing out on class trips. Well, we know Eric is a problem, but who do you like in your class? Who do you play with at recess?*
JAMES: *I like to play with Ronald, but he doesn't always want to play. (Worker: Anybody else?) No, those kids just like to mess with me. (He noticed the duck the therapist had made out of the play dough and wanted to make one, too.)*
WORKER: *Recess is a lot more fun if there is someone to play with. Maybe this is something else you and I could figure out—how you can get to play more with other kids. That's a nice-looking duck you made. Shall we make a pond to put them in to swim? (James flattened a piece of dough to make a pond.) James, if you could make three wishes for anything at all you wanted, what would you wish for?*
JAMES: *A Nintendo and Ronald could come over to play after school. (Worker: You have one more wish.) I wish I could go to camp and go swimming.*
(James moved over to the cabinet, where he began playing with the toy hospital.)
JAMES: *What's this (pointing to the stretcher)?*
WORKER: *That's the stretcher. That's what people lie in when they get hurt and need to go to the hospital. It goes inside the ambulance.*
JAMES: *Oh yeah. I rode in an ambulance once. I had to go to the hospital for my leg (pulls up his pant leg to display his leg brace). I got hit by a car.*
WORKER: *What a scary, awful thing to happen to a little guy (James says emphatically "yeah"). What's it like now with the brace? Are you able to run and play?*
JAMES: *I can run, but not as fast as the other kids.*
At this point, James became intensely involved in repeatedly placing a doll in the stretcher, fastening it, and taking it to the hospital in the ambulance. His level of absorption in the activity was high and he was minimally communicative, stating only in response to a question about who was going to the hospital that they were kids who got hurt. He nodded his head affirmatively when a comment was made about the kids being scared. By the end of this play, there was a change in demeanor. He seemed less tense and brittle and calmer as he headed out to sit in the waiting area while his mother was interviewed.

Intake Interview with Parent (Mrs. G)

WORKER: *I enjoyed meeting with James. He really is quite an engaging kid, the way he gets so intensely involved in activities and can talk so easily about what he's thinking. My impression matches his teacher's, which is that he is a bright boy.*

MRS. G: *Really! You enjoyed him! All I ever hear is what a terror he is. Nobody but me seems to enjoy him (tears filled her eyes).*

WORKER: *I can see that this makes you sad. What in particular makes you so sad?*

MRS. G: *It makes me sad that James is so bright and he's probably going to end up in a special ed class. I thought James would be my child to do well in school. I could see when he was little that he was so quick to learn new things. I thought that he would be the one to finish school, maybe go to college. Damien never liked school. I was real upset when he dropped out of school. I didn't want him to end up like his father, but I knew school was hard for him. I don't know why James can't behave himself in school, why he can't get his work done.*

WORKER: *I can see now why it was so important for you to come in at this time. Worrying about James being placed in a special education class when you had such dreams for him has to make this a tough time for you. I think you, Ms. T, and I see the school situation the same way. It looks like James has the ability to do the schoolwork, but the fact that he gets so easily frustrated and distracted and doesn't know how to get along with other kids keeps him from succeeding in school. I have the impression that James is baffled, too. He wants to get along with other kids, but he doesn't seem to know how to do it. What we all want is to figure out how to help him with this behavior, but to do that I am going to need to hear from you a little bit more about what things are like with him at home and some more about his earlier life before we come up with a plan.*

Mrs. G at this point provided the above developmental history and information about his relationship with his father (he has seen his father little since his father's incarceration). Treatment options were then discussed.

WORKER: *As I said before, I think we are all in agreement that James's behavior problems are interfering with his academic performance. However, there are several problem behaviors, so we need to choose where we want to begin working. It appears from our discussion that the problem that is of most concern to you is his failure to complete his schoolwork, so I would suggest we start there. How does that seem to you?*

MRS. G: *I think that's a good idea. Ms. T said that if he paid attention to his work and got it done and stopped fighting with other kids he could go on to first grade. I don't want him placed in special ed.*

WORKER: *In talking to James, it appears that he very much wants to have friends and to be able to go on school trips. We can ask him which one he wants to work on first when we bring him in. In terms of finding ways to help him complete his work, we should consider medication as a way of helping him to focus and pay attention better. However, I would like to wait a while on that, because I'd like to observe him a little longer to see if another form of treatment might be helpful to him. One of the things I could see today is that James is a very anxious, worried kid. It appears that some of this anxiety is tied to his accident, so I would like to see if having some time to talk about what happened to him might be helpful.*

MRS. G: *You think that he might still be bothered by the accident?*

WORKER: *It certainly is possible, given how serious and frightening an event it was. It would be hard for an adult to handle, but for a 4-year-old you could expect that it would be harder for them to deal with it.*

MRS. G: *He has mentioned it from time to time, but we never really talked about it, except when it was time to see the doctor about his leg. Do you think I should talk to James about the accident?*

WORKER: *You can certainly let him know that he can talk to you about this. There may be a children's book that deals with this subject. Let me check this out for you. So we are going to wait a bit before we consider medication. In the meantime, I'd like to meet with Ms. T and set up a plan for helping James to complete his work. It will be a plan that will give James rewards for focusing and sticking to a task. After we set that up, you and I will discuss how you can follow the same plan at home. How does this all sound to you?*

MRS. G: *It sounds good to me. I just didn't realize that James could still be bothered by the accident.*

WORKER: *Well, kids seem to bounce back so quickly. They go right back to playing, so it's not easy to see that they might be bothered, until they start having some sort of behavior problem. When we start meeting regularly for the 15 sessions your benefits package allows, about half of the time I will be meeting with James alone to help him with his worries about being safe. Let's invite James in to discuss what we are planning to do. (James indicated that he wanted to work on going on a field trip, which we would begin working on the next session.)*

The treatment that followed this session was primarily a Level I intervention in that it emphasized behavior modification, social skill development, and resource development, but there was also an expressive play therapy component related to the resolution of the Post-traumatic Stress Disorder. Weekly objectives on the control of aggression, frustration tolerance, concentration, and staying on task were addressed through behavior modification plans. These plans were coordinated between the NA baby-sitting group, the school, and

Assessment–Intervention Exercise with a Child: Jessica

Use the following vignette to answer the questions in this exercise.

Jessica, an 8-year-old girl, was brought by her maternal grandmother for an evaluation because she was becoming increasingly socially withdrawn and mute. The quality of her schoolwork was also declining, and she was exhibiting a number of tics. The symptoms began 2 months before, after Jessica and her younger sister witnessed the death of their father. He managed to push them out of the way before being struck and killed by a speeding automobile as they were crossing the street. Although Jessica's parents were divorced, she and her sister spent every weekend with their father. They attended their father's funeral, but his death has been little discussed since then. Prior to the accident, Jessica appeared to be developing normally and to be doing well socially and academically.

The girls are taken care of by their grandmother while their mother works, and they are quite attached to her. The grandmother and girls are actively involved with their church, and in this environment Jessica is less symptomatic; that is, her tic movements are less frequent. Jessica continues to enjoy reading, but has come to prefer this solitary activity to playing with her sister and friends.

1. *With a 12-session limit, design a multisystem, multimodal crisis intervention plan that will address the PTSD and bereavement issues.*
2. *How could family and community resources be used to aid in the trauma recovery process?*
3. *What play therapy techniques could be employed to help Jessica process the trauma and loss of her father?*
4. *How could Jessica's areas of competency be used to help in the processing of the trauma and loss?*

Answers to this exercise appear in the Appendix.

---

home. James met his first goal of attending a field trip. As James was able to join an after-school program and summer camp, these programs were incorporated into the behavior modification plans. The play therapy sessions initially centered on the trauma, with James using the toy hospital to work through the trauma and his fears about his safety and his family members' safety. Later the focus shifted to social skill development.

There was steady progress in treatment, in large part due to Mrs. G's affection and commitment to her son as well as the support and cooperation of the teacher and NA members. The play therapy appeared to lead to a significant reduction in anxiety, which in turn enabled James to better meet the behavioral objectives. Treatment occurred over a 6-month period. After James met his long-range goals of being promoted to first grade and being able to attend camp, treatment was phased out. The follow-up session and telephone calls through the first 6 months of first grade found James performing well academically and getting along well with classmates.

Summary

A number of changes in the conceptualizations of stress reactions, coping responses, and resiliency have altered approaches to working with families and children, particularly in time-limited work. In addition, there have been paradigm shifts in policy and practice methodology resulting from parental demands for help that is nonjudgmental, flexible, and responsive to parents' need for concrete assistance with emotional and behavioral problems. Consequently, brief treatment with children and families is a strengths-based, reality- and action-oriented, multisystem approach to practice. The Levels of Intervention model for working briefly with families and children was outlined in this chapter, and the use of the model over the course of treatment was illustrated with case examples of work with children and adolescents.

Recommended Reading

Berg, I. K. (1994). *Family based services: A solution-focused approach.* New York: W. W. Norton.

Katz, M. (1997). *On playing a poor hand well.* New York: W. W. Norton.

Kilpatrick, A. C., & Holland, T. P. (1995). *Working with families: An integrative model by level of functioning.* Needham Heights, MA: Allyn & Bacon.

Webster-Stratton, C., & Herbert, M. (1994). *Troubled families, problem children.* New York: J. Wiley & Sons.

WORKING BRIEFLY WITH COMPLEX CLINICAL PROBLEMS: COMMUNITY MENTAL HEALTH CARE

Introduction

Community mental health care has been an evolving treatment paradigm during the second half of the 20th century. Its central premise is the public health concept that the chronicity of psychiatric disorders could be prevented through provision of comprehensive mental health services to targeted populations or communities. The central premise has endured, but the philosophy and modes of service delivery have changed (Breakey, 1996). This chapter examines the evolution of community mental health care to provide both the context and rationale for the brief treatment approaches advocated for working with complex problems that have traditionally been treated on a longer term basis. Treatment issues related to severe and persistent mental disorder, culturally sensitive practice, and dual disorders will be examined in this chapter. The brief treatment of depression will be examined in greater depth, since this disorder is a significant treatment issue in each field of practice. The brief treatment models relevant to community mental health work—that is, crisis intervention, psychoeducation, combined biological and psychosocial therapies, and phased interventions—will be described. The brief treatment principles and techniques of working with complicated clinical problems will then be demonstrated in the treatment of three clients, one with schizophrenia and multiple substance abuse, one with borderline personality disorder, and the third with major depression.

History of Community Mental Health Care

In the three decades since the formation of the community mental health care system, the clinical population served has come to include more vulnerable clients with more complicated problems. As a consequence of deinstitutionalization and federal laws stipulating services to vulnerable populations, clients with severe and persistent mental illnesses or with dual disorders of mental illness and substance abuse complicated by other stressors such as medical illness, poverty, unemployment, racism, immigration, old age, and homelessness now represent the majority of clients being served by community mental health centers (CMHCs).[1] Such centers were originally conceived of in 1963 under the Community Mental Health Centers Act as being part of a network of comprehensive services that would enable hospitalized individuals with mental illness to return to their families for care within their communities and would provide services to families, children, and adults suffering from stress-related disorders (Breakey, 1996). However, 15 years after this legislation was passed, a presidential commission found that many vulnerable groups were either not being served or were underserved—for example, the poor, minorities, and people with chronic mental illness. In response to this report, the National Mental Health Systems Act of 1980 (Public Law 99-660) mandated that services to these groups become priorities for the community mental health system.

The decades of the 1980s and 1990s also brought changes in the political system and health care delivery systems. There was a move away from federal and state funding for mental health services toward managed mental health care. This has placed community mental health care systems under greater pressure to deliver services in a more cost effective and efficient manner and to seek alternative sources of funding, particularly through participating in managed mental health care provider networks. The mandate to serve clients with severe and persistent mental disorders while at the same time meeting current requirements for cost efficiency and accountability has meant that CMHCs had to shift from expressive, insight-oriented psychotherapeutic methods that had been favored in the first two decades of their existence to more activist, problem-solving, brief, and crisis intervention methods (McGovern, Lyons, & Pomp, 1990).

Planned brief treatment has always been a part of the repertoire of interventions employed in community mental health centers. Short-term inpatient care and 24-hour emergency crisis intervention services were two of the five essential services that CMHCs were required to provide under the Community Mental Health Centers Act of 1963 (the other three services were consultation, education, and day treatment) (Hargrove, 1992). In addition, the mandate to provide mental health services to everyone in designated catchment areas meant that there was a significant increase in the number of people seeking mental health services. To serve this increase in clients and to reduce waiting lists, CMHCs were pioneers in the development of brief treatment models. However, until recently, the preferred mode of treatment for most mental health center clinicians, who by and large were psychodynamically trained, was long-term treatment. "Most of these centers were staffed by people who were much more interested in insight-oriented psychotherapy with neurotics than in

---

[1] Acronyms introduced in this chapter: CMHC, community mental health center; NIMH, National Institute of Mental Health; BPD, borderline personality disorder; CI, crisis intervention; CES-D, Center for Epidemiologic Studies Depression Scale; SIS, Suicide Intent Scale; IPT, interpersonal therapy; SSRIs, selective serotonin reuptake inhibitors.

case management or rehabilitation of schizophrenics" (Cutler, 1992, p. 8). Consequently, CMHCs have had to train their staffs in new intervention strategies as they transformed their clinical management (as well as marketing, operations, and financial management) strategies to address the changes in clientele and in funding (Hargrove, 1992).

Service Delivery and Practice Methods

Meeting the needs of underserved, vulnerable groups required CMHCs to make changes in the type of treatment programs offered by community mental health care systems and the ways in which these services were delivered, and to reformulate intervention strategies. To meet the treatment needs of people with chronic mental illness, for example, there needed to be a recognition of the biological and social dimensions of psychiatric disorders. That is, the existing psychotherapy services were not set up to deal with clients who were taking medications with significant side effects, had many complicating medical problems, were self-medicating with addictive substances, and lacked adequate living situations and family and community supports (Pollack & Cutler, 1992). These clients were at high risk for relapse and repeated hospitalizations because they tended to be inconsistently compliant with treatment, were highly vulnerable to stress, lived stressful lives, and were nonresponsive to traditional passive methods of treatment (Santos, Henggler, Burns, Arana, & Meisler, 1995).

The needs of people with chronic mental illness are generally long term, but the question is whether the need is for long-term psychotherapy or whether other treatment modalities are more appropriate. Research, in fact, has indicated that intensive psychotherapy might have adverse effects on individuals struggling with schizophrenia (Drake & Sederer, 1986). Meanwhile, community-based psychosocial rehabilitation and psychoeducational interventions were proving effective in reducing hospitalizations, improving treatment compliance, and improving clients' quality of life (Primm, 1996). Moreover, as the biological origins of severe psychiatric disorders became better understood, the emphasis in treatment shifted from uncovering the psychological origins of the illness to stabilizing the individual on medication and assisting in his or her adaptation to the illness (Eaton, 1996). The appropriate, empirically derived psychotherapy for severe and persistent mental illness thus came to be defined as short term, intermittent, across the lifespan, and active; focused on immediate problems in living; and directed toward enhancing competencies for remaining in the community (Rothman, 1994).

Practice Models

The changes in practice models and delivery methods for people with chronic mental illness were predicated upon paradigm shifts in etiologic and behavioral theories of mental illness. Linear causality etiologic models, such as the psychogenic or adverse early childhood experiences model, have been replaced by interactive, biopsychosocial models of severe and persistent mental disorders. Thus, the diathesis/stress or vulnerability/stress etiologic model and the ecological model of behavior have become the dominant paradigms influencing practice approaches with vulnerable clients. The vulnerability/stress model postulates that the symptoms of mental disorders are likely to become manifest when relevant stress factors intersect with vulnerability factors to overwhelm the individual's coping capacities (Falloon & Fadden, 1993). Vulnerability can be any factor (genetic propensity, cognitive style, trauma history, etc.) that predisposes an individual to develop a particular disorder, but it is the interaction between genetic vulnerability and stresses that has the greatest implications for mental health services for people with chronic mental illness.

In addition, individuals with a predisposition to severe and persistent mental disorders have an increased vulnerability to responding symptomatically to negative life events and everyday life stresses. The first implication of the vulnerability/stress model for treatment of clients with chronic mental illness was that management of stresses as a way of preventing relapses needed to be emphasized. Increasing the repertoire of coping skills of people with chronic mental illness has been found to reduce the chances of a stress-induced relapse (Wallace & Liberman, 1996). Crisis intervention at times when the individual shows prodromal signs of becoming overwhelmed by stresses was also found effective in reducing the incidence of rehospitalization (Eaton, 1996).

According to this conceptual framework, the clinician's primary role is to support and empower the client to optimize his or her areas of strength and functioning and to maximize the client's social support system as a buffer against stresses. As Gunderson (1997) describes it, the therapist's role is that of a clinician-manager helping patients to manage their daily lives and to deal with problems such as an inadequate living situation, lack of social supports, inadequate vocational and social skills, and so on. Therefore, adequate treatment plans for this clinical population requires a combination of biological, psychological, and social interventions individualized for each client.

Another implication of the vulnerability/stress model is that effective stress management is considered a lifelong process that generally will require a consistent case management approach that addresses the medical, psychological, vocational, and housing needs of vulnerable clients. Finally, there is an appreciation for the reciprocal nature of the mental illness and environmental stresses. That is, the client's illness is stressful for family members and others in the client's work and social environments. They may react to the illness in ways that create additional stresses for the client. Therefore, stress management interventions should include family members and should encompass skills for coping with work and interpersonal stresses (Falloon & Fadden, 1993).

The ecological framework postulates that behavior is a function of the continuous, reciprocal interactions between person and environment. Each transaction between person and environment presents risks and opportunities that can result in adaptation or disequilibrium and dysfunction. When there is a goodness of fit between person and environment, a niche is created within which the individual can function competently (Germain, 1991). One of the consequences of the adoption of the ecological model of behavior for program planning, service delivery, and intervention strategies with vulnerable populations is the dual focus on improving individual competencies and remediating or enhancing environmental resources. Therapy or counseling is not focused on insight or emotional or personality growth but on helping the client to function competently in his or her community through gaining skills in living—for example, social, vocational, and daily living skills. Furthermore, the clinician works not just at the individual (micro) level, but serves to link the client to resources and support at the family or community (meso and macro) levels (Rothman, 1994).

Case management and multiple helpers are characteristic of an ecologically informed practice model. Also characteristic are targeting of the community for mental health intervention (Breakey, 1996) and a community-based approach to mental health service delivery. Thus, at CMHCs the emphasis in service delivery is on maintaining clients in their communities through outpatient day treatment, supervised residential programs, and crisis intervention services. With the more recent community support programs developed under National Institute of Mental Health (NIMH) grants, there is an even greater emphasis on community-based services. Thus, the central treatment components of programs such as the Assertive Community Treatment program are crisis intervention and intensive care services, outreach services, mobile treatment teams, and supervised residential treatment programs (Falloon & Fadden, 1993).

Services to Culturally Diverse Groups

Ethnic minorities were another population group that was identified in the 1978 Presidential Commission on Mental Health report as being underserved. To meet their needs for mental health services, it was necessary to reformulate practice approaches and means of delivering service. This reformulation took into account language and cultural differences and a general reluctance of members of these groups to seek mental health services. Several factors were identified as contributing to certain ethnic minority groups not utilizing services and to the high rates of attrition for other ethnic minorities after entering the community mental health system. This underutilization was especially significant in view of the fact that these groups might be expected to be experiencing higher rates of stress-related disorders, given the multiple stressors in their lives.

Among the factors cited as contributing to this service delivery problem were language and cultural differences, preference for family or community resources, distrust of professional institutions, inaccessibility of services, the stigma attached to mental health services, and therapist discomfort in working with ethnic minority clients (Primm, Lima, & Rowe, 1996). However, the reason most often cited is that misunderstanding and miscommunications arise because clinicians are not familiar with the values and life experiences of ethnic minority groups since their training was primarily developed for members of the dominant culture. Consequently, several assumptions of clinical social work may need to be reassessed, such as "relying mainly on verbal skills in the language of the host society, focussing on the individual client who is expected to express problems and feelings and then arrive at a satisfactory solution using our help" (Legault, 1996, p. 65). Otherwise, ethnic minority clients may continue to find mental health services disempowering or unhelpful.

Several changes in program design and service delivery at CMHCs have been proposed or put into place to remove some of these barriers to service. Changes include a shift from institutional delivery of services to community-based services. The ideal in service delivery for these populations is to locate such services within or near existing community agencies, schools, shopping centers, and general health settings, and within easy proximity to public transportation (Land, Nishimoto, & Chau, 1988). Since they are frequently consulted first, community leaders, primary health care providers, and family members are considered key to linking minority individuals with the mental health system and to sustaining them in treatment (Primm et al., 1996).

The informal support system is very important in ethnic minority, immigrant, and poor communities because there tends to be a high degree of interconnectedness within the social support network. This means that emotionally distressed people turn first to family and community members for help. Family members provide information, advice, or support, or the distressed individual will consult traditional healers until such time as the individual's distress or distressing behavior overwhelms the family's ability to cope with the behavior. Family members may then play a key role in getting the individual to the mental health center or field office. They may pool financial resources to pay for the service and provide the instrumental and emotional help to continue in treatment (Land et al., 1988). The primary care health provider is also considered a key individual because help for distress is often sought first from the medical sector. This is because emotional distress is frequently expressed somatically in ethnic minority groups, and traditional beliefs about illness and treatment often stress organic or somatic causes for emotional distress (Rogler & Cortes, 1993).

Hiring bilingual and minority therapists and other staff has been another important way of removing barriers to service at CMHCs. Besides facilitating the engagement process with minority clients, linguistic and cultural congruity is likely to result in more accurate assessments and rapport in treatment (Primm et al., 1996). However, since matching client and worker by ethnicity is not always a realistic goal, and outcome studies on the effectiveness of matching have been inconclusive, there has been greater emphasis on training clinicians to gain a measure of cultural competency. To avoid an ethnocentric bias in assessment and diagnosis and problems in establishing a good working alliance, clinicians are now being trained to become aware of their own cultural beliefs, assumptions, and values (worldview) and the ways this worldview may differ from that of clients from diverse backgrounds. "The first step in training consists of lectures or courses aimed at informing . . . practitioners in the numerous life-styles that make up human experience. A simple awareness of different child-raising methods, marriage forms, social organization, and world views contributes greatly toward removing ethnocentric blinders" (Westermeyer, 1993, p. 140).

Ethnically Sensitive Assessment and Intervention

Misdiagnoses and ineffective treatment plans are additional problems that have complicated the delivery of community mental health services to ethnically and socioeconomically diverse populations. Cross-cultural assessment models have been developed to ensure a greater degree of accuracy in the assessment and diagnosis process. The *Diagnostic and Statistical Manual of Mental Disorders* (American Psychiatric Association, 1994), for example, has included an Outline for Cultural Formulation and a Glossary of Culture-Bound Syndromes in its fourth edition, and Ramirez (1991) in *Psychotherapy and Counseling with Minorities* offers an assessment model that takes into account acculturation and cultural identity issues.

These assessment models direct attention to the cross-cultural dimensions that influence the clinical picture and the coping capacities the client can bring to resolving these difficulties. Information is gathered about (1) the client's cultural explanations of his or her distress, illness, or problems; (2) the stresses associated with migration, acculturation, and socioeconomic status; (3) the supports or stresses in the client's social environment; and (4) the degree of adherence to traditional norms with regard to gender roles, family relationships, social hierarchies, and spirituality (Corcoran & Vandiver, 1996).

Knowledge about cross-cultural variations in symptom presentation and culturally specific syndromes is also crucial to arriving at an accurate diagnosis. For example, it is important to know that somatic complaints are more common as signs of depression with many ethnic minority individuals than the cognitive and affective signs and symptoms emphasized in most depression inventories. Secondly, since recent immigrants and those who are more traditional in culture are likely to express their distress in culturally determined ways, it is worthwhile for the clinician to become acquainted with common cultural syndromes. Two examples of commonly occurring illnesses among Latinos are *susto,* a state of fright with symptoms similar to PTSD, and *ataque de nervios,* a state of distress in which the person feels out of control. Finally, errors in judgment can be reduced if the clinician is also aware of the possible range of differences in the presentation of self with regard to eye contact and verbal and emotional expressiveness (Westermeyer, 1993).

A culturally sensitive assessment should result in a treatment plan that makes sense to the client and fits his or her expectation of help. For example, there is a better chance for treatment and medication compliance if a family modality is employed with ethnic minority clients, many of whom have an interdependent view of relationships and respect for a strong family hierarchy. Thus, therapy that is centered upon the interactions between family members and provides the whole family with a framework for understanding and managing illness is likely to be more intelligible to and supported by the client's family members (Yamamoto, Silva, Justice, Chang, & Leong, 1993).

For clients who adhere to traditional health beliefs and practices, indigenous health care providers can be consulted and incorporated into community mental health programs and individual treatment plans. The indigenous healers and religious practices often provide tension and stress relief and could be combined with interventions that normalize and explain stress reactions and offer instrumental help in dealing with stressors such as housing, employment, health care, and so on (Land et al., 1988). Home visiting, referral to existing community mutual-aid groups, and liaison work with community leaders to inform them about and collaborate with them on community mental health programs can serve to reduce the stigma of using CMHCs and can provide early intervention and prevention services (Primm et al., 1996).

Since it is not possible to gain more than a superficial knowledge of the many ethnic groups in this country, most models of cross-cultural practice place more emphasis on the elimination of ethnocentric biases and the development of a receptive attitude toward other cultures. Other approaches to ethnically sensitive practice eschew culture-specific techniques in favor of relatively culture-free interventions, such as cognitive-behavioral or self-help strategies (Ramirez, 1991). Sue and Zane (1987) also recommend that "presumed" culture-specific techniques be discarded because they are likely to be applied in oversimplified or inappropriate ways. Instead, they recommend that clinicians employ interventions that will give immediate relief or an immediate gain so that skeptical minority clients will be persuaded that this form of help will meet their needs. In general, the evidence suggests that therapy that is brief, active, and focused is a better match for ethnic minority clients because it fits their expectations of help.

Services for Dual-Disordered Clients

Individuals suffering from both psychiatric disturbance and substance abuse came to be identified in the 1980s as a group whose needs were not fully understood and for whom existing services were not very effective. Two societal forces came together that had begun in the 1970s: deinstitutionalization of people with chronic mental illness and the upsurge in availability and use of illegal drugs. CMHCs struggled to treat clients who were difficult to diagnose, resisted treatment except in crisis, and had high rates of hospitalization and attrition (Ryglewicz & Pepper, 1992). In addition to being difficult to engage in treatment, the dually disordered client presented with more at-risk behaviors due to negative and complicating interactions between the mental illness and the substance abuse. In this population there was a higher incidence of volatile, violent, and criminal behaviors as well as self-endangering behaviors. Dual-disordered clients also had more difficulty than those with single disorders in managing money and employment, and they were more likely to have unstable living arrangements and to become homeless (Drake, Osher, & Bartels, 1996).

Among the changes that took place to better serve the dually diagnosed client was an integration of mental health and substance abuse treatment systems that had developed separately and that individually were not effectively addressing the needs of these clients. This prompted the direction in community mental health toward (1) greater coordination between mental health and substance abuse programs, (2) location of dual-disorder services within each system, and (3) development of separate dual-disorder units (Ryglewicz & Pepper, 1992).

With the changes in program structure, there has also been a change in the principles of service delivery and in intervention strategies with dual-disordered clients. In service delivery, there is a greater emphasis on an activist role for clinicians and on enhancement of client competency. For example, clients who are trying to manage their feelings and social interactions by means of substance abuse are helped to develop alternative coping strategies. The clinician in the dual-diagnosis program actively intervenes by conducting outreach efforts to identify and reach dual-disordered clients, by monitoring and promoting treatment adherence, and by providing instrumental help and linkage to community support services (Hunter, 1995). There is now a recognition in program planning that comprehensive services such as transitional-living housing, education, and vocational training are needed in order to provide the structure and stability in these clients' lives that are essential to recovery and functioning within the community (Ryglewicz & Pepper, 1992).

Drake et al. (1996) indicate that research and clinical experience support a longitudinal, stages-of-treatment model for working with dually disordered clients, as opposed to the more traditional intensive inpatient stay with minimal follow-up. The stages-of-treatment approach addresses the chronic, relapsing nature of both substance abuse and mental illness and ensures that the appropriate interventions are applied at different points in the recovery and stabilization process. The stages identified by Drake et al. are (1) engagement, where the focus is on the establishment of a trusting relationship; (2) persuasion, in which the client is assisted in identifying and understanding the adverse consequences of his or her symptoms and substance use; (3) treatment, in which the client's efforts toward change are supported and advanced; and (4) relapse prevention. This model for treatment of dual disorders clearly has much in common with the Prochaska-DiClemente model of motivation to change.

The intervention strategies that have evolved for working with dually diagnosed clients are similar to the motivational interviewing techniques that Miller developed for working with substance abusers. These intervention strategies, unlike the traditional alcoholism treatment methods, are nonconfrontational; instead, they are educational, supportive, and empowering (Sciacca, 1997). At the same time, the clinician is also more active, functioning more in a case management than a therapeutic mode—for example, providing information and feedback about the negative interplay between mental illness and substance abuse while teaching skills such as stress management or interpersonal relationship management (Ryglewicz & Pepper, 1992).

In recognition of the obstacles that dual disorders present for engaging and maintaining clients in treatment, and in recognition of the fact that treatment is not available on demand, harm reduction and relapse prevention models have grown more popular. "Sobriety and recovery are always the ultimate goal, but realistic steps along the way to that goal are promoted, such as cutting down on use, encouraging the use of clean needles, . . . and identifying situations that trigger substance craving and employing a type of behavior modification to avoid these situations (relapse prevention)" (Cabaj, 1998, p. 125).

Although "dual disorder" refers to the coexistence of any psychiatric disorder and substance abuse, the term is used most often to emphasize the treatment needs of abusing individuals with the psychiatric (Axis I) disorders of schizophrenia, bipolar disorder, and major depressive disorder. However, the coexistence of substance abuse with personality disorders, particularly antisocial and borderline personality disorders, can result in the same sort of treatment complications as with the major Axis I disorders—that is, resistance to treatment except in crisis, noncompliance, high rates of attrition, and volatile behavior. For this group, as with clients with severe mental illness, the use or abuse of substances is a serious hazard, as it can exacerbate the vulnerability to mood swings, impulsivity, self-destructiveness, suicidality, and brief psychotic episodes that characterize severe personality disorders. Substance use or abuse by these individuals can also precipitate a decline in functioning that may result in loss of job, relationships, housing, and financial stability (Ryglewicz & Pepper, 1992).

This group of dual-disordered clients often presents in crisis. Clients with borderline personality disorder (BPD) are particularly likely to be seen in treatment following a suicide attempt or threat of suicide or after self-destructive, self-mutilating acts. These clients are likely to be perpetually in crisis "because of their rigid and limited repertoire for shouldering stresses, their vulnerability to attachment and abandonment challenges, and their susceptibility to induced and reactive brief psychotic episodes" (Turner, Becker, & DeLoach, 1994, p. 27). Normal or severe life stresses tend to create intolerable feelings of anxiety, anger, fear, or depression that the borderline individual seeks to relieve through drug and alcohol abuse or self-destructive acts.

Brief Treatment of Personality Disorders

Intervention strategies with personality disorders have undergone several changes in recent years, particularly in the case of the client with borderline personality disorder. This type of case will be used in the following discussion to illustrate these changes in strategy and service delivery. As empirical evidence for the origin of BPD in trauma and other knowledge was gained from retrospective studies about the natural course of the illness, there were significant shifts in the treatment approach and methods recommended for use with clients with BPD. Fifteen years ago "borderline psychopathology was conceptualized as a form of personality organization, and virtually all treatments involved long-term psychoanalytic therapies. However, the borderline construct has been revised to the extent that it is now recognized as a form of personality disorder with a complicated biogenetic substrate and multifactorial environmental contributions" (Gunderson, 1997, p. 225). Chief among these environmental contributions was a childhood history of abuse (in about 60% of cases), two-parent psychopathology, and chaotic family life, including separation from or loss of caregivers (Links, Boiagoa, Huxley, Steiner, & Mitton, 1990). Furthermore, BPD clients with such histories were more likely to experience dissociative episodes, to self-mutilate, and to present repeatedly in crisis for treatment (Gunderson & Sabo, 1993).

The implications of this childhood history for the treatment of BPD have been that several nonpsychoanalytic methods of treatment are now recommended as ways to help these clients manage the ambient and extraordinary (often self-initiated) stresses of their lives and to reduce the vulnerabilities that make them highly reactive to stresses. These include all techniques outlined above under crisis intervention (CI), psychoeducation, case management, and social and vocational rehabilitation group work efforts. Many workers favor an approach with clients with BPD that involves differential levels of treatment, with the initial phase of treatment addressing the impulsive, self-destructive, chaotic, crisis-ridden lifestyle of these clients (Koerner & Linehan, 1992; Saunders & Arnold, 1993; Turner et al., 1994; Gunderson & Links, 1996).

In the first level of intervention with clients with BPD, the primary goals are the establishment of a good working alliance and reduction of risk behaviors. Close attention is paid to suicidal, parasuicidal, and impulsive behaviors, substance abuse issues, and destructive relationships; in other words, the focus initially is on safety and stabilization. Cognitive-behavioral interventions related to impulse control, affect dysregulation, interpersonal skill deficits, and stress management are key interventions in the first stage. Case management interventions related to housing, employment, job training, health care, social supports, substance abuse treatment, and coordination of services are also important in this phase of the treatment (Gunderson, 1997). Psychoeducation interventions are particularly important because they help clients with BPD to develop the skills to recognize stresses and personal vulnerabilities that make them prone to react to stress in self-defeating or self-destructive ways. It helps them to gain a sense of control and personal efficacy instead of always feeling victimized or wildly out of control.

For clients with BPD, the second level of intervention, after a solid working alliance has been established and the client's life situation and symptoms have stabilized, is to reduce the lingering effects of childhood abuse and neglect. In this stage, psychodynamic exploratory and expressive methods may be useful, as are cognitive restructuring efforts, particularly around dysfunctional beliefs about relationships and self-in-relationship (Koerner & Linehan, 1992). "In the second stage, the therapist is less a teacher than a witness and ally, helping patients to bear traumatic memories of victimization along with direct or indirect betrayal by nonprotective family members" (Saunders & Arnold, 1993, p. 199). The final stage is devoted to a consolidation of selfhood and a solidification of positive self-esteem and respect for self. It is the period when memories are neither overwhelming nor avoided and a broader view of self beyond victimhood is possible. Clearly, in their initial contacts most clients with BPD will not get beyond the first level of intervention. The usual pattern for clients with BPD is to drop in intermittently for treatment through adolescence and early adulthood and not to be ready to settle into treatment and move beyond crisis intervention work until middle adulthood. As Stone (1990) found in examining the natural course of the illness, clients with BPD tend to do reasonably well once they have survived the turbulence and risk of young adulthood. The stage approach to treatment provides a way of matching interventions to the developmental needs of the client, that is, keeping them alive until the normal developmental processes can occur.

Brief Treatment of Borderline Clinical Problems

Sarah, a 36-year-old administrator, was seen shortly after she was released from the hospital. She had been hospitalized for a suicide attempt following the breakup of her third marriage. Sarah had been hospitalized several times since the age of 18 for suicide attempts related to relationship problems. The current suicide attempt occurred after a month of severe depression in which Sarah was unable to work or attend to pressing financial problems that had been created by her husband. She had been placed on antidepressant medication in the hospital, but she was still significantly depressed and having difficulty functioning at the time of the referral. Sarah had been intermittently in treatment over the past 10 years but had never remained in treatment for long because, as she reported, she had never found the therapy helpful and therefore had never committed herself to it. Her past treatment had focused primarily on her feelings of abandonment and rejection by her mother and husbands and to a lesser degree on sexual abuse by her stepfather and physical abuse by her husbands and boyfriends.

Sarah's husband is an alcoholic who verbally abused and financially exploited her. She is the mother of two teenage children, both of whom are experiencing some emotional and behavioral difficulties. Sarah also exhibited strengths, including intelligence and a capacity for problem solving. She had shown considerable perseverance and ingenuity in getting a college education in spite of her family's lack of support and being a single parent. She had also performed well in her current position and had advanced to a mid-level supervisory position. Although she was estranged from her family, she had a good support network of friends, coworkers, and members of her church.

The following excerpts are from the initial assessment–crisis intervention session and the fourth session of a 13-session treatment course. They illustrate the phased approach to treatment with clients with BPD.

WORKER: *I'm glad you were able to come in today. When you were late, I was concerned, because Dr. W called to say that it was important for you to be seen today.*

SARAH: *(speaking slowly and in a monotone, but well-groomed and attractively dressed) I didn't think I was going to make it in. I didn't think I was going to be able to get out of bed.*

WORKER: *But you did make it. What do you think made it possible for you to get out of bed and get here?*

SARAH: *Well, I can't stay like this. I need help. I've got to go to work. If I don't, I'm going to lose my job. I already got a notice from the director before I was in the hospital that if I didn't go back to work immediately I would be fired.*

WORKER: *Going back to work will be important. We'll talk later about what can be done to help you to return to work. We can get the medical leave form signed for the time that you were in the hospital and let your director know that you are now in treatment here for depression, if you like. That will protect your job for now. (Sarah indicated she wanted to submit the medical leave form.) Before we talk about what we can do to help you with your troubles in getting out of bed, I'd like to learn more about your depression and about your suicide attempt. Do you think about wanting to be dead or about wanting to kill yourself now?*

SARAH: *I think about it sometimes, but not for very long. It's not like it was before when I thought about it all the time, but I feel just as bad as I did then (said with a tone of resentment).*

WORKER: *What's it like for you when you feel bad? What are you thinking about? What are you doing?*

SARAH: *I'm not doing anything. That's the problem. I can't get out of bed. I don't want to get out of bed. I don't know how I'm going to deal with everything I have to deal with, so I just stay in bed.*

WORKER: *What are the things that you have to deal with that you don't think you can handle?*

SARAH: *I have to get back to work, but I can't do it. Even if I don't lose my job, I need to go back to work for the money or I'll lose my house. I owe 3 months on the mortgage and I got a shut-off notice for the gas and electric. My husband didn't pay the bills even though I gave him the money.*

WORKER: *So the major problems that you are dealing with are a depression that makes it difficult for you to get up out of bed and take care of business and your financial problems that make your depression worse. Are these the problems that you would like help with here?*

SARAH: *Yes, but what I really need help with is figuring out what's wrong with me. What am I doing wrong that men always leave me? That's the cause of all my problems. If I could get my husband back, I wouldn't be depressed.*

WORKER: *Could there be other reasons why your husband left? I understand from Dr. W that he had a serious drinking problem.*

SARAH: *He does have a drinking problem. He finally went into the hospital after I had been begging him to do it for a long time, but that's where he met her. She was working at the hospital. He left the hospital and moved in with her. There has to be something wrong with me if he left me for someone he just met. If I could just figure this out, maybe he would come back home.*

WORKER: *Well, we can certainly try to figure out why your relationships haven't worked out for you. Maybe you will want to work on some of the ways you could change in how you relate to men, but we can't work toward a goal of getting your husband back, because this isn't something you have control over. We can only work on things that you can change—you don't look happy with what I've said. Are you angry because I said that we can't make him do anything or because I'm questioning whether he might have left for other reasons than there's something wrong with you?*

SARAH: *I'm angry because you don't seem to get it that there has to be something wrong with me if every one of my husbands has left me.*

WORKER: *I'm glad that you were able to tell me what I was saying that was upsetting to you. You are the expert on your life and if I'm not getting it right, then we need to clear up that misunderstanding right away. So, in addition to the depression and financial crisis, you would like to change some things about your behavior? (Sarah nods her head yes.) Does it make sense to you that we first focus on the things that have to be taken care of right away, like getting you back to work and dealing with your bills?*

SARAH: *Yes. I've got to start taking care of business. My kids are suffering, especially my daughter. She's going to need to be seen here if I don't start taking care of them. My daughter had to call 911 and she's still upset about that.*

WORKER: *Wanting to take care of your children is an important reason to work on solving these problems. Let's start with getting up in the morning. You know from your previous experience with antidepressant medication that it will take a few more weeks before you'll start feeling better, and then taking care of tasks won't be so hard. In the meantime, though, we'll work on other ways to help you to take care of the most pressing problems you're facing. So let's look more closely at what made it possible for you to get up this morning and get here. Did you do anything different than other mornings when you couldn't get up?*

SARAH: *Last night, I asked a friend to call me. She did, and that helped, although it still took me a long time to get up.*

Sarah was then encouraged to use friends and coworkers as supports in the same way so that she could return to work by the following week. Resources in her church and community were employed in the same way to assist her in paying her utilities and to arrange an alternative payment plan for her mortgage. Treatment was scheduled for twice weekly to address the moderate to low level of risk for self-harm, the severity of depression, and the crisis nature of her living situation. Sarah responded well to a crisis intervention, problem-solving approach. Building on her predepression problem-solving skills, she made steady progress with her financial problems and returned to work within a week. However, her black-and-white thinking, particularly with regard to her husband, threatened to undermine the progress she was making. Thus, cognitive therapy techniques were added to prevent revictimization by her husband and to alter Sarah's negative view of herself within relationships, which was prolonging her depression. The excerpt from the fourth session illustrates this.

SARAH: *Keith called last night. He said that I owed him money because he made the last month's payment on my car. I told him I didn't have the money to pay him back because I had to pay the gas and electric and put aside money for the mortgage. (Worker: What did he say?) He got really angry and just started yelling at me.*

WORKER: *You didn't discuss the fact that he spent the money you gave him to pay the mortgage and utilities and what a difficult financial situation that left you in?*

SARAH: *(furious) No! Of course not. It wasn't his fault. He was drinking and didn't know what he was doing. You make it sound like he's to blame for my problems, but I shouldn't have given him the money in the first place.*

WORKER: *It seems like I upset you whenever I raise the possibility that there might be another view of you and your husband. You get angry if I seem not to understand that you are the one at fault and that your husband is blameless. I can appreciate how that would make you upset, because this is the way you have always seen yourself and it's like someone is now telling you that what you have always believed is wrong. But, I wonder if we can move past who's right or wrong about you and Keith and look instead at what happens to you when you think you are at fault. Let's look at last night when Keith called. What happened after you hung up? What were you thinking?*

SARAH: *I was angry with myself that I didn't have the money to give him because of missing a month of work. I kept thinking that he'll never come back if I don't show him I'm different now, that I'm not always screwing up.*

WORKER: *How did you feel when you were thinking this way?*

SARAH: *Depressed. Discouraged. Like nothing is ever going to change. I wanted to get in bed, but my girlfriend called to ask me to pick her up for work because her car is in the shop. We talked for a while about work and then she had to hang up.*

WORKER: *How did you feel at that point?*

SARAH: *(surprised) I actually felt a little better. It took my mind off Keith to talk about work. The two of us are working together on a big project. It's a lot of work, but it's going well.*

WORKER: *Maybe it also felt good to be reminded of what you've been able to accomplish: going back to work while you were still feeling depressed and finding ways to start paying your bills. It appears that when you're thinking bad things about yourself, you feel depressed and hopeless, but when you start thinking about what you've accomplished you feel better.*

SARAH: *I guess that's true. It makes sense to me.*

The rest of the therapy continued to focus on the personal price Sarah was paying for holding onto a view of herself as worthless and of her husband as ideal. The origins of these views in her childhood relationships and adult relationships with men were examined briefly once her job and financial crises diminished. However, the focus of the treatment was on Sarah's current interpersonal interactions, particularly within the therapy. Gradually her view of herself in relationships was restructured. This altered view of self in relationship was evident in her refusal to take her husband back after he had to move out of his girlfriend's home and in her unwillingness to rush into another relationship because she wanted to continue to work on herself. Clearly she had reached the stage in her borderline condition in which she was ready to stay with treatment (she never missed an appointment), move past a crisis-ridden existence, and begin to develop a more positive, realistic view of self. At termination, she was struggling with the impact of her illness on her children but was ready to see how she might handle things on her own until the following year when she would again have psychotherapy benefits. At follow-up Sarah continued to be depression-free and was coping well.

Brief Treatment Models

Crisis Intervention

The preceding description of the community mental health system's mission, clinical populations, and evolving service delivery models and funding challenges provides the context for the following discussion of brief treatment models currently in use or suitable for use in the community mental health system. From this review, it was possible to discern an emerging consensus as to what are effective practice approaches for the types of clinical problems that vulnerable client populations presented. These evolving practice guidelines influenced the selection of the brief treatment approaches presented here. The first brief treatment approach described, the crisis intervention model, is a set of techniques designed to restore functioning or to prevent further sustained decline in functioning in clients who are exhibiting signs that they are being overwhelmed by the psychosocial challenges in their lives. It is a time-limited approach designed for the duration of the client's acute reaction to stresses. It requires active interventions on the part of the clinician and active involvement by the client in the accomplishment of a series of tasks designed to resolve the crisis and increase coping skills (Hepworth, Rooney, & Larsen, 1997).

In view of the fact that clients with severe or persistent mental illness are biologically and psychologically vulnerable to stress and have a number of stressors in their lives, it is not surprising that many of the CMHC clients enter or reenter the system at points of crisis in their lives. Crisis intervention (CI) services had been one of the basic services required by the federal government when the community mental health system was set up. However, the original concept of CI was that it was a means for returning the "ordinarily intact, well-functioning" individual back to his or her previous level of functioning by helping him or her master a "predictable series of coping tasks" (Lukton, 1982, p. 277). In reality, the bulk of the individuals seen in crisis units were people with preexisting psychiatric disorders, some with severe problems in functioning before the stressful events. In addition, the shift in emphasis to serving more vulnerable individuals meant that more clients would be presenting in crisis and that crisis intervention strategies would need to be employed at some point in the course of the treatment (Cutler, 1992).

Although, as Cournoyer (1996) has noted, brief treatment and crisis intervention methods have converged, there remain some distinct features of CI that make it a particularly useful approach for vulnerable clients. These features are (1) the emphasis placed on understanding the nature of the immediate precipitant and its impact on and meaning to the client and (2) a here-and-now focus in treatment aimed at relieving the client's distress and restoring a degree of equilibrium through active, direct interventions at all levels of the client's ecosystem. Given this population's high reactivity to stresses, limited coping strategies, and vulnerability to decompensation, timely and active interventions are needed to keep the client safe and to avoid hospitalization. In *dumb* addition to safety and stabilization goals, crisis intervention presents an opportunity for these clients and their families to learn problem-solving and other coping skills, to learn about the nature and course of mental illness and how to manage it, and to establish a plan for continuity of care over the client's lifetime, including connecting the client with community support resources (Falloon & Fadden, 1993).

Typical crisis situations for this clinical population include situations of self-harm and suicidal actions, hostile or aggressive behaviors, clashes with the law, onset or relapse of psychiatric symptoms or substance abuse, a decreasing ability to manage the daily tasks of living, and loss of domicile. Sometimes the request for help represents the inability of the client's family or support system to continue to cope with the client's symptoms or behaviors. The precipitant to a crisis may have been an accumulation of stresses, a significant loss event, or a disruption in their lives, such as a change in relationships or loss of employment (Perris & Skagerlind, 1994).

The first tasks in crisis intervention are to rapidly establish rapport with the client in crisis and to get an accurate assessment of the dimensions of the problem—that is, what is distressing to the client and why; what the consequences are for the client and family of the stressful, precipitating event and the client's reactions to it; and what it will take to restore equilibrium. Falloon and Fadden (1993) stress the extreme importance of rapidly establishing rapport in working with clients with major psychiatric disturbance because they often present in a panic or cognitively disorganized state and are feeling coerced into coming to treatment. Bellak (1992, p. 83) describes this as the need to connect with the client psychologically, "to throw him an anchor that will buoy him, make him feel more secure and understood." If the client is exhibiting psychotic or dysfunctional thinking, the clinician needs to empathize with and validate the client's distress and underlying concerns without either disputing or supporting the client's distortions in thinking.

Falloon and Fadden (1993) also stress the importance of completing a functional assessment and having a problem-based focus to the crisis intervention. The functional assessment determines the key issues that are both contributing to problems in functioning and also are most amenable to rapid resolution. To identify these key issues requires a complete assessment of biological vulnerabilities; psychosocial stressors; the stress-related cognitive, affective, and behavioral impairments; and existing coping strategies. The assessment should also include an evaluation of the caregivers' coping capacities and reactions to the crisis as well as their willingness to become involved in the resolution of the crisis. Involvement of the family or significant others is very important in working with this population because they are considered key to reducing or buffering the stresses that have overwhelmed the client (Bellak, 1992).

The next task for the CI worker, once the details of the crisis situation have been elicited and a tentative case conceptualization and intervention plan have been formulated, is to arrive, jointly with the client and his or her family, at specific strategies for problem resolution. Because of the clients' preexisting vulnerabilities and the severity of their reaction to stresses, the worker initially may have to take an active, directive role in the problem-solving process. The worker guides the client and family in identifying individual and family coping strategies that may not be evident to them at a point of crisis, and the worker will help the family use these strategies to deal with current difficulties (Myer & Hanna, 1996).

Additional CI tasks for this population will be efforts to stabilize the client on medications through referral for evaluation or reevaluation of medication needs and through analysis and remediation of compliance problems. The central CI task is the implementation of the plan of action for resolving the crisis. This plan will generally entail several goals addressing needs at a number of different levels of the client's system. For example, with a suicidal client a series of tasks and problem-solving steps needs to be taken to preserve the client's life. The first is to restore hope by expanding the client's alternatives to suicide and by offering alternative solutions to problems—that is, restructuring the client's helpless and hopeless cognitions. Other types of problem-solving steps that can be taken in suicide management include developing effective deterrents; removing means for committing suicide; reducing stresses, particularly interpersonal stresses, while increasing support through therapist availability; and enlisting the aid of the client's social support system while providing the client with the tools for crisis management (Reinecke, 1994).

Clients who are having a severe, disorganizing reaction to stresses will likely find it beneficial to have a written, step-by-step problem-solving plan for dealing with at-risk situations, such as when the client is tempted to use drugs or alcohol or engage in self-harming behaviors (Turner, Becker, & DeLoach, 1994). A written contract that spells out agreed-upon tasks for each family member and for the worker can also bring a sense of organization and direction at a time of confusion and demoralization. Once the client is safe and there is a decrease in the level of distress and an improvement in functioning, the tasks are educational. That is, the client and family learn to recognize risk situations, learn to identify signs of impending crisis or decompensation, and learn ways of reducing the severity of stress reactions through stress management techniques (Falloon & Fadden, 1993).

Psychoeducation and Family Work

The psychoeducational approach to family work in the last 20 years has become the preferred method of working with families of clients with severe and persistent mental illness. It has been found to be effective in helping these clients to resolve crisis situations, maintain gains in therapy, and prevent relapses and rehospitalizations. Although originally developed as a response to the needs of families of people with schizophrenia who became the primary caregivers following deinstitutionalization, it has evolved into an approach for working with individuals and families needing lifetime skills in management of an illness or needing living skills. Thus, the psychoeducational approach is used separately or as part of another treatment program with a wide range of presenting problems, from mood disorders to marital conflict and parent-child conflict (Hardley & Guerney, 1989).

Psychoeducation tends to be defined in vague terms that are open to interpretation, but generally speaking it refers to interventions that provide individuals or families with information, skills development, and support. Hardley and Guerney (1989) distinguish psychoeducational approaches from the traditional medical model's approach to psychotherapy as follows. In the medical model, the process of problem resolution begins with defining the problem as an illness that needs to be diagnosed in order to define a prescription for its cure. From the psychoeducational perspective, the problem would be defined as a value or goal choice held by the family or individual such that with instruction the client can be motivated to change to reach a new level of goal satisfaction. Problem resolution is thought of as the acquisition of knowledge and skills rather than the removal of deficits.

Psychoeducational interventions with families of people with mental illness are designed to be time limited. Different programs emphasize different combinations of skill development and support, but all share the goal of helping families to cope better with the illness and the impact of it on their lives. Some programs focus on education about mental illness and relapse prevention. Others promote development of stress reduction and communication and problem-solving skills while providing support around the emotional, financial, and medical stresses families face (Simon, McNeil, Franklin, & Cooperman, 1991). Differing types of structure are used to provide support and education. For example, family members may be seen alone, with the patient, or in multi-family workshops. Marley (1992) advocated for the family and patient to be seen together in order to resolve problems in communication. He also urged a psychoeducational approach that informed the family about the latent content of the patient's communications, so that the family could have a better understanding of the conflicted feelings and thoughts being expressed in the symptoms. The family might then have a greater degree of empathy for the patient and less anger and hostility. A reduction in expressed emotion is considered a desirable outcome, given that high levels of expressed emotion are associated with higher rates of rehospitalization.

When psychoeducation is employed individually with clients with major psychiatric disturbances, the focus is on helping them understand the nature of their illnesses and the role they can play in managing the illness. Clients are educated about the stress/vulnerability model of mental illness—that is, about the relationships between stressors, individual vulnerabilities, coping styles, and symptoms. For example, a client might learn to make the connection between an increase in hallucinations and withdrawing behaviors, his hypersensitivity to criticism, and an encounter when his landlord asked him to mow the lawn. Part of the psychoeducational approach to working with problems related to chronic mental illness involves cognitive restructuring interventions around erroneous beliefs, learning stress management skills such as relaxation training to cope with insomnia, and development of interpersonal skills (Heinssen, Levendusky, & Hunter, 1995).

Interventions need to take place within the context of a therapeutic relationship that is respectful, empathic, validating, and reliable. All of the above treatment approaches have emphasized the importance of establishing a strong working alliance with high-risk clients, who are highly reactive to relationship disruptions (Rothman, 1994). The worker has multiple roles when working in a time-limited fashion with high-risk clients; chief among them are the roles of advocate for clients who have multiple needs and vulnerabilities and facilitator of empowerment—that is, a person who helps the client to learn coping skills, including learning to access resources on his or her own (Klein & Cnaan, 1995). The worker will most often be involved with these clients when they are highly symptomatic and in need of intensive counseling to stabilize them. Thereafter, the long-term management of the illness will be followed by the case manager or by the facility that provides social and vocational rehabilitation. The following case vignette illustrates this approach with a client with severe and persistent mental illness and substance abuse problems.

Combined Treatment Modalities with a Dual-Disordered Client

Neal, a 23-year-old man, was referred for follow-up care after a brief hospitalization for auditory hallucinations that were directing him to kill himself. He presented in the first interview as an extremely anxious, frequently incoherent, but affable young man who wanted to be cooperative in the interview. However, he was too thought disordered to communicate clearly what he was experiencing or how he had been managing since his discharge from the hospital 3 days earlier. Neal had been diagnosed as having schizoaffective and multiple substance abuse disorders. The most recent hospitalization was his sixth since his first psychotic episode when he was 19 years old. This hospitalization followed a period of homelessness and noncompliance with treatment, including discontinuing his medications, that culminated in an emergency room visit for acute suicidal feelings.

Neal was seen over a 6-month period using a time-sensitive format in which sessions were scheduled according to his level of functioning. Initially, a crisis intervention approach was used, with two or three sessions per week due to Neal's state of high distress, his problematic living situation, and his previous multiple failures to engage in treatment. Later, as he stabilized and moved into a long-term case management situation, the sessions were spaced further apart. Staying focused on his concerns and safety needs appeared to help Neal become more organized in thought and speech. Gradually, over the course of two sessions, he was able to identify that his chief concern was about his ability to remain abstinent, particularly since he was living with two drug addicts. He wanted to continue to attend AA, which he had begun attending in the months prior to this hospitalization. Maintaining his recovery and stabilizing his living situation thus became two of the goals of treatment. Neal agreed that his hallucinations had become worse since leaving the hospital and that they posed a significant risk for him. Therefore, another primary goal was to reduce the intensity and frequency of the hallucinations. Neal also responded well to questions about his personal experience of illness. He expressed considerable distress about disappointing his parents and not being able to function. He blamed himself for his illness and for the conflicts he had with his parents. Therefore, a fourth goal was set of improving his and his family's understanding and management of his illness.

The first phase of treatment involved intensive counseling around the auditory hallucinations and the negative signs of schizophrenia—that is, his inertia and social withdrawal. Through the careful tracking of when the hallucinations were worse and the times when they were less intense, it was possible to identify conflict with his parents as the source of his intense anxiety and increase in command hallucinations. Psychoeducational work separately with Neal and his mother reduced the level of conflict with his family and diminished the frequency of hallucinations, while altering the message from commands to kill himself to less troubling ones. Focusing on the details of his daily life, Neal came to recognize how unsafe he felt in his current living situation and the risk it posed to his sobriety. He therefore was motivated and able to move. Examining his daily routine made it possible to devise strategies for overcoming inertia and apathy, such as setting up activities that he had found pleasurable in the past, like taking a walk, to motivate him to get out of bed before late afternoon. Strategies were also devised to help him take his medication consistently and to attend to daily tasks of living. As he gained confidence in his ability to manage the activities of daily living, Neal was able to consider entering a partial hospitalization program, which he had never been able to do before. In the past he did not think he could drive or participate in such a program. His regular attendance at AA made it possible to build on that group experience to restore interpersonal skills and self-confidence.

The second phase of treatment involved extending and solidifying connections with the community agencies that would provide long-term social and vocational rehabilitation services to Neal. Neal and his parents were able to develop more realistic expectations of him, which enabled them for the first time to do long-term planning for him instead of living from crisis to crisis. They arranged for psychological and vocational testing and found a supervised-living apartment that had on-site social services. The final stage of treatment involved Neal and his family constructing an alternative narrative of his illness, one that did not place blame for Neal's illness on any family member, but that took into account all their survival skills and a more optimistic but realistic future for him.

Brief Treatment of Depression

Depression is the most commonly occurring psychiatric disturbance, and it can also be among the more lethal disorders if the severity of the depression and the risk of suicide are not accurately assessed and treated. Depression is the most important contributing factor in attempted and completed suicides. Major depression was found to be present in 40% of suicide cases and a combination of major depression and alcohol abuse in 60% of cases (Clark, 1995). Depression is frequently found in combination with other disorders. However, its presence can go undiagnosed when the other disorder is more disabling or compelling in presentation, as in certain personality disorders. Failure to recognize the presence of depression can lead to ineffective treatment for both disorders.

Depression is understood to be the result of an interaction between a biological vulnerability for depression and personally stressful life events. Some depressive conditions have a stronger biological contribution, while others are thought to have a stronger psychosocial contribution. Bipolar disorders and major depression appear to have a stronger biological contribution, and medication has been shown to be the most efficient and effective treatment; psychopharmacology then is the preferred modality of treatment, with other modalities being adjunctive. Cyclothymia and dysthymia are considered to be midway on this continuum and appear responsive to a combination of pharmacological and psychosocial interventions. Adjustment reactions and depressions reactive to interpersonal difficulties are considered to be mainly psychosocial in origin and therefore may be responsive to psychotherapy alone (Mays & Croake, 1997).

Effective brief treatment of depression is predicated upon an accurate assessment of the scope and severity of the illness and on the selection of the appropriate level of intervention. Another fundamental principle in the brief treatment of depression is that distressing symptoms should be ameliorated as quickly as possible because of the negative impact of depression on role functioning, cognitive functioning, physical well-being, self-care, self-esteem, and interpersonal functioning. Therefore, medication and cognitive-behavioral interventions, which have proven to be effective in rapidly reducing symptoms, are usually part of the initial treatment plan. The brief treatment approach to the treatment of depression also recognizes that depression is more often a recurrent or chronic condition than a single episode. Therefore, treatment is geared toward lifetime management of stresses and vulnerabilities.

The interpersonal context of the depressed individual's life is also an important focus in brief treatment because of the reciprocal interaction between depression and social environment. Marital and family discord have been linked with the onset or exacerbation of depression. For example, 30% of couples in one study of marital discord had one depressed spouse (Clarkin & Haas, 1988). Depression, in turn, can increase marital and family discord or provoke family members to withdraw or become unsupportive because of the difficulty of living with a depressed person. Anger, irritability, resentment, hostility, low frustration toleration, a sense of entitlement, clinging dependency, and social withdrawal are some of the common signs of depression that can have a devastating impact on relationships. The result may be that the depressed individual has less support at a time when he or she needs more support (Mays & Croake, 1997).

Assessment of Depression

To ensure a full and accurate assessment, a semistructured clinical interview or standardized measures of depression and suicidality, or both, are recommended. Instruments such as the Beck Depression Inventory (BDI) and the Center for Epidemiologic Studies Depression Scale (CES-D) are self-reports that are easy to score and therefore easy to use in everyday practice. If there appears to be a risk of suicide, instruments such as the Suicide Intent Scale (SIS) can be helpful in assessing the seriousness of the wish to die, particularly for patients who have made a previous attempt. The Beck Hopelessness Scale is useful for determining how negatively clients are feeling about themselves, their life situations, and their future (Beckham & Leber, 1995). A comprehensive assessment of suicide risk would include an evaluation of the degree of helplessness and hopelessness that the individual is feeling, the degree of attachment to significant others, the availability of social supports, behaviors that might indicate suicidal intent such as collecting pills, and access to deadly instruments such as a gun (Ackermann-Engel, 1992).

A semistructured interview is one in which the patient is assessed for the physiological, mood, and cognitive symptoms of depression, as outlined in structured formats such as in DSM-IV, but it is also flexible enough to allow the individual to tell his or her story of what the experience of depression is like and what the illness means to him or her (Meichenbaum, 1996). The interviewing process with a depressed person can be challenging because the depressed person may have difficulty following and answering questions and may be unresponsive in general. Patience, empathic statements about the pain of depression, and a brief explanation of the nature of depression and its treatability may enable the patient to participate more in the interview. Careful attention to the client's experience of depression may also help increase receptivity to the interviewing process. The lived experience of depression directs the clinician to what is meaningful and motivating to the patient, where the risks are, and what the priorities in treatment need to be in order to stem the disturbance and disability associated with depression. This is a particularly important dimension of the assessment when working cross-culturally, where for many people depression is not experienced as an affective disturbance. Instead, depression is predominantly experienced as bodily complaints, such as backaches, headaches, or in more culturally specific forms of somatic distress, such as *el calor* (intense sensation of heat), found among Central American women (Jenkins, 1995).

The information provided by the depressed individual needs to be understood as coming through the distorting prism of depression; therefore, other sources of information can help provide a more accurate picture of the client's situation. Interviews with family members or significant others separately or with the client can also provide a more complete picture of the client's functioning and social history. When the depressed individual is an immigrant or a member of an ethnic minority, the social history should include an inquiry into socioeconomic stressors as well as the client's migration experiences, losses endured, and acculturation strains. With recent immigrants from Southeast Asia and South and Central America, among others, the clinician should also be alert to the possibility of trauma—for example, experiences of torture or witnessing violence and violent deaths of loved ones (Bernier, 1992). Family structure, gender roles, socialization patterns, and child-rearing patterns should also be examined to determine if oppression, power differentials, or significant clashes between the traditional culture and the dominant culture exist and may be contributing to the onset or maintenance of the client's depression (Jenkins, 1995).

Intervention Strategies

"Focused," "practical," "supportive," and "interpersonal" are terms that apply to most brief treatment models. The central goals in the treatment of depression in these models are a rapid reduction of disabling symptoms and behaviors and an increase in functioning. The distinctions between long-term and short-term treatment of depression also relate to the role and activity level of the therapist, the emphasis on interventions at the interpersonal level, and the use of extratherapeutic resources, medication, and didactic methods of intervention. The therapist in short-term work is more active in reducing the impact of disabling symptoms—for example, recommending medication or employing cognitive-behavioral interventions that will increase the client's activity level, diminish rumination, ameliorate sleep and appetite disturbances, and so on (Mays & Croake, 1997). The clinician will also take a more active role in educating clients about depression and the impact it has on their functioning, relationships, and self-esteem. In addition, the clinician may have to actively guide clients during periods when they are in the grip of distorted beliefs and desire to escape from painful feeling states. At these times clients may feel impelled to take actions that they hope will make them feel better but which in the end may make their situations worse, such as leaving a marriage or a job. The clinician will have to actively engage the client around these decisions, using his or her professional credibility to place such decisions on hold until the depression subsides (Shuchter, Downs, & Zisook, 1996).

The therapist's activity level is greatest when the client is at risk of harming self or others. There are two main goals with clients who are at risk for suicide: first, ensure their safety; and second, effectively treat the depression. The first step, then, for clients who are at moderate to high risk is to remove the means for committing suicide. For the client at high risk this generally involves a period of stabilization in a hospital setting, particularly if the client cannot work collaboratively to reduce the risk of suicide and there is no one in the community to contain the client's suicidality (Ackermann-Engel, 1992). For clients at moderate risk for suicide, the intervention strategy centers on interrupting the client's suicide plan by engaging the client in treatment and activating his or her support system. Family members, friends, or coworkers must be able to cooperate in removing pills, guns, and so on, and in supervising and supporting the client until the suicidal feelings abate. This strategy also requires an active stance on the clinician's part in countering the client's suicidal thoughts, feelings, and impulses. Depressed patients, in general, "need therapists who will provide structure, help them direct and correct their thinking, and actively support the strengths that they themselves cannot perceive or utilize," but this stance is even more essential with suicidal clients (Shuchter et al., 1996, p. 143).

The clinician must simultaneously seek to understand and validate the client's experience of depression and suicidality and perspective about his or her life situation, and at the same time to expand the "tunnel vision" of seeing only one solution that is characteristic of depressed suicidal people (Bellak, 1991). That is, the clinician must allay the client's very real feelings of pain, while conveying a conviction to the client that this distress is temporary and that they can get through this crisis. A psychoeducational approach, in which the client is provided with information about the nature of depression and about the connections between depression, feelings of helplessness and hopelessness, and suicidal wishes, is useful at this point. Clients should also be informed about the treatability of depression and about the treatment options available to them.

The initial session should also include a review of past coping efforts, particularly previous efforts at overcoming suicidal impulses. Reminding clients of past successful efforts in dealing with problems equivalent to their current stresses can challenge the negative, rigid views that depressed clients hold of themselves and their future, and it can engender hope that alternative solutions are possible (Shuchter et al., 1996).

The conditions of safety within the therapeutic relationship can also be demonstrated by the willingness of the clinician to be available to the client during this period of crisis. Other ways of solidifying the therapeutic alliance are to offer more frequent visits; telephone availability by the clinician or an on-call worker; immediate problem-solving techniques such as a preestablished, detailed plan for dealing with anticipated points of stress (e.g., for a divorced parent, the time when the children return to the other parent after a visit); and an orientation to the future by bridging sessions through homework assignments that build on session discussions and are linked to the next session. For many clients it may be useful to negotiate a written contract "that the patient will not hurt him- or herself for a specific period of time" and instead will follow through on contacting the therapist or designated substitute when he or she is feeling desperate or impulsive (Jobes & Berman, 1996, p.76). The contract, however, is only as good as the rest of the safety plan, especially the establishment of a sound therapeutic alliance, and therefore it should not be seen as the primary deterrent.

Rapid resolution of the depressive episode is essential to resolution of the suicidal crisis when the suicidality is associated with major depression, as the suicidal impulses are artifacts of the depression. The profound dysphoria, anhedonia, anergia, feelings of hopelessness and helplessness, cognitive impairments, and sleep and appetite disturbances need to be aggressively treated. In addition, interventions that provide some measure of relief from distressing symptoms motivate the client to continue in treatment and help to solidify the therapeutic relationship. For example, anxiety and sleeplessness are among the most distressing and disabling symptoms to the depressed, suicidal patient. These are symptoms that medication can alleviate; a sedating antidepressant or one with anxiolytic properties might be useful in helping the client to get some restful sleep. The amount of medication available to the client during the height of the suicidal crisis should generally be limited to the number of days between scheduled visits (every day or every few days for the first few weeks). Family members or friends who can reliably supervise the administration of the medication should be enlisted in the treatment plan. Helping the client to reestablish social connections that became attenuated during the period of depression is an important part of the crisis intervention plan, because renewed attachment bonds can provide the necessary opposition to suicide that may have been lacking at the point that the client felt hopeless and could see no other solution than suicide (Hoff, 1995).

Once a safety plan has been put into place and a working alliance is form-ing, the primary crisis intervention strategies for the depressed, suicidal client are countering of cognitive distortions that are impelling the client toward sui-cide, enhancement or development of problem-solving skills, and enhancement of the client's social support network. To counter the client's hopelessness, it is useful to employ cognitive therapy techniques such as challenging dichoto-mous thinking ("He left me because he is a wonderful man and I can't do any-thing right") by eliciting more complete and complex views of people and sit-uations. Other useful techniques for combating hopelessness are helping the client to recognize logical inconsistencies in his or her belief system and to eval-uate rationally rigid beliefs and search out alternative explanations for events ("I don't deserve to live. It's my fault that my brother died. If I had insisted that he go to see a doctor, he wouldn't have died.").

Helplessness and hopelessness can be countered with behavioral tech-niques that foster a sense of competence and reduce depressogenic thoughts and activities. A depressed client who is isolating and ruminating might be helped by self-monitoring, activity scheduling, and graded task assignments. These techniques help clients to become aware of behaviors that exacerbate depressive and suicidal thoughts and feelings, such as use of alcohol or drugs as a coping strategy. The clients can then be helped to move into activities that can distract them from their self-preoccupation and rumination about all that is wrong in their lives. Suicide is often seen as a necessary solution to problems; therefore, better problem-solving skills need to be imparted—for example, as-sisting clients in clearly defining problems, generating alternative solutions, im-plementing a solution, and problem-solving when obstacles arise (Ackermann-Engel, 1992). Treatment can be understood as the process of coming up with an alternative solution to the suicidal imperative. "Suicidal thoughts and plans may mean that something needs to die, but it shouldn't be the patient. It may be a job, a relationship, a view of oneself, a goal, or a plan, but not the patient" (Mays & Croake, 1997, p. 183).

Interpersonal therapy (IPT) is a brief treatment approach that was devel-oped to address problems in interpersonal relationships that create and main-tain depression for some individuals. The theory of interpersonal therapy is based on the premise that the reason individuals become depressed is that there is conflict, dissatisfaction, and frustration of their needs in their intimate relationships. The therapy is directed toward identifying and resolving such problems as interpersonal conflicts, social skill deficits, role transitions, and un-resolved grief so that the depressed individual can begin receiving the social support that he or she needs to overcome depression and prevent or diminish the severity of relapses (Klein & Wender, 1993).

In the treatment of less severe or more chronic forms of depression, there has also been a move to combined forms of therapy—that is, a combination of medication, psychotherapy, psychoeducation, and community and family support work. Until the advent of selective serotonin reuptake inhibitors (SSRIs), medication was considered inappropriate or ineffective in treating the chronic, mild, intermittent, or atypical forms of depression because these disorders were considered to be characterological in origin. Now SSRIs appear to be effective with dysthymia. In one research study, two-thirds of dysthymic individuals treated with SSRIs reported being free of depression and half showed improved social adaptation (Akiskal & Cassano, 1997). Use of SSRIs in combination with other therapies should thus be considered a best-practices approach.

Treatment of depression under managed care is often a team or interdisciplinary effort. It is not assumed that therapeutic work is performed only by the therapist. Instead, contributions to the treatment may be made by primary care physicians, community leaders, church organizations, self-help groups, health maintenance or health education groups, and so on. In addition, didactic intervention strategies are a significant part of many brief treatment approaches to depression. For example, in the first session, interpersonal therapy "explicitly inducts patients into the sick role, with accompanying psychoeducation about the nature of depression" (Markowitz & Weissman, 1995, p. 379). This is done to provide patients with some immediate relief.

Eclectic brief treatment approaches use psychoeducation to provide patients with a framework for understanding their experiences of depression; that is, they learn about what precipitates, maintains, or aggravates the disorder for them and the ways in which they attempt to avoid the painful feeling states of depression. The goals of this psychoeducation are to motivate patients to comply with treatment, particularly medication, until symptoms subside and to provide patients with the knowledge and skills to recognize and monitor their symptoms of depression. The family or spouse is also provided with information about depression and made aware of the connection between the depression and the behaviors of the depressed individual that may have been distressing to them, such as irritability or lack of interest in socializing or participating in former activities (Shuchter et al., 1996). This approach is intended to increase the family members' empathy and support for the client and allows them to plan for how they will respond to distressing behaviors in the future so as to limit the damage the depression is taking on a family's functioning.

When severe symptoms subside and the client is able to work and manage interpersonal relationships better, and if sufficient time remains, there can be a shift from the crisis intervention, psychoeducation, problem-solving methods of Level I interventions to those of Level II (expressive, exploratory) or Level III (narrative reconstruction approaches). In cases of depression associated with bereavement, a combination of crisis intervention and expressive therapies may be the most helpful approach. For example, at the crisis stage of the loss, providing information about the nature and course of grief, helping the client problem-solve around immediate instrumental tasks, and improving social supports are important first interventions. The other tasks of grief work—for example, ventilating painful feelings of loss, reorganizing one's identity, mastering shifts in roles, and searching for new definitions of well-being—can then be addressed by expressive techniques from psychodynamic, gestalt, humanistic, or other therapies. In brief treatment, however, it is recognized that the clinician's role is that of a catalyst or guide to how the client can move through the bereavement process. The majority of the grief work will take place after therapy ends, with the assistance of the enhanced social support network (e.g., self-help groups, such as Compassionate Friends).

Relapse Prevention

When provided with information about the nature and course of a depressive illness, family members are in a better position to help the depressed individual monitor and cope with the negative, regressive consequences of depression. Enhancement of the social support system and development of skills for the identification and monitoring of depressive symptoms are important parts of relapse prevention for depression, because the absence of social supports and high levels of environmental stress are risk factors for relapse. Rates of relapse for depression are quite high. At a 2-year follow-up, about 50% of patients treated for an initial episode had a return of symptoms, and for longer periods, the rate approached 80% (Ludgate, 1995). Therefore, relapse prevention or, perhaps more accurately, lifetime management skills need to be considered an important component of the treatment plan.

Many of the general relapse prevention strategies described in Chapter 5 are applicable to reducing vulnerability to recurrent episodes of depression. Strategies that improve the client's sense of efficacy and help the client develop skills for coping with stresses are particularly important interventions, because the major factor associated with depression relapse is life stress. Thus, general coping skills such as stress management, problem solving, conflict resolution, and effective communication reduce everyday stresses and thus reduce vulnerability to depression. Further, wherever possible, clients should be encouraged to anticipate sources of stress and to plan for how they will manage them. The depression treatment approaches described above are also useful for developing a sense of efficacy because of the emphasis placed on patient and family responsibility for identification and monitoring of symptoms and countering the regressive pull of the depression. Helping clients to manage the symptoms of depression with techniques such as relaxation, guided imagery, and distraction to reduce rumination and painful feelings is also a way of warding off the full return of symptoms. In essence, clients learn how to tolerate a measure of discomfort and how to be their own therapists when symptoms return (Ludgate, 1995; Granvold & Wodarski, 1994).

Given the natural course of depressive illnesses, termination needs to not only include the lifetime management perspective but also be seen as open-ended in the sense that the client may need to be seen again in brief contacts throughout his or her lifetime. Termination sessions focus on the skills and knowledge gained by the client and how these can be used in self-therapy. Gradual fading out of sessions and planning of a booster session are useful ways for clients to practice skills on their own and to come to see themselves as responsible for their recovery from depression. It is also helpful, if family members or friends have not been involved beyond the assessment, to have them in for part of the final session to review what they have learned about depression and to reinforce any positive changes in interactions with the client. Finally, the clinician should provide clear information about when and how the client should seek treatment in the future should the need arise (Lebow, 1995).

Crisis Intervention in a Case of Major Depression

When Barbara called, she asked for an immediate appointment because of her concern that she was going to lose control at work or with her 15-year-old son, Jim. Barbara, a 35-year-old divorced social service worker, stated that she was in a constant state of rage and resentment toward her supervisors for making impossible demands on her for increased productivity, and toward her son because he had become disobedient and irresponsible. Barbara was seen later that same day. She indeed looked very angry and tense. She sat with her hands clenched, speaking in angry tones as she described the stresses she was experiencing at work and home. Twice in recent weeks she had been reprimanded for mistakes in calculation, which at first she attributed to the increased workload—that is, the agency's expectation that more clients should be processed in a shorter period of time. The completion of a depression inventory indicated the presence of problems with decreased attention, concentration, and memory, insomnia, early morning awakening, fatigue, decreased appetite, and headaches. While not actively contemplating suicide, Barbara did have suicidal thoughts that took the form of wishing she were dead so that she wouldn't have to deal with her life situation anymore. In addition to feeling irritable, Barbara stated that she was impatient with everyone and everything and "basically didn't want to be bothered with anyone." She had stopped socializing with family and friends and was too exhausted to go to church.

Barbara reported several explosive confrontations with her son Jim in recent weeks about his refusal to do his schoolwork and about staying out late. She got so angry with him at these times that she worried about doing serious harm to him. Barbara was also concerned about not paying enough attention to her younger child, 12-year-old Sean, because of her problems with Jim, working at two jobs, and putting in extra hours at her first job to try to get caught up. She felt overwhelmed and hopeless about her situation because her efforts to try to resolve her problems by working overtime and sternly disciplining her son were not working. In examining the family's past coping efforts, Barbara stated that she and her sons had managed to cope with having to start over after having been burned out of their apartment 3 years before. However, she felt that Jim, who had been burned in that fire, never fully recovered from the trauma, because he was very self-conscious about the scars on his back and arms. She wondered if this might be the cause of his difficult behavior now. Also, their financial situation was precarious because the cost of replacing their household had exceeded her means and she was still in debt.

Barbara gained some relief from learning that she was clinically depressed and that many of the areas of difficulty that she was concerned about, such as her irritability, poor concentration, poor memory, and difficulties on her job, were a function of the depression. Information about the nature and course of the illness and the treatment options were provided to her. She agreed to an initial treatment plan that included a medication evaluation, individual therapy that would focus on problem solving and stress management, and an evaluation interview with Jim in order to determine the best approach for dealing with the conflict between them. Barbara was given an emergency medication evaluation that day and placed on an antidepressant. A 1-week medical leave from her job was arranged for her, and she arranged for Jim to live temporarily with his father. She was given an appointment for 3 days later and provided with a 24-hour emergency number.

When Barbara returned 3 days later, she reported that she was sleeping better and that the anxiety and tension had diminished. She had not had any suicidal wishes. The pressure had diminished, and she no longer felt that she was going to lose control of her anger, but she worried about what would happen when she returned to work. She was encouraged to use a problem-solving method in which she generated options for managing her problems at work. Barbara opted to speak with her union representative about a temporary transfer to another division until she was stabilized on the medication.

Each session began with a check-in on how she was feeling so that her depression could be carefully monitored for risk of self-harm or harming others and so that she could see the progress she was making. Homework tasks centered on reestablishing social contacts and supports. Since her ex-husband could not keep Jim longer than 3 weeks, the next two sessions focused on preparing for managing discipline problems when he returned home and on learning stress management techniques like deep breathing and progressive relaxation. She also learned to restructure her views of her supervisors' requests in terms other than the absolutist ones she tended to use, so that she wouldn't become so anxious and angry with the supervisors. She agreed that she needed to stop overreacting to her son's behaviors and to find ways to de-escalate or walk away from confrontations before her anger got out of control. In session, Barbara practiced ways of responding differently to typical conflict situations such as Jim not cleaning his room or not doing his homework; for example, she could make the request, move away from the situation to cool down, and then repeat the request, with consequences if he wasn't compliant. An appointment was made for Jim to be seen before he returned home from his father's house.

Jim presented as a bright, friendly kid. He expressed regret about the conflicts between himself and his mother. However, he felt his mother was always angry with him and was always telling him what to do. He conceded that his behavior was making her very angry, and he didn't understand why he kept "messing up" when he knew that this would lead to a big fight between them. In reviewing the impact of the fire on his family and his hospitalization for burns, Jim reported that he had talked with someone at a youth center for a while and that this had been helpful in his returning to school and in participating in after-school activities. He accepted the suggestion that he again meet with the youth counselor to talk about the problems he was having in getting along with his mother. When Jim and his mother were seen together, they were both initially tense and angry with each other, but they became calmer as they reached agreement that they wanted to get along better and that each would work with a counselor to achieve this. Barbara was able to talk with Jim about her depression, which allowed for a discussion of the impact of depression on family life, including her irritability and impatience with him.

By the third week of treatment, with reduction in the depression, sessions could be spaced further apart. Barbara also made steady progress in mastering stress management, even though there were always financial stresses because of her limited income and her degree of indebtedness. With each financial crisis, she was encouraged to use the problem-solving model. For example, when her refrigerator broke and she had no means of replacing it, she found a charitable organization that provided her with a replacement. Jim continued to see his counselor and was making good progress in school and in his schoolwork, although he still had trouble keeping his curfew. Barbara felt she was handling this situation better than she had in the past. She had enlisted his father's help in dealing with problem behaviors by getting him to follow through with disciplinary consequences when Jim was visiting his father. She also no longer saw his behavior as a catastrophe but as typical adolescent behavior that she needed to address in a calm, reasonable manner.

The final two sessions were used to review her experience of depression in order to pinpoint the stresses that she was highly reactive to and the warning signs that she was becoming overwhelmed or depressed. At the end of 7 months (12 sessions), her depression remained in remission, she had achieved a sometimes tense but workable relationship with her son, and she had returned to her position, in which she felt no more stressed than her coworkers about the demands placed upon them. Barbara knew that she could return the next calendar year, which was a few months away, and that I would follow up with her in 3 months. At 3 months follow-up, she did not feel the need to return, but she indicated that she would have no reluctance to reapply should she become depressed again or if the situation with her son deteriorated.

Exercise in Selecting a Focus When Working with Severe Mental Illness: John

Use the following vignette to answer the questions in this exercise.

John is an 18-year-old high school senior who was referred by his primary care physician after he had a second car accident in a year. Both accidents were associated with drinking and appeared to be deliberate attempts to harm himself, as both times he had driven off the road into a tree. John also revealed during the intake session that he had cut himself several times over the past 2 years. The cutting, drinking, and car accidents had occurred after fights with his girlfriend or after episodes when they had broken up.

John is the youngest of three boys. One brother, 20, is in college, and the other, 23, works as a mason. John's father is a fireman, and his mother works as a secretary. Both parents are described as steady, heavy drinkers, although both deny having a drinking problem. Their marriage had been in difficulty in the past, related to his father having an affair. After a brief separation, they reconciled and have lived peacefully together for the last 10 years, but with an increase in drinking and a lack of closeness. John complains of a lack of closeness with both parents, but especially with his father, who he believes is scornful of him because of the problems John has had over the years. John was described as always having been a restless, "antsy" kid. He began exhibiting academic problems due to poor attention and concentration about the time of the parents' separation. Treatment was recommended at that time but not followed through on, because the parents did not accept the recommendation for marital therapy. John has performed adequately in the vocational track in high school and is planning to attend community college. He works part time and also frequently as a disk jockey at parties and weddings.

John presented as an extremely anxious, confused, and needy young man. He focused much of his attention on his girlfriend, with whom he had reconciled again, and indicated that all his problems would be solved if he could only work out the problems in their relationship. He saw his girlfriend of 2 years as his primary support, as he had no close friends, although he had several friends he regularly hung around with, and he did not get along well with his brothers. His parents expressed considerable concern about John but were baffled and overwhelmed by his problems and about how to help him.

1. *Why now? Speculate on the interpersonal, developmental, and/or existential factors that might be utilized to enhance motivation to remain in treatment and to change.*

2. *Speculate on the healthy strivings behind John's symptoms. What individual and family strengths and resources could be drawn on to help reduce the risk for self-harm?*

Exercise in Selecting a Focus When Working with Severe Mental Illness: John (continued)

 3. *Using the I-D-E model, select a focus for brief treatment.*
 4. *Select the level of intervention and develop a treatment plan based on the selected focus and level of intervention.*

Answers to this exercise appear in the Appendix.

Summary

The features of time-limited work with clients with severe and persistent mental disorders can be summarized as being a structured, goal-directed, multi-stage, multisystem, problem-solving, stress reduction, skills development and relapse prevention approach. This approach is based on a stress/vulnerability conceptualization of mental illness, in which interventions are directed toward reducing the number and severity of stresses while increasing the client's resources and capacities for managing life stresses. Thus, the focus of treatment is first and foremost on stabilization (e.g., living situation, social support network, and medication), symptom reduction, treatment of substance abuse, and ensuring the client's safety. The establishment of a solid working alliance is an essential part of this process and at the same time is likely to be a consequence of paying attention to the client's immediate, pressing needs. Client understanding of unconscious affects and motivations may help in the reduction of symptoms and self-destructive behaviors, but exploratory, expressive methods are secondary to alliance building and the stabilization methods that are part of case-management, cognitive-behavioral, and psychoeducation approaches.

Recommended Reading

Corwin, M. D. (1996). Early intervention strategies with borderline clients. *Families in Society, 77*(1), 40–49.

Cournoyer, B. R. (1996). Converging themes in crisis intervention, task-centered, and brief treatment approaches. In A. R. Roberts (Ed.), *Crisis management & brief treatment: Theory, technique, and applications* (pp. 3–15). Chicago: Nelson Hall.

Mays, M., & Croake, J. W. (1997). *Treatment of depression in managed care.* New York: Brunner/Mazel.

Rothman, J. (1994). *Practice with highly vulnerable clients: Case management and community-based service.* Englewood Cliffs, NJ: Prentice Hall.

BRIEF SOCIAL WORK PRACTICE
IN HEALTH CARE

Social Work and the Health Care Revolution

Brief treatment has always been a significant modality used by social workers in health care settings because contact with medical patients is limited by the nature of the host setting. In the past, social work with medical patients generally took place in acute care settings, where the opportunity for contact tended to be limited by the length of stay in the hospital, or in outpatient clinics, with time determined by the length of the medical treatment for an acute illness or injury. Although the focus in health care has shifted from treatment of acute illness to that of complex, chronic health problems, other forces—both economic and technological—are certain to result in the continuation of time-limited interventions as the predominant mode of social work practice in health care settings. For example, managed care's restrictions on inpatient stays and outpatient mental health services and the use of DRGs (diagnosis-related groups)[1] as the basis for payment for Medicare and Medicaid patients have both limited the time that social workers have to work with patients and families (Berkman, 1996).

Advances in technologies for diagnosis and treatment have also contributed to reduction in the length of hospital stays and to the movement toward ambulatory care for many procedures that formerly were performed in the hospital. This trend has led to an oversupply of inpatient beds, hence financial difficulties and subsequent downsizing or closing of facilities. Social work departments in medical centers and hospitals have been negatively affected by downsizings, mergers, and institutional restructurings of hospitals. Social work positions have been lost to layoffs, attrition, and assignment of social work functions to persons who are not social workers. Job insecurity is widespread, and this has added to the high degree of stress that social workers in health care were already experiencing from the adaptations required by very brief hospitalization stays (Dhooper, 1997).

Changes in patient demographics have also contributed to the change in health care from an emphasis on acute, episodic care to one of long-term

---

[1] Acronyms introduced in this chapter: DRGs, diagnosis-related groups; SST, single-session therapy.

management of chronic health problems. Increases in the elderly population, people with chronic illness, and patients with medical problems related to psychosocial problems such as domestic violence and homelessness are posing new challenges to the health care delivery system (Moffat & Kay, 1996). This demographic shift is expected to lead to a greater emphasis on prevention of illness and promotion of health and adaptive coping, and on psychosocial consultations and interventions. Medical cost offset research, which has demonstrated that the cost of brief psychosocial interventions is offset by savings in the use of medical services, reinforces the move toward psychosocial consultations and interventions in health care (Seaburn, Lorenz, Gunn, Gawinski, & Mauksch, 1996).

Other significant demographic changes in patient populations have contributed to the turn toward the biopsychosocial model in medicine. Due to changes in immigration patterns over the past two decades, health care consumers have become more ethnically diverse. These changes have presented challenges to health care providers to find ways to overcome intercultural misunderstandings that can lead to ineffective treatment or noncompliance. Cultural factors influence patients' perceptions, their experienced meaning of symptoms, and beliefs about the causes and appropriate treatments for illnesses. Ethnic minority patients may hold beliefs about how and why people become ill and what an illness means that are different from those embedded in the biomedical model and from the dominant cultural views held by many providers. In addition, there are likely to be sociocultural and socioeconomic factors that influence the patients' ability to comply with recommended treatment and maintain their health. Therefore, health care providers now recognize that it is important for them to understand the context of ethnic minority patients' lives and to reduce barriers such as language and conflicting views of medical roles, so that miscommunication can be avoided and treatment interventions modified when necessary (Julia, 1996).

Psychosocial assessment—that is, the contextualizing of a patient's life for health care providers—has been a long-standing function of social workers in tertiary medical care, where the acuteness or intensity of a medical condition requires a specialized medical setting such as a hospital acute care unit (Dhooper, 1997). At the primary care level of practice (where the patient is presymptomatic or in early symptomatic stages) or the family medicine level, social workers have also functioned as consultants, educators, and collaborators with health care providers to incorporate the person-in-environment perspective into medical practice. In these settings, social workers have provided or trained health workers in the "basic skills of obtaining relevant social data, being sensitive to resources or deficits in resources, formulating an integrated view of the patient and understanding how community services complement community-oriented primary care" (Zayas & Dyche, 1992, p. 250).

Social Work Roles in the New Health Care Environment

Discharge Planning

With the emergence of the new health care ideas, there should be expanded roles and opportunities for social workers, because the new biopsychosocial paradigm is congruent with basic social work principles and practice approaches. However, concern has been expressed for the future of social work in health care, because new positions have not yet developed in the primary care, community health care, and ambulatory care settings to replace the number of hospital social work positions lost to mergers and downsizing (Berkman, 1996). Dhooper (1997) sees the acceptance of the biopsychosocial model by the medical profession as, paradoxically, partly responsible for this outcome. That is, with the integration of the psychosocial with the biomedical, there has been a blurring of the distinctions between professions. Physicians, nurses, and psychologists, along with social workers, are performing psychosocial assessments and interventions, discharge planning, and interdisciplinary collaboration related to patient care in both primary and tertiary care settings. On inpatient psychiatric units, psychiatrists have taken on more of the work with families, conducting the family evaluations and family therapy provided by social workers in the recent past (Farley, 1994).

It is becoming clear that social workers will need to take a more assertive approach to job development and job security in health care settings, as well as in social service and mental health settings. All these areas are undergoing major changes in structure, function, priorities, and methods of financing. For social workers to adapt to and find a place for themselves in the emerging ambulatory, community-based health care system, they will have to change the perception of social workers as discharge planners and case managers to the more expansive roles of educator, consultant, collaborator, and co-provider. Social workers will need to expand their skills so as to be able to create new roles and be able to move easily across departmental lines. They will have to be more assertive in carving out roles that match the emerging service challenges (Seaburn et al., 1996). Social workers historically have had to take a proactive stance when working in host agencies. Social work services can easily be ill defined or narrowly defined, poorly understood, and misused if the role definition is left exclusively to the host agency. In a similar fashion, social workers in the changing health care environment will have to take the lead in defining their roles and finding ways to integrate those roles into a system in which the hierarchy will be flattened and outcomes will be emphasized over professional roles (Globerman & Bogo, 1995).

Time-Limited Social Work Practice

Case Management

Traditional hospital social work functions are already being transformed in response to the changes in the health care environment. For example, discharge planning now involves coordinating care for patients with chronic or complex health problems who will need long-term, comprehensive care. Consequently, social workers now need to know how to design a continuum of care that involves community-based nonmedical services as well as the more traditional medical follow-up care. This comprehensive care approach requires a full, multisystem assessment, but the compressed time frame of short hospital stays makes such a comprehensive assessment and discharge plan difficult to complete. One suggested method for maximizing the use of time is to do pre-admission screenings of patients around areas of risk and need in order to start the process of identification and linkage with community resources before discharge. Another suggestion is for workers to take the time to develop an in-depth knowledge of community resources and establish relationships with key service providers based on mutual support of each other's service objectives (Berkman, 1996).

Case management is another traditional hospital social work function that will continue to be a central one in the emerging health care environment, but in a modified form. The central objectives of case management are ensuring continuity of services, linking of clients with needed resources, and coordinating and monitoring those services. Case management developed as an intervention approach to assist patients with complex medical and psychosocial problems, who needed help from a number of providers and assistance in dealing with the fragmented, confusing health and social service delivery systems (Austin, 1990). The requirements of managed care that duplication of services be eliminated and that services be coordinated to maximize cost savings will ensure that case management will continue to be an important modality in the new health care environment (Ballew & Mink, 1996).

Traditionally, the basic case management approaches have included (1) outreach, case finding, and screening; (2) comprehensive assessment of the client's medical, psychosocial, financial, and level-of-care needs and multisystem assessment of resources; (3) development of an individualized care plan of the services and resources necessary for maintaining the client in the community; (4) referral, linkage, advocacy, and coordination of services; (5) direct provision of services—for example, counseling and education; and (6) monitoring and evaluation of services and reassessment of client's needs (Goering & Wasylenki, 1996). Modifications in the case management approach as a result of changes in funding and service delivery methods are likely to include an increased responsibility for cost containment and an expanded role in monitoring the quality and cost effectiveness of the contracted care (Berkman, 1996).

Another modification due to managed care will be in the use of time. In the past, case management was considered to be a long-term approach, because many of the clients served by a case manager were considered to be vulnerable and to have chronic problems. However, under managed care and capitated programs, case management services will need to be time sensitive. For example, case management services are likely to be intensive at the beginning or at points of crisis and then be titrated downward as the client is stabilized in the community (Hoyt & Austad, 1992). Even intensive case management, where there is a high frequency of contact (from daily to weekly contact) and a high staff-to-patient ratio, is likely to follow this phasing of treatment approach (Goering & Wasylenki, 1996).

Clinical Social Work

In hospital social work the direct practice role or the "clinical specialist" position remains, but in a considerably altered form. In the past, clinical social workers often provided the psychosocial family assessment pieces of the evaluation and sometimes provided individual and family therapy or conducted groups. The clinical social worker role will continue to include psychosocial assessments and interventions and the translation of the psychosocial dimensions of a patient's illness to other members of the medical treatment team. However, much of this work will be very brief, often single-session work. In addition, workers will have to function more independently—that is, with minimal supervision and without a social work department (Globerman & Bogo, 1995).

Social workers have been and will continue to be a part of acute ambulatory care and emergency departments to provide crisis intervention for patients experiencing medical crises and psychosocial emergencies. Over the past decade, social workers have had to develop expertise in such areas as domestic abuse, homelessness, and substance abuse in order to deal with changing health care needs. They have had to develop the particular skills for intervening effectively in these emergency situations, such as trauma intervention skills for helping families deal with medical emergencies or death and for assisting victims of domestic violence (Myer & Hanna, 1996).

In ambulatory care settings, social workers are increasingly serving in a consultant role with other members of the medical team about psychosocial issues that could affect the course of the medical illness or injury. This kind of collaborative role will assume even greater importance in primary care settings, where the emerging goal is to integrate primary care and mental health services as a way of improving the effectiveness of both services and of gaining the medical cost offset benefits of good mental health. In the consultant role, the social worker might assist the physician in early discovery of patients with depression and anxiety that are manifested in somatic complaints, thereby saving the plan unnecessary expense for diagnostic procedures. With the same patient, the worker might then serve as a co-provider of health services, providing such services as crisis intervention, brief therapy, psychoeducation, or case management (Seaburn et al., 1996).

Single-Session Therapy: Acute and Nonacute Settings

In hospital social work and acute ambulatory care, a single contact with a patient or with a patient's family is not uncommon and may become increasingly common with shorter hospital stays. Therefore, the particular assessment and intervention skills of single-session work are essential social work skills in the health care setting. The goals in single-session work are of necessity more limited in scope than in longer-term work, but there is research evidence that a single contact can have beneficial effects. Several of the medical cost offset studies, for example, found that "one therapeutic interview, with no repeat psychological visits, reduced medical utilization by 60% over the following five years, and that the reduction was the consequence of resolving the emotional distress that was being reflected in physical symptoms" (Bloom, 1992, p. 255).

Single-session therapy (SST) is used in crisis situations such as are found in emergency departments or acute ambulatory care settings. It may be used for less acute situations, where patients or their families elect to have only a single contact, or where circumstances such as short hospital stays allow for only one session. SST or a single-contact consultation is fundamentally eclectic and pragmatic in approach; that is, the nature of the problem will determine the therapeutic approach. There are, however, several factors that characterize single-session therapy. These common factors are (1) a view of each session as being complete in and of itself, with an emphasis on quickly gaining clarity about the work that needs to be accomplished in the session—that is, identifying a focal problem that can be realistically addressed in the session; (2) rapid establishment of a positive working alliance; (3) facilitation of coping or problem resolution as central goals; (4) an emphasis on here-and-now problem situations; (5) an emphasis on creating a solution that the client feels will be useful and that builds on existing client strengths and resources; (6) an opportunity within the session to acquire or reinforce the skills that the client will need to cope or make changes; (7) use of feedback or education to increase the client's sense of mastery; (8) flexibility in setting length of session, with most single sessions running longer than the usual 45 to 50 minutes; and (9) a relatively high level of therapist activity, matched to the client's needs and the therapy process—that is, a higher level of activity for clients in crisis but a lower level of activity at the beginning of the session to give the client an opportunity to tell his or her story (Hoyt, 1995; Bloom, 1992).

Given the more modest or circumscribed goals of single-session work, the assessment process is adjusted to allow sufficient time for the intervention process. In the noncrisis situation, there is less of an emphasis on a comprehensive assessment and more concern with having sufficient time to help the client identify current stresses and needs and find ways in which the therapist might be helpful to the client in reaching his or her goals. The health care social worker conducting a single session or consultation with a client who is dealing directly or indirectly with a serious or chronic health problem will still need to gather information about the illness or disability, the client's personal and family resources for dealing with the illness, and his or her coping skills. However, the formal assessment occupies a smaller portion of the session than it might in first sessions in longer term work, although the assessment process will continue throughout the session. From the beginning of the session, the focus is on determining what personal or environmental resources clients will need to deal more effectively with their situation—for example, concrete assistance, validation, reassurance, support, a change in perspective, meaning revision, motivation to interrupt nonproductive behavioral patterns, skill instruction, and so on (Hoyt, Rosenbaum, & Talmon, 1992).

This client-centered, problem-focused approach, in conjunction with the use of rapport-building techniques such as attentiveness, concern, respect, and genuineness, aid in the rapid establishment of a positive working relationship. Given the higher level of therapist activity in single-session therapy, the positive relationship is essential for the client to be able to make use of the advice, guidance, or direction the therapist is likely to give. The positive relationship may be the central new experience, and the introduction of a new experience is the sine qua non of all successful single-session work. A "new experience" can be described as one in which "the patient passes through his or her habitual, self-limiting patterns of thinking, feeling, and acting . . . resulting in the patient having a sense of increased freedom and hope" (Hoyt, 1995, p. 147). This approach to single-session work is illustrated in the case study below.

Single Session: Crisis Intervention

Mrs. A was referred by her primary care physician for a mental health evaluation. This happened after she requested a medical leave of absence from her job as a crossing guard because the job had become too stressful for her. The director of her unit had recommended the leave because he was concerned about Mrs. A's "fixation" about her supervisor and her ability to function while so distressed. For the previous month Mrs. A had grown increasingly agitated and suspicious of her supervisor. She accused him of constantly checking up on her because he blamed her for a child having been hit at her corner even though she was off duty at the time. Her supervisor denied this.

Mrs. A, who is 57 years old, married, and the mother of five grown children, presented as anxious, confused, and concerned about her current emotional state. The assessment revealed that she was having increasing difficulty in concentrating, sleeping, and eating. She was spending increasing amounts of time ruminating about her supervisor's alleged harassment of her and was withdrawing from many of her usual social activities because she was afraid that people were getting tired of hearing her complain about her supervisor's unwarranted surveillance of her. Before this episode, Mrs. A had never sought or needed counseling. She had always functioned very well in her 25 years as a crossing guard (according to the director, who was contacted during the interview). She was also highly esteemed in her community (according to her husband, who was also contacted during the interview). She had been very active in her church her whole life (her father had been the minister) and in community activities. People in her neighborhood turned to her for advice and for help in resolving neighborhood problems. Children in her neighborhood called her "Grandma" and came to her for comfort and help with family problems.

Although highly anxious, Mrs. A showed no signs of depression and, apart from her preoccupation with her supervisor's negative view of her, she showed no signs of thought disorder. She was able to reflect on the accuracy of her perceptions about her supervisor's behavior and on her reactions to her perceptions of him. Mrs. A readily responded to a cognitive restructuring intervention, as illustrated below.

WORKER: *Mrs. A, I want to see if I'm understanding correctly the way you see things. You said that you know that you were not responsible for this child getting hit, because it occurred after you were officially off duty. However, you think that your supervisor doesn't believe that and that's why he keeps circling around in his car checking up on you. Is that how you see things? (Mrs. A nodded affirmatively.) Okay, can you think of any other reasons why he might be driving around in his car other than checking up on you?*

MRS. A: *Well, I guess he could be making his rounds checking up on everybody. That's what happened the last time that a child got hurt, but I don't think that's why he's coming around now. He says he's not coming around more than before, but I know what his car looks like and I've seen him circling the block. He thinks it was my fault, but it's not my fault.*

WORKER: *What would make you feel better? How would you like things to turn out in this matter?*

MRS. A: *I want him to believe me that it wasn't my fault.*

WORKER: *How are you going to know that? He's already said that he doesn't think it was your fault, but you don't believe him.*

MRS. A: *I never thought about that. I guess I can't ever really know.*

WORKER: *No, you can't know, and you can't control what he thinks or get him to change his mind. As you look at this situation, what do you think can change?*

MRS. A: *I don't know. I just go round and round. I sit at the kitchen table and keep thinking about how unfair this is for him to blame me.*

WORKER: *What happens to you at those times when you're sitting at the kitchen table stewing about him. What are you feeling?*

MRS. A: *(tears in her eyes) I feel terrible. I get so upset, I can't sit still. I just walk back and forth in the kitchen. My husband and kids try to coax me to get out of the house, but I can't go. I'm too upset.*

WORKER: *So when you start thinking about your supervisor, you can't do the usual things you enjoy and it makes you feel what? Worried, angry, sad?*

MRS. A: *Tense, I feel tense like my nerves are jumping out of my body.*

WORKER: *Do you feel better when you are doing something that takes your mind off of the problem?*

MRS. A: *Yes, but it doesn't last long. It seems like this situation is always on my mind. It's getting so that all I do is sit and think about it.*

WORKER: *It's going to be important for you to get back involved in the activities you enjoyed before. You're going to feel better, be able to eat and sleep better, if you stay busy doing things instead of sitting at home brooding. We can discuss how to do that in a little while. But first there's something that's puzzling me. I don't quite understand why what your supervisor thinks of you is so important. What he thinks seems to have taken over your whole life and left you miserable. Why is that?*

MRS. A: *Well, you don't want people to think you're a bad person. You want people to like you, to think highly of you.*

WORKER: *Yes, that's true, but what happens if you know that you didn't do a bad thing, but somebody else sees it differently?*

MRS. A: *I don't know. I think I would keep trying to convince him that he's judging me unfairly.*

WORKER: *You know, Mrs. A, I think you and I are coming at this from two different perspectives because we come from different backgrounds. When I started kindergarten, my father told me that old saying, "In this life, some people like you a lot and some people not at all. No rhyme, no reason. That's just the way it is." I wonder what your father told you when you went off to school.*

MRS. A: *(laughs) I wish he had told me that. I don't remember him saying anything, but I just knew that, as the preacher's kid, I was expected to always be good. I had to be an example, someone people could look up to and respect. Until now no one has ever thought bad things of me.*

WORKER: *Never? That's pretty amazing. That must be part of the reason this has thrown you for such a loop. You haven't had any experience coping with people not liking or not approving of you. Maybe we could use the rest of our time today figuring out ways of coping with this situation. Let's see what we're dealing with here. The facts are you know you didn't do anything wrong. You think your supervisor believes otherwise, but you don't have control over what he thinks. And thinking all the time about what your supervisor thinks is taking a terrible toll on you. So it's going to be important to find things to get your mind off of him.*

MRS. A: *It does seem foolish now that I think about it that I've been spending so much time worrying about what he thinks. I've got better things to do.*

WORKER: *Like what?*

MRS. A: *Well, my kids have been unhappy that we haven't had our usual Sunday family dinners for the last 3 weeks. I haven't felt up to it. I probably should try it again.*

WORKER: *It's a choice. Sitting at the kitchen table brooding and feeling worse and worse or having a good meal with your family. What kinds of dishes do you like to fix for Sunday dinner? What are your family favorites?*

The rest of the session (which totaled an hour and a half) was spent planning this dinner, including sharing a pie recipe that Mrs. A was proud of and planning how she would deal with seeing her supervisor driving by. Mrs. A became noticeably less anxious and was relieved that she was "feeling so much better" as we discussed distracting techniques and alternative ways of viewing her supervisor's behavior. We agreed that she should not take a leave and that her husband and director should be brought into the plan. They could be helpful in reminding her to focus on something else whenever she got stuck in her thinking. We also agreed that she would call first in 2 days and then in a week to see if she continued to feel better. Finally, a follow-up appointment was set for 1 month. When Mrs. A called in, she reported that she was feeling like her old self. She was sleeping and eating as before and back involved in her church and community activities. Mr. A confirmed this. The 1-month follow-up visit was a short one because Mrs. A had returned to her previous level of functioning.

Single Session: Consultation

Single-session work is not conceived of as a cure or "quick fix," nor is there any expectation that the patients' presenting problems will be totally resolved by the end of the session. Instead it should provide patients with a helpful experience, which may or may not be all the help they require or want. However, it is hoped that such positive experiences will enable patients and their families to make good use of other medical services; to be able to follow through with recommended treatment, discharge, and referral plans; and to be receptive in the future to additional treatment when needed (Hoyt et al., 1992).

Pollin and Kanaan (1995), writing about medical crisis counseling, also see a single session, the consultation, as potentially a pivotal event that can enable clients to regain control of their lives at a time when they are feeling that everything is beyond their control. The single contact or the consultation can give some clients all they need to be able to cope for the time being. From the one contact, clients can gain some clarity about the scope of their situation, sort out what their unexpressed concerns are, have their coping skills affirmed and resources identified, and learn about the professional help available to them if needed down the road. Clearly, single-session therapy would not be the treatment of choice for patients with severe and persistent mental disorders, substance abuse disorders, eating disorders, or symptoms arising from early and sustained trauma or abuse. However, SST can be an effective and cost-saving method for clients with circumscribed problems, good coping skills, and a functional support system. It can also serve as an introduction to mental health services for involuntary or reluctant clients (especially male clients or clients from culturally diverse backgrounds who, studies show, may be especially reluctant to get involved with mental health or social services), because it meets the client where he or she is in the help-seeking process (Hoyt et al., 1992).

In acute care settings or when the client is in crisis, the format of single-session therapy will need to be modified to meet the higher level of risk and care. In emergency departments, for example, the social worker is likely to be dealing with families who are faced with such traumas as acute illness, injury, violence, and abuse. The worker must assess the immediate psychosocial needs of the patient and his or her family—that is, how overwhelmed they are, what personal resources they have to cope with the crisis, and what will be necessary to ensure the safety of the patient, family, or others.

Once the family's immediate needs have been determined and the immediate shock and fear have subsided, a more comprehensive but focused assessment of how the patient and patient's family are functioning in crisis will need to be undertaken. The assessment process can be streamlined by having a conceptual framework to guide the inquiry or through the use of rapid assessment instruments. Pollin and Kanaan's (1995) medical crisis counseling model and measures such as the Family Crisis Oriented Personal Evaluation Scales (Fischer & Corcoran, 1994) are useful guides for gathering data on the cognitive, affective, and behavioral reactions to a crisis and how these reactions will likely affect individual or family functioning in the short and long term. Assessment of past coping responses and family resources is particularly important because individual and family strengths and resources are significant in determining what level of intervention would be most helpful.

Pollin and Kanaan's model is based on the eight expectable issues that patients and families typically contend with when faced with long-term disability or illness. These are loss of control, self-image, dependency, stigma, abandonment, anger, isolation, and death. The Family Crisis Oriented Personal Evaluation Scales, on the other hand, help clinicians identify a family's problem-solving and coping strategies by reviewing their ways of acquiring social support, their capacity to reframe stressful events to make them more manageable, their use of spiritual support, their capacity to seek and accept help, and their ability to tolerate painful or nonresolvable situations (Fischer & Corcoran, 1994).

After the degree of risk has been evaluated, sufficient rapport has been established, and a working assessment has been completed, the remainder of the session is devoted to providing immediate psychosocial assistance. This may involve helping the patient or family to develop a realistic, accurate understanding of the medical crisis and what will be needed to cope with the consequences of the illness, disability, or trauma; lending support for the expression of feelings; and helping the patient or family to weigh options, develop a plan of action for dealing with the current situation, or mobilize formal and informal support systems (Dhooper, 1997). Depending upon the degree of risk, level of need, and personal and environmental resources, the worker will need to provide varying degrees of direct assistance. Patients or families with lower levels of risk and cognitive or affective disorganization may need only supportive counseling and education about the illness or injury and care plan.

Other patients with a history of poor coping, with limited personal or family resources, conflicted family relationships, and no previous experience with serious illness would likely need the full services of the crisis social worker. These services would include (1) advocacy within the medical setting and within the community to gain the resources and services that the client will need to resolve such a crisis situation—for example, advocating with hospital personnel or managed care reviewers for hospitalization; (2) case management services, including the formulation of a care plan for managing the immediate consequences of the illness or trauma and referral to community health and social services for long-term management issues; (3) education for patient and family about hospital procedures, medical care, and lifestyle adjustments to illness or injury and consultation with medical personnel about the family's psychosocial needs; and (4) counseling to reduce emotional distress and foster problem solving (Myer & Hanna, 1996).

Brief Treatment of Medical Crises

The issues and themes that characterize single-session work are also present in the brief treatment of medical crises of chronic illness and disability. The roles that social workers have traditionally played in health care are also found in short-term ambulatory care—for example, assisting the patient and family in making decisions and in accomplishing the psychosocial tasks necessary for adapting to illness; working with the patient or family and health care specialists to overcome obstacles for managing the recommended treatment plan; identifying and addressing caregivers' needs; counseling patient and family about loss issues; and serving as a liaison for the patient and family to the physician and other health care specialists in addressing medical care and psychosocial issues (Abramson, 1992; Berkman, 1996).

Brief treatment of individuals in ambulatory care is characterized by a focus on the medical condition and by the use of task-centered, problem-solving, structured approaches for assisting patients and families with the psychosocial and physical problems resulting from the medical condition. In this practice model it is expected that patients will be able to make good use of a time-limited approach at times of crisis—that is, when the patient has received the diagnosis or has been discharged from the hospital, or when there is an exacerbation of the chronic condition, and that interventions targeted to the specific problems and concerns associated with the medical condition will be most useful to patients and their families. Implicit in this practice approach are certain assumptions about the nature of a medical crisis and its resolution. One assumption is that there are normative reactions and predictable psychosocial adjustments to chronic illness and disability. The strengths perspective (the need to engage the client's usual coping strategies in the resolution of the medical crisis) and the crisis theory principle (of a crisis as being an opportunity to learn new coping strategies) are also implicit in this practice approach (Abramson, 1992).

In the first session of brief medical counseling, the clinician will need to explain the purpose of the consultation, the focus of the assessment, and the services that the health care social worker can offer. This is particularly important with patients referred by their primary care physicians or specialists or by other family members and who might be reluctant to accept social work or mental health services. Encouraging patients to discuss their thoughts and feelings about the referral and their expectations and concerns about the process is a good place to begin. In addition, an educational approach in the first session can be a useful way of diminishing fear or stigma about illness or mental illness that may be making the individual hesitate about accepting services. For example, reluctant clients can gain some relief from hearing about the kinds of changes in lifestyle and concerns and feelings that people typically experience: concerns about being able to comply with the demands of a rehabilitation program, distress about limits to vocational or social activities, and feelings of confusion and anxiety about these lifestyle changes. In addition, focusing on the normative and predictable responses to illness rather than on preexisting personal or interpersonal difficulties can also reduce anxiety and fear about entering treatment (Moffat & Kay, 1996).

The focus in the assessment is on the impact of the medical condition on the functioning of the patient and the patient's family. Therefore, the assessment should begin with what the patient sees as the problem(s) stemming from the illness or disability, in an unstructured manner that allows him or her to tell his or her story. Thereafter, the worker can ask targeted questions that will help the patient recount his or her experience with the medical problem. Following a semistructured interview such as the one developed by Seaburn et al. (1996) enables the interviewer to do a complete biopsychosocial assessment. The interview generally begins with the history of the medical problem, including the earliest symptoms; reactions to the problem by the patient, family, and friends; hospitalizations; diagnosis; and current health status. Next the impact of the illness on the patient is elicited. Details of changes in daily functioning, including work and interpersonal relationships, should be noted, along with the client's expectations of the course of the illness and the future. Data should also be gathered on the client's past coping strategies and the client's view of how he or she is coping with the medical crisis.

Information on the impact of the condition on the patient's family should also be gathered from the patient or family. This can be derived by looking in detail at changes in family functioning and in relationships—for example, what changes in relationship have occurred; who has been most affected by the difficulty; who is the chief caregiver; how much financial, emotional, and physical support is being given, from each person's perspective; and whether the family can discuss the medical condition (Seaburn et al., 1996). Since caregivers often show physical, emotional, and social evidence of increased stress related to their caregiving, an ecomap can be a useful instrument for quickly gathering information on the family's resources and vulnerabilities and the degree of support that is available to the patient (Abramson, 1992). Finally, the meaning of the illness to the patient and family should be assessed to determine if dysfunctional beliefs or a self-defeating narrative might be compromising adaptation. Examples would be a belief that the illness is a punishment, that the patient is no longer lovable, or that illness or disability must inevitably lead to helplessness, betrayal, or abandonment (Druss, 1995).

The assessment of the patient's adjustment to illness or disability and the formulation of goals should also take into account such factors as the phase of the patient's illness, the influence of cultural beliefs on the experience of the illness, the patient's and family's past experiences of illness and loss, and where the patient and family are in terms of life cycle stages (Rolland, 1994). Finally, it is important to assess whether psychological problems such as depression, anxiety, substance abuse, or dementia are interfering with the patient's ability to adapt to the challenges of the illness or disability and with his or her ability to make decisions required for adaptation.

Once the patient and the therapist have reached a mutual understanding of the problems and needs of the patient, they will need to set goals that are specific and attainable. Realistic goals facilitate the process of adaptation and help clients gain a sense of cognitive and emotional control at a time when they are losing physical control. Examples of achievable goals are (1) finding additional social supports among relatives or in the community, (2) reducing tensions between particular family members, (3) learning how to express one's needs in a direct manner, and (4) locating needed financial, housing, or health care resources (Pollin & Kanaan, 1995).

An eclectic approach to intervention planning is generally favored in the brief treatment of medical crisis situations because the needs of patients facing chronic illness are so diverse and also change over the course of the illness. One or more practice models such as task-centered, cognitive-behavioral, case management, psychodynamic, psychoeducation, and family models might be selected over the course of the treatment, which generally lasts six to ten sessions. The Levels of Intervention model might be useful here for making that selection. Thus, a patient whose illness or disability has brought about major changes in physical, occupational, and social functioning, who is experiencing major depression and anxiety, whose family has a history of having difficulty coping with illness or loss, and who will need to move is someone who will need the concrete assistance, guidance, symptom reduction, educational, and stabilizing interventions of Level I. Many clients, however, with good coping strategies and support networks will be able to make use of both Level I and the exploratory, expressive interventions of Level II as they proceed with adaptation and grief work.

Level I interventions in medical crisis situations would address the fundamental instrumental and psychosocial tasks for reducing distress and fostering an accommodation to the changed life circumstances. Clients may first need to be guided through the problem-solving process, because their level of emotional distress is interfering with their usual capabilities or because they lack problem-solving skills. Thus the first step in the intervention process would be to help them prioritize problems, generate possible solutions, and identify the resources and the tasks that would be involved in each possible solution. In these circumstances, the problems often have to do with inadequate information about the patient's medical condition and about resources and how to access them. The social worker might need to educate the family about the course of the illness or refer the patient or family to a support or health education group. Another way to help the family get the necessary information would be to arrange a conference with the physician or home care providers and, if necessary, coach the patient and family about how to get their questions answered by health care providers (Abramson, 1992).

Other problems that may need to be addressed in the early sessions are difficulties in making decisions about treatment and long-term care arrangements, problems with the continuity of care and coordination of medical and social services, and caregiver stress. While the social worker serves as a broker, advocate, or mediator[2] for the family with health care organizations and social service agencies, the goal remains that of empowering the patient and his or her family with the skills to obtain information and resources over the course of the illness and to problem-solve. Thus, educational and psychoeducational approaches are important interventions in health care counseling, because these are the methods by which the client can gain knowledge and skills for the long-term management of the illness or disability. The psychoeducational approach generally involves a structured teaching model. The steps in this model are identification of a needed skill or skills—for example, stress management, communication skills, time management, and so on; explanation of the purpose for mastering the skills; presentation of behavioral guidelines and the necessary steps to mastery; coaching in the practice of the skill; and assignment of homework to develop competency in the new skills and to generalize learning to other areas of functioning (Hardley & Guerney, 1989).

In brief treatment, the worker provides support and a sense of direction for how these tasks will get worked through (i.e., the worker serves as a catalyst), but the work will go on perhaps throughout the course of the illness. Some of the psychosocial tasks are specific to the medical crisis, but several are tasks facing anyone passing through a major transition in life. The general tasks are (1) dealing with feelings of loss and longing for the way things were before the crisis (2) struggling with feelings of tension and anxiety about having to make decisions and to choose new directions and new ways of doing things, and take on new roles; (3) adjusting to any changes in status or position that accompany the transition; and (4) adopting a new standard of well-being and accepting a period of transition to the new standard (Golan, 1981).

The psychosocial tasks particular to chronic illness and disability center on the typical emotional and interpersonal adjustment issues faced by individuals. These issues have a greater or lesser degree of salience depending upon whether the illness or disability had an acute or gradual onset, is progressive or episodic, and is incapacitating or fatal. Rolland (1994) notes that the intense affects that are common with chronic medical conditions can undermine a patient's or family's ability to cope with the many practical, instrumental tasks and decisions that they face. The patient and his or her family struggle with fear and anticipatory grief as they experience a loss of control over their lives, loss of bodily control, loss of key roles (worker, athlete, etc.), and ultimately the loss of the relationship. The anticipation of loss in and of itself may unbalance the family equilibrium.

---

[2] *Broker:* One who works to link clients with needed resources and services and to facilitate the referral process.

Advocate: Someone who works with and on behalf of clients to help them obtain needed resources and services and who works toward improving oppressive social conditions.

Mediator: In the role of mediator, the worker seeks to resolve obstacles to obtaining services and resources when there is a conflict about or denial of services (Hepworth, Rooney, & Larsen, 1997).

The decision to work with the patient individually, with the family, or some combination of both is dependent upon the assessment of where the greatest need is, what will be most beneficial, and what the patient and family members feel will be most helpful to them in resolving the problems they have identified. Involvement of the family in the evaluation process and at termination is very likely to be beneficial, even if the choice is for individual counseling. Some families may seek help on their own because of their concerns about the patient and about the feelings (such as depression and anxiety) they are experiencing in coping with the patient's needs. Having the opportunity to express their concerns and feelings, to hear each other's concerns, to problem-solve as a family, and to develop tolerance for their differing styles and pace of grieving can reduce the degree of stress they are experiencing.

Coping with a Child's Chronic Illness

Mr. and Mrs. L applied for marital counseling at the suggestion of their pediatrician, who was treating their 10-year-old son, Jason, for asthma. They had received this referral 6 months earlier but only decided to come in after having had a fight, during which Mrs. L asked her husband to move out. The couple had been married for 21 years, but they had been having increasing difficulty getting along over the past 3 years. The most recent fight was over something that they had fought about many times before, the amount of time Mr. L was spending with friends. Mr. L insisted that he was not spending an inordinate amount of time with friends, and besides he needed time out after working two jobs and spending much of his remaining time on their son's health care needs. Mrs. L, on the other hand, complained about the burden of their son's care falling to her, even though she worked 30 hours a week and did most of the housework. The most recent argument was about Mr. L using his day off to spend the day with friends when Mrs. L had expected him to stay home and help her get caught up with the household tasks that had piled up during their son's most recent hospitalization for severe asthma. The hospital was located an hour away and Mrs. L had spent all of her nonworking hours at the hospital.

Jason had suffered from asthma since early childhood, but his condition had worsened over the past 3 years. He required daily supervision of his medical care and often wanted his parents' companionship because his outside physical activities were increasingly restricted. In addition, there had been a number of frightening trips to the emergency room during the past 3 years. Jason is their youngest child. They have two older children, 20 and 21, who are not living at home and who intermittently help out. A few family members live nearby, but they are not able to help much. Mr. and Mrs. L reported that, as their son had become more disabled, they had had less time for friends and church and therefore did not have the support network that they once had. Mr. and Mrs. L essentially relied only on each other for Jason's care and for support, although they had not been able to give each other much support in recent years. When queried about any advice or guidance they might have been given about how to manage the stresses of dealing with a chronically ill child, they reported that they had not received any, either through the medical centers or through their HMO. They had received assistance in getting insurance coverage and some education in the management of the illness, but no one had ever asked them about the impact of the illness on their lives.

A review of their individual and marital history revealed they were a couple with many strengths. They had been effective in coping with the normal stresses of living and child-rearing. Initially, they had worked well together in dealing with Jason's asthma attacks even though his medical care had created financial strains (both parents worked in relatively low-paying jobs). However, as the severity and frequency of the attacks increased, they found they were arguing more and enjoying each other less and less. Both acknowledged that they did not want the marriage to end and wanted to work on resolving the conflicts they were having.

The remainder of the first session was spent on validating their efforts and accomplishments in caring for a severely ill child, as well as in normalizing for them the tensions and fears they were experiencing. The focus was placed on how to deal with the medical crises and on examining their feelings about their son's relapsing medical condition. Neither one was certain what to expect about the course of the illness, and both clung to the idea that, if they followed medical advice, Jason would eventually get better. However, they were demoralized and frightened by the fact that he seemed to be getting worse rather than better. Both Mr. and Mrs. L were feeling helpless and angry about not being able to prevent the asthma attacks and about the toll the illness was taking on their lives. Mr. L, in particular, felt badly about Jason not being able to run and play like other kids. He admitted wanting to get away from what he perceived to be Jason's unhappy life. Both agreed that they needed some respite from caring for Jason, but Mrs. L found it difficult to leave Jason with anyone but her husband.

Mr. and Mrs. L were relieved to learn that many of the marital problems they were experiencing were common responses to the extraordinary demands a child's chronic illness place on a couple. They indicated that they would like to find additional ways of coping with the stress of Jason's illness since they were both feeling under tremendous strain. Six sessions were contracted for, with the goal of achieving a better balance between caring for Jason and for themselves and for their relationship. The objectives were exploring options for respite care; learning to communicate better about child care and household tasks; getting more information about caring for asthma, particularly from other parents with asthmatic children; and finding ways to support each other in the way they had before Jason's asthma worsened.

At the end of the six sessions, the goal and objectives had been met. Mr. and Mrs. L reported feeling less stressed about Jason, even though they knew that his condition was going to be a chronically relapsing one. They attended a workshop for parents of asthmatic children, where they learned about how other parents sought to balance child care and their own needs.

They felt more comfortable in asking friends and family for assistance with child care, particularly as Mrs. L was socializing more. They were engaging in some of the activities they had enjoyed before Jason's illness began to occupy all of their time and attention, and they were able to resolve conflicts about sharing responsibilities, using a problem-solving method learned during the course of treatment. At the 3-month follow-up, Mr. and Mrs. L were still adequately coping.

Group Therapy for Medical Crises

Group therapy may be the treatment of choice for either or both the patient and the family members. Groups have been found to be very effective in reducing emotional distress and in improving functioning of individuals and families struggling with chronic medical conditions, whether the groups are medical information groups or social support groups. Groups offer patients the opportunity to view their feelings and adjustment difficulties as normal and to share experiences and feelings. Group members can offer each other valuable insights and information about how to cope with the particular problems that illness entails or how to access resources. Time-limited groups for individuals with medical conditions are often homogeneous; that is, the members have (or are related to persons having) the same medical condition and are at the same stage in the course of the illness. These commonalties usually facilitate the development of affiliation, trust, and empathy so that the group coheres more quickly. However, groups with heterogeneous medical conditions can also work within a time-limited framework. Here the group leader must be more actively involved in bringing commonalties into group awareness (Moffat & Kay, 1996). Finally, whether the individual or family was seen individually, in family, or in group, referral to a self-help group can help the individual or family sustain the gains they made in treatment and provide them with ongoing support.

Caregivers' Group

A 6-week psychoeducation and support group was established to assist individuals in their roles as caregivers for spouses or parents who had Alzheimer's type dementia. The five individuals were referred by their primary care physician after they sought help for what appeared to be stress-related physical complaints, anxiety, and mild depression. The group was a closed one that used a combined structured and unstructured format—that is, one in which the first half of the session focused on imparting knowledge about the nature of Alzheimer's disease, the course of the illness, and the medical care of Alzheimer's patients and on developing stress management skills, while the second half was an open discussion of the participant's experiences in caring for their loved ones. A nurse and social worker were co-leaders of the group, with the nurse assuming responsibility for providing information about the disease and both group leaders assisting in the development of skills for coping with stress and in the facilitation of discussion and the development of mutual aid among the participants. The information and skills-building portion of the group sessions consisted of presentations by the nurse, videotapes, and a guest lecture by a previous group participant.

The first presentations on the diagnosis and prognosis of the disease prompted many questions and points of discussion, as well as some expression of anger with medical professionals for not being sufficiently forthcoming or responsive to their concerns. The guest lecture by a former participant, however, opened up the group to a fuller discussion of the impact of caring for someone with dementia on their lives. Among the themes that developed through the remaining sessions were the sense of isolation, confusion, chronic uncertainty about the appropriate level of care needed, guilt, anger, concern about the impact of the strain of caregiving on their spouses and children, the loss of freedom, and sadness about the loss of the parent or spouse they had known. The final sessions focused on working toward achieving a better balance between caregiving and caring for themselves. Group members shared with each other techniques they had discovered that worked for dealing with some of the day-to-day difficulties such as gaining cooperation around the taking of medications. They also shared stress-relieving strategies. In the last session, when they were asked what they had gained from the group, most members cited the support they had received for their feelings and the information they had gained about how to deal with typical problems in caregiving. Most also noted a welcome reduction in guilt, knowing that others shared their same feelings of frustration, anger, and resentment about the changes in their parents or spouses and the resultant changes in their own lives.

Brief Interventions with Victims of Violence and Abuse

Acute Care Settings

"Victims of violence are heavy consumers of health care. It is estimated that 30% of all emergency room visits by women may be the result of battering and that 1.4 million physician visits per year are for treatment of battering-related injuries" (Dhooper, 1997, p. 41). In response to the increasing number of patients who are victims of random violence or domestic violence, many hospitals have set up procedures and protocols for handling suspected abuse of children, and some have them for spousal and elderly abuse. In addition, screening for possible victimization and risk of danger to self or others has been incorporated into routine assessments in many emergency departments for patients presenting in crisis (Hoff, 1995). This discussion of single-session therapy and brief treatment will focus on the treatment of the abused woman, but the general practice approach described, the problem-solving, client-determined approach, is applicable to working with victims of random or stranger violence.

Social workers in emergency departments are called upon to provide crisis intervention services to patients and their families when the need for medical care is the result of violence or when abuse or violence is suspected. They also serve as consultants for the other members of the emergency department team, providing them with the psychosocial information that will help them in making treatment decisions such as whether or not to hospitalize or if the treatment plan needs to be modified because the patient's or the family's degree of distress or dysfunction would interfere with their ability to follow the recommended treatment (Berkman, 1996). Contact with the victim and his or her family in emergency departments is often a single contact, with a follow-up visit if the patient is admitted to the hospital, or a follow-up call if the patient will be seen on an outpatient basis or in the community.

The worker's most immediate task in working with a victim of violence is to determine lethality (whether there is an actual or potential threat to the life of the patient or the lives of others) and the degree of dysfunction (whether the patient is in danger of losing his or her home, job, or social supports as a consequence of not being able to cope). To make this determination, the worker looks at the balance between coping responses and signals of distress. Typical signals that a client is not coping well with stress are (1) difficulty in dealing with negative feeling states, (2) exhibiting suicidal or homicidal tendencies, (3) abuse of drugs or alcohol, (4) violations of the law, and (5) inability to make use of available resources or help (Hoff, 1995). It is vital to have an accurate assessment of risk; therefore, it is important to establish rapport with the patient and patient's family and to provide them with a sense of calm and safety in order to obtain complete information. These conditions are more likely to develop if the crisis worker has a nonjudgmental attitude, an openness to learning the client's views on his or her situation (particularly with clients from backgrounds different than the worker's own), and a willingness to move quickly and actively to provide distress relief—for example, normalizing the client's reactions and validating his or her fears and anxieties. Listening actively and empathically, paraphrasing, lending support for emotional expression, helping the client to organize thoughts and gain cognitive clarity, and conveying a sense of direction and hope are also useful for establishing rapport and good communication (Myer & Hanna, 1996).

If victimization has been determined or if there is a risk of violence toward self or others, then the central task for the remainder of the crisis session is developing a plan of action that addresses the risk of future abuse. A more detailed assessment of personal and family strengths and limitations and of the risk and protective factors in the victim's environment will be needed in order to determine the level of care needed and the feasibility of putting a plan into action. In a situation of partner abuse, for example, setting realistic, achievable goals that reflect the woman in her situation and her point of view is more likely to lead to a positive outcome than an intervention plan that, no matter how well intentioned, is more reflective of the worker's perspective. This does not negate the importance of the worker being clear about his or her concern for the victim's safety or directives about what steps are necessary to ensure safety, but rather requires that the plan of action fit the patient's psychosocial reality and that she make her own decisions, thereby empowering her and increasing the chances that she will succeed (Walker, 1995). Thus, the plan of action should take into consideration the degree of the victim's emotional and economic dependence on the abusing partner; her usual coping strategies (productive and counterproductive); the degree to which denial and minimization have become survival strategies; the degree to which self-esteem and sense of efficacy have been impaired by the abuse; any cultural and family restrictions on the victim's options for dealing with the abuse; and the degree of helpfulness or conflict in the victim's social support network (Dziegielewski & Resnick, 1996).

In addition to collaborating with the patient on the formulation of a plan of action, the key intervention strategies in this single contact are (1) offering an alternative perspective on the abuse, (2) educating the victim about the abuse cycle, and (3) linking the victim with community resources. The introduction of a novel or alternative perspective begins with validating the abused woman's feelings of fear, anxiety, and anger and respecting her views on her relationship with the abuser. The validation and respect, in conjunction with a collaborative approach to problem solving, can serve as a disconfirming experience; that is, it challenges the victim's negative assumptions about her powerlessness within relationships that have been internalized as a result of the abusive relationship. Similarly, in the process of arriving at goals and an action plan, the patient can learn to differentiate between what is under her control (her own actions) and what is not (his abusive behavior) and what steps are necessary to ensure her own safety. In addition, education about the patterns of violence in abusive relationships, in general and specifically in her own relationship, can provide the woman with a different perspective on her situation. The pattern of violence is one of escalating violence and psychological manipulation, with typically a three-stage cycle to the violence (building tensions, acute battering incident, and loving-contrition stage). Asking for details about the abuse that brought the woman to the hospital and other abuse incidents helps her to identify the tension-building cues that can alert her to when she is in potential danger (Walker, 1995).

The process of arriving at a plan of action should also be an empowering one for the abused woman. That is, personal strengths should be identified and incorporated into the plan. Options should be identified and the pros and cons of these options for her weighed—for example, a shelter for battered women versus a personal safety plan, or individual therapy versus a support group. If the woman is not yet ready to leave the relationship, a preliminary, basic personal safety plan can be devised based on her understanding of the tension-building signs in the abuser. This would include an escape plan and a plan for dealing with the abuser—for example, telling him beforehand that she will leave for a cooling-off period when tensions are building (Walker, 1995).

The final step in this process would be to link the client with the community resources that she has decided would be helpful to her. The role, if any, that the patient would like the social worker to play in the referral process—for example, advocate, broker, or mediator of services—should also be negotiated. At the end of the session, time should be allotted for summarizing what has gone on, with an emphasis on the decisions that the woman has arrived at and time for the patient to reflect on the session. This end-of-session summarizing and feedback time provides an opportunity for correcting misunderstandings and clarifying details of the action plan. This is especially important in working with victims of violence, who may be emotionally overwhelmed and having difficulty achieving cognitive clarity on the issues under discussion. Finally, an agreement on the time for a follow-up call should be negotiated (Dhooper, 1997).

Nonacute Settings

The crisis intervention or brief treatment (6 to 12 sessions) of trauma or violence in ambulatory care settings would begin with many of the same interventions described above for a single session: establishment of a safe therapeutic environment and rapport, assessment of lethality, evaluation of personal and environmental risk and protective factors, education about abuse, determination of level of care, development of an immediate plan of action, and referral to needed medical or social services. However, there may need to be differences in emphasis in the first session, because the presenting problems may not be directly or obviously linked to trauma or abuse. That is, victims of abuse or violence may not present with physical injuries as they would in an emergency room, but instead present with somatic complaints or noninjury medical problems. "Victims of abuse are much more likely than non-victims to have poor health, chronic pain problems, addictions, problem pregnancies, depression, and suicide attempts" (Dhooper, 1997, p. 181). Problems with substance abuse, anxiety, depression, or behavior problems with their children may then surface, but the abuse may be denied or minimized upon routine inquiry. Women who are being abused may go to considerable lengths to conceal the abuse, in part because of fear of retaliation or pessimism about others being willing to help them (Hamberger & Hotzworth-Munroe, 1994). Even if the abuse is acknowledged, it may not be seen as a problem that needs to be addressed, because the abused women may see the behavior as justified (e.g., "he's under a lot of stress") or blame themselves for provoking the attack. Such abused women will need more time to see the abuse from a different perspective and to accept their right to be free from harm (Walker, 1995).

The first sessions in the brief treatment of trauma or abuse are essentially Level I interventions that address problems of safety, substance abuse, stresses, and stability through focused, problem-solving interventions. In single-session contact, a basic personal safety plan is developed for the woman who does not want to leave the relationship with the abuser. In brief treatment this plan is elaborated upon, covering more contingencies and thereby increasing its effectiveness. The plan focuses on "how the victim can escape, where she can go, and who can help her. This should be laid out in terms of very specific behaviors, including such items as which phone she would use, where she could keep some clothes and an extra set of car keys, and more" (Dziegielewski & Resnick, 1996, p. 123).

Developing a safety plan involves reviewing specific details of past abuse situations and discussing specific steps needed to get to a safe place. This process serves as a consciousness raising intervention for abused women who are using denial and minimization as survival strategies. When details are elicited for putting together a safety plan, cognitive dissonance can develop when the woman's beliefs about the abuser and her own responsibility for the abuse conflict with the reality of the abuser's behavior and her actual degree of danger. Exploration of past coping strategies in developing the safety plan can also begin to challenge the woman's belief about her lack of power and efficacy in her life. As Walker (1995) indicates, the two primary goals of therapy with victims of abuse are ensuring their safety and restoring a sense of control in their lives. The two goals can be mutually reinforcing.

For clients who are dealing with multiple stressors, Level I interventions may be the only appropriate ones for the course of the treatment. Thus, the young woman in the following vignette, who had recently moved to the area with her boyfriend, was best served by a task-centered, case management, cognitive restructuring approach for the first 9 of 12 sessions. This was because the client lacked a support network, housing, and secure employment, was abusing alcohol, and either denied or minimized her boyfriend's abusive behavior while blaming herself for his rages. With such clients, the middle sessions are devoted to finding and connecting the client to resources, reviewing the safety plan, and resolving obstacles to task accomplishment, including dealing with the unconscious fears and assumptions that make it difficult for the client to take actions on her own behalf. Other abused women with fewer stressors, more resources, or a limited history of abuse may be ready by the third or fourth session to examine their thoughts and feelings toward the abuser and about themselves—the losses they have experienced as a result of the abusive relationship—and grieve for the impending loss if they are moving in the direction of leaving the relationship (Hoff, 1995).

For both groups of women, restructuring of dysfunctional beliefs appears to be an essential component of the therapeutic process because of the degree to which disabling cognitions such as "I can't survive without him" or "If I hadn't done_____, he wouldn't have hit me" inhibit the woman's ability to protect herself. Moreover, fear and anxiety create cognitive confusion such that good judgment and decision making are compromised. For the woman to be able to accept that the abuse is not her fault and that she does not deserve mistreatment, these "cognitive rules" will need to be challenged through the cognitive-behavioral techniques of guided discovery, examining the evidence, challenging absolutes, labeling of distortions, de-catastrophizing, challenging dichotomous thinking, and so on (Freeman, Pretzer, Fleming, & Simon, 1990). Thus, a belief such as "I can't survive without him" is first identified as being significant, for example, in the woman's decision-making and as having emotional and self-esteem consequences. The client is then guided in the exploration of the evidence that supports or disconfirms this belief (e.g., evidence of competency in other roles). It can also be a useful challenge to this absolute belief to examine its origins in the threats of violence and verbal abuse from her partner and the process of socialization into dependency in a relationship. The client is then encouraged to compare the consequences of maintaining this belief and giving it up. Homework that offers an opportunity for disconfirming experiences should be assigned—for example, talking with family and friends about support that might be available to her if she chooses to leave her partner (Granvold, 1996).

A similar process can be used when such dynamics as conflicted motivations prevent the woman from following through with referrals to needed services such as substance abuse treatment programs or employment agencies. Practical issues that interfere should not be overlooked—for example, lack of baby-sitting or financial resources. Enhancing the effectiveness of the client's natural social supports is another important task in the middle and termination stages, as the client is likely to have become isolated from family and friends, and their support will be essential to her being able to sustain gains in self-care and self-sufficiency. Meeting with family members or friends before termination can be very useful, as is connecting the client to ongoing support groups for battered women in the community. In the final session, time should be spent on reflecting on the difficult work the client has had to face and the progress she has made in this brief contact. This is an important part of correcting the client's negative self-image and motivating her to seek help in the future when needed (Dziegielewski & Resnick, 1996).

Domestic Violence

> Sonia, a 28-year-old administrator, was referred by her primary care physician, who suspected that she was being battered. Sonia had consulted her physician for an anorexia of several weeks' standing. She acknowledged many stresses in her life related to her recent move to the state, including employment uncertainty for her, her boyfriend's inability to secure employment, living in temporary housing, and frequent arguments with her boyfriend over their financial problems and other problems associated

with the move. Sonia denied physical abuse but could not give convincing explanations for bruises found during the physical exam. She readily accepted a referral for mental health services, stating that she wanted to get couple therapy because she wanted her relationship with her boyfriend to return to the one they had had before they moved from Georgia.

When Sonia and Dan came for the first interview, Sonia was first interviewed alone, which she objected to, insisting that she only wanted to be seen with Dan. At first Sonia focused only on the stresses and strains in the relationship related to the move and the fact that their job situations were not working out. She did eventually acknowledge that part of the motivation to leave Georgia was related to conflicts with her family over her relationship with Dan. Her family had emigrated from an Eastern European country and settled in Atlanta into a tightly knit ethnic enclave, which did not approve of marriage outside of the group. Her family did not approve of Dan because he was an outsider and not college educated, as Sonia was, and thus Sonia and Dan had moved to get away from the pressure her family was placing on her to get out of this relationship. Sonia stated that their arguments generally took place after they had been drinking and that they were mainly verbal fights. Dan had hit her only twice, she insisted. However, in going over the details of their most recent fight, it became clear that Dan's anger was explosive and while this time his slamming her against the wall had only caused bruises, the potential was there for greater injury. I expressed my concern about her safety and provided her with information about help for women who are being battered and with telephone numbers including the clinic's 24-hour number. She took the information but insisted she didn't need these services.

Dan also minimized the extent of the violence, stating that he only grabbed Sonia when she was becoming verbally abusive during one of their frequent fights. He expressed concern about the fact that they were no longer getting along, but mainly he wanted to justify his actions and blame Sonia for provoking the fights and his attacks on her. He denied any previous problems with controlling his anger or hurting anyone, except during his service in Vietnam, where he had been a member of a Special Forces unit. He did acknowledge a psychiatric hospitalization for depression and PTSD shortly after returning from Vietnam, but he had not received treatment since then. Dan appeared to expend considerable effort to try to control the interviewer's impressions of him.

The joint interview quickly revealed the degree of conflict between them and their lack of ability to resolve their conflicts. They quickly launched into criticizing and blaming each other for their financial and housing problems. They knew a few people, who were friends of Dan's from his army days, but Sonia did not want to spend time with them because she suspected that they were involved in shady activities. Dan's involvement with the friends was a constant source of friction between them, as was the fact that Sonia did not feel that Dan was doing enough to find a job.

The recommendation for treatment was for each of them to be seen separately, because of the degree of stress each was experiencing in adjusting to the move and the need to end the violence in their relationship. In addition to individual sessions, it was recommended that Sonia join a support group for women and Dan join an anger control group for men. Both Sonia and Dan expressed disagreement with the assessment. However, they agreed to think over the treatment options and to call back within a week about their decisions. Before the week was over, Sonia called the 24-hour emergency call-in service at 2:00 A.M. Sonia reported that she and Dan had had another fight, and this time he had grabbed her by the hair and slammed her head into the wall. She indicated that she didn't need to go to the emergency room but would see a doctor that day, and that she was safe for the night. A meeting was arranged at another office because of her concern that Dan would be angry if she came in alone.

A safety plan was devised at the first session. It specifically addressed the hazard to her of drinking with Dan. She was not ready to consider going to a shelter or moving to another apartment, but she agreed that she needed to find some place to stay at those times when they were having arguments. She wasn't ready to give up on the relationship, but she could now acknowledge that there was danger for her in this relationship and that she needed and deserved to be safe. In this session and for the next eight sessions, the focus was on her worries and fears about leaving Dan. These centered on being in a strange community without a secure job or support network. She also didn't want to go home and admit to her parents that they were right about Dan. She had been trying for years to establish her own life and worried that if she returned home, she would again be subject to their control. At the end of the first session, Sonia contracted to attend the 12 sessions her HMO plan allowed. The primary goal was to ensure her safety and the secondary goal was to reduce the anxiety and depression associated with the stresses of being in an abusive relationship and with moving.

Although Sonia exhibited some of the dysfunctional beliefs that many abused women exhibit—for example, that she caused and deserved the abuse and that she could not live without Dan, these were not firmly entrenched. She also had several areas of skill and accomplishment that could be drawn on to counter her current low self-esteem. Therefore, Sonia was able to change these beliefs, as she could see other options for herself. During this period the supports that she would need to leave the relationship were put into place: securing steady employment, joining a church, and researching other communities.

By the eighth session, she was concerned enough about her safety and about illegal activities that Dan might be getting involved in that she decided she needed to move, but without Dan's knowledge. She had fears about Dan's reaction to her leaving and that his army training might enable him to track her. With the assistance of a social worker at a women's shelter, a plan for moving was devised. The worker also invited Sonia to join a women's group, which she did after she moved into her own apartment. The final sessions focused on helping Sonia deal with the sadness she felt at the loss of Dan, whom she had expected to marry. She also reassessed what her relationship could be to her family. She had contacted her sister and that had gone well, and she was now working toward talking with her parents. Time was also spent on reviewing and reinforcing the gains she had made in stabilizing her employment situation, starting a new support network, and gaining a greater respect for her ability to function well on her own, as she had before she met Dan. With her connection to the self-help group at the women's center and the knowledge that she could get additional help from the clinic in the future if she needed it, Sonia felt comfortable about terminating. At follow-up 3 months later, she had not been found by Dan and was adjusting to her new job and apartment and making friends at work and in her church.

Case Management Exercise: Duane

Use the following vignette to answer the questions in this exercise.

Duane O is a 5-year-old boy who was referred for an evaluation by a pediatrician in the outpatient pediatrics clinic after no physical cause could be found for his severe encopresis and after attempts at diet management had not resulted in any improvement. Duane had been toilet trained, but at age 3 he had begun wetting and soiling again after a 6-month foster home placement where he had been physically abused. He and his brother Troy, age 6, had been placed in foster care after their mother had been badly injured in a car accident and was unable to care for the children, then 2 and 3 years old. Over the last 2 years, the soiling had increased until Duane was soiling over a dozen times per day, including during school hours. At that point, his school felt that they could not manage his problem and were requesting a special education placement.

Mr. and Mrs. O were baffled about how to deal with the soiling and were concerned about Duane not being able to attend school until a special placement could be found. Mrs. O appeared overwhelmed and unable to cope, while Mr. O reported feeling very stressed by the demands placed upon him by his wife, who remained partially disabled, and by Duane, as well as the fact that his job occasionally required that he be away a day or two at a time. In the play therapy evaluation session, Duane presented as a friendly child, pleasant but very anxious, behaviorally and emotionally constricted, acting younger than his stated age. Over the course of two sessions, the source of his anxiety became clear. In his selection of play material, repetitive play activity, and projective drawings, Duane appeared to be expressing excessive concern for his mother's well-being. When his brother Troy was brought into the session, the two children were able to talk about their worry about their father hurting their mother, because he was beating her.

Case Management Exercise: Duane (continued)

> When Mr. and Mrs. O were given the results of the evaluation and told about the relationship between the high anxiety and the encopresis, Mr. O acknowledged the violence and expressed great concern for his children's well-being and remorse for his treatment of his wife. The antecedents to the violence appeared to be his rage at the state of chaos he found the home in when he returned from his business trips. His wife was unable to keep up with the housework or with the extra cleaning that the encopresis presented, in part because of her disability and apparent depression. A home visit was scheduled to assess the family's need for homemaking assistance and a referral was made to a program for male batterers, which Mr. O readily accepted.

1. Select the appropriate level of intervention and your rationale for that approach.
2. Develop a multisystem treatment plan, specifying the community resources that would be utilized to address the current crisis and to provide long-term support to this family. Include a plan for coordinating and monitoring services.
3. Identify individual and family strengths and indicate how you would make use of them in addressing the child's severe symptoms and the domestic violence.
4. Plan how you would use an 8- to 12-session time limit in a flexible, effective manner.

Answers to this exercise appear in the Appendix.

Summary

Health care settings have traditionally employed brief treatment approaches because the nature of the patient's medical condition and treatment time places time constraints on therapy. In addition, since therapy in a health care setting is conceptualized as assisting the patient with medical needs—that is, helping in the recovery process, in following recommended treatment, and in adapting to the challenges of chronic conditions, the health care needs provide a ready focus for brief treatment. This chapter has outlined the traditional roles and functions of social workers and described the changes in roles and functions in the evolving health care environment. It also presented three brief treatment approaches that are particularly useful in health care settings: single-session work, crisis intervention with trauma and abuse, and brief medical counseling.

Recommended Reading

Dhooper, S. S. (1997). *Social work in health care in the 21st century.* Thousand Oaks, CA: Sage Publications.

Hoyt, M. F., Rosenbaum, R., & Talmon, M. (1992). Planned single-session therapy. In S. H. Budman, M. F. Hoyt, & S. Friedman (Eds.), *The first session in brief therapy* (pp. 59–86). New York: Guilford Press.

Pollin, I., & Kanaan, S. B. (1995). *Medical crisis counseling.* New York: W. W. Norton.

Brief Treatment in Health Maintenance Organizations and Employee Assistance Programs

HMOs and Managed Mental Health Care

Health maintenance organizations (HMOs) and employee assistance programs (EAPs) are two forms of capitated,[1] self-contained, managed care organizations that provide mental health services to their subscribers. HMOs and EAPs were the earliest types of managed care organizations in this country, and many of the service delivery methods that have come to characterize managed care practice were developed in these organizations. Today, like all of managed care, they are in a state of evolution in terms of structure and delivery of mental health services (Cummings & Sayama, 1995).

The prototype HMOs were organized along a staff or group model in which comprehensive health care services were provided by in-house staff for a set premium. Mental health services were generally limited to consultation and referral. The goal of the early nonprofit HMOs, which were often union sponsored, was to provide equitable and affordable health care. The HMO Act of 1973 was designed to introduce competition to the predominantly fee-for-service American health system by subsidizing the creation and expansion of HMOs. Profit-making prepaid group practice models were seen as a way of containing costs and controlling the quality of care (Bennett, 1989). After 1973, HMOs adopted a managed care approach to service delivery. They sought to contain costs while ensuring that patients were receiving necessary, appropriate, quality care through such practices as employing primary care physicians as gatekeepers; negotiating fee agreements with preferred hospitals; requiring precertification for hospital admission; and utilizing the techniques of concurrent review, case management, and retrospective chart review (Winegar, 1992). Mental health care benefits (up to 20 sessions) were added to the benefit packages in order to take advantage of federal subsidies that were available to

---

[1] *Capitation* is a business practice in which the providers are paid a set amount of money per member per month.

organizations that met federal requirements under the Community Mental Health Center Act for inpatient and outpatient crisis intervention services. In the late 1980s, in an attempt to gain control of spiraling mental health and substance abuse (MH/SA)[2] treatment costs, HMOs contracted with behavioral health care companies to provide mental health and substance abuse services or to manage the cost and quality of the services. These "carve-out" companies "assume some risks for program costs" and use mental health and substance abuse specialists for managing the utilization of the HMO mental health and substance abuse treatment benefits (Garnick, Hendricks, Dulski, Thorpe, & Horgan, 1994, p. 1203).

The number of Americans receiving their health care through HMOs has increased dramatically, exceeding 79 million members in 1999. This growth has taken place primarily in the newer, open-system models. The traditional closed staff or group models have come to occupy a decreasing proportion of the market. By 1996, staff and group model HMOs served only 27% of the total HMO enrollment, while open system models, independent practice associations (IPAs), network models, and mixed models serving 73% of enrollees were the fastest growing types of HMO (Medical Source, 1999). In the open system models, mental health professionals are loosely affiliated across a wide geographic area, and their practices may include fee-for-service patients. An IPA consists of providers who have agreed to sell their services through the IPA, and the network model consists of groups of providers who have independently contracted with an HMO.

The trend in HMOs will probably continue in the direction toward open system models, with more plans offering point-of-service (POS) options in which the subscriber can decide at the time of receipt of services whether to choose a network provider, with financial incentives to do so, or a nonnetwork provider. Cummings and Sayama (1995) predict, on the basis of several decades of experience with HMOs, that the next generation of HMOs will be complex exclusive provider organizations (EPOs) that are provider-participant owned and accountable to the communities in which they are located. Certainly there will be an increase in membership as more Medicare and Medicaid recipients join HMOs. These changes are likely to spur further developments in practice and delivery of mental health services beyond those outlined below, including a greater emphasis on developing ecosystemic and culturally sensitive practice approaches.

---

[2] Acronyms introduced in this chapter: MH/SA, mental health and substance abuse; IPA, independent practice association; POS, point of service; EPO, exclusive provider organization; CRA, Community Reinforcement Approach; CAGE, from words in the four questions (Lyons et al., 1997); HIV, human immunodeficiency virus.

HMO Mental Health Services

Staff and group model HMOs have been in the forefront in the development of brief psychotherapy approaches and techniques, because mental health services were always time limited in these health care plans. HMOs such as Harvard Community Health Plan and Kaiser Permanente were innovators in the areas of brief family and group therapy, combined biological and psychotherapeutic treatment, empirically based practice, and development of brief therapy principles and techniques. Because facilities using the staff and group models employed a full-time staff of clinicians, there was an opportunity for interdisciplinary cooperation in the development of innovative and efficient mental health services (Hoyt & Austad, 1992).

Among the contributions that HMOs made to the practice of brief therapy was providing an empirical basis for time-limited practice. For example, medical cost offset studies conducted at several HMOs generated evidence that brief treatment was effective and identified some of the characteristics of effective brief therapy. These studies looked at the impact of brief psychotherapy on utilization of medical services to determine if there was a cost savings associated with the offering of mental health services. Kaiser Permanente experimented with combinations of practice approaches (e.g., cognitive-behavioral, psychoeducational, family systems, and psychodynamic) and with combinations of modalities (e.g., individual and group). These were then matched to specific conditions, with medical cost offset used as the criterion of effectiveness of the intervention strategy. On the basis of these experiments, they determined that the most effective treatments in terms of diminishing utilization of medical services were those that were focused, that were oriented toward solving problems in the here and now, and that provided information and skills (Cummings & Sayama, 1995).

Based on such research and clinical experience, there was a central paradigm shift about the role of therapy and of the therapist in HMO mental health services. Therapy came to be seen as a means for facilitating change rather than as a mechanism for the development of insight or the healing of past hurts. At the same time, the therapist's function was reconceptualized as being a catalyst for change rather than an analyst or interpreter of the client's thoughts and feelings about the past (Bennett, 1989).

By the late 1980s, the following principles came to characterize HMO therapy: (1) an emphasis on problem solving; (2) organizational support for rapid response to clients in crisis; (3) an emphasis on an active partnership between therapist and client, culminating in an agreement on a treatment plan with defined goals; (4) a differential and flexible use of time according to the client's changing needs; (5) collaborative, interdisciplinary relations to facilitate combinations of treatment methods in order to maximize positive treatment outcomes;

(6) flexible, integrated, and combined treatment modalities tailored to the patient; (7) treatment conceptualized as brief and intermittent throughout the life cycle; (8) the therapist as catalyst—that is, the therapist setting a process into motion, with the significant changes in the client's life taking place outside of therapy and after the end of therapy; (9) acceptance of utilization management as essential to containing costs and assuring quality of care; (10) an emphasis on outcomes rather than on roles, therefore favoring the use of interdisciplinary teams and community resources for efficient, effective treatment; and (11) a belief that prepaid services (capitation) allow for innovative practice, as the therapist is not bound by what will be reimbursed and therefore can offer services such as home visits, school consultation, and prevention programs such as stress management and parenting groups (Hoyt & Austad, 1992; Cummings & Sayama, 1995)

Certain practice approaches were deemed a better fit with the HMO orientation and therefore have become preferred practices in HMO therapy. These are crisis intervention, cognitive-behavioral intervention, solution-focused therapy, group work, family work, psychopharmacology, case management, psychoeducation, and outpatient substance abuse treatment (Hoyt, 1995; Winegar, 1993). As an example, groups have become an important part of HMO practice not only because they are cost efficient, but also because of their intrinsic power to facilitate and maintain change. With regard to substance abuse treatment, employers' dissatisfaction with the high cost and high rate of recidivism of traditional inpatient substance abuse programs led to a search for alternative treatment methods that are less costly and more effective. In addition, research studies found that traditional 28-day inpatient programs were no more effective than less restrictive outpatient programs (McCall-Perez, 1994). The Institute of Medicine of the National Academy of Sciences in 1993 recommended a move from the one-size-fits-all traditional inpatient substance abuse programs to more flexible, briefer, community-based programs. Consequently, HMOs and other managed care organizations have been developing intensive outpatient programs and contracting with chemical dependence units that offer variable-length-of-stay programs (Johnson, 1995).

EAPs and Managed Care

Employee assistance programs have been in existence since the early part of the 20th century. They began as employee-sponsored counseling programs for employees with alcohol abuse problems. Over time, particularly during the 1960s and 1970s, when many employers began adding EAP services, the counseling came to include assistance with a wide variety of personal problems that might affect an employee's job performance or safety. Four main types of EAPs emerged. Two types are in-house models, with one limiting services primarily to diagnosis and referral and the other having more comprehensive services such as crisis intervention and short-term counseling. The other two types of EAP services are external contractor models, in which EAP firms provide services to a number of employers through a network of counselors and case managers and offer either limited or more comprehensive services (Fleischer & Kaplan, 1988). Most of the EAPs also provide other services for employers, such as educating supervisors about mental health and substance abuse issues and training supervisors in how to recognize and refer troubled employees. EAPs in these educational and service brokerage roles were also a significant force in reducing some of the stigma surrounding psychological and substance abuse problems (Winegar, 1993).

Prior to the emergence of managed mental health care concepts and practices, EAPs focused mainly on identifying and obtaining care for employees with substance abuse or mental health problems. In the traditional EAP (before managed care), the EAP counselor might provide case management services (e.g., monitoring patient care, coordinating services, supervising follow-up services, etc.), but the emphasis was on advocating for and management of services for the client and not on the use of case management to contain costs and manage the MH/SA benefits. Most employers recognized the benefits of EAP services in terms of improved worker performance and morale and in the reduction of wrongful-dismissal suits related to personal problems. By the late 1980s, though, with the costs of their MH/SA programs escalating rapidly, employers began to demand cost savings as well. Therefore, the organization and functions of EAPs also underwent transformation in response to the desire of employers for both utilization-of-benefits management and high-quality MH/SA services that assure good outcomes and that also offer prevention and health promotion services (McCall-Perez, 1994).

Managed mental health care organizations are now offering EAP services as a component of an integrated system of health care delivery that includes "claims administration, specialized utilization management, employee assistance programs, and provider networks all offered by one vendor" (Garnick et al., 1994, p. 1204). In-house EAPs and EAP firms have also started to offer more integrated services, though more slowly than managed mental health care organizations. For example, more EAPs are providing prospective and concurrent utilization review services, in contrast to the mainly retrospective review services they offered in the 1980s. They are also coordinating MH/SA admissions: selecting the doctor, hospital, or provider; monitoring the patient's care; and, in some cases, assuming responsibility for payments to the provider. EAPs may now use detailed triage protocols that stipulate the appropriate level of care for particular types of problems. They may also employ practice guidelines to assure that a proposed plan of care is likely to be the most effective one for the patient's presenting problems (Winegar, 1993).

EAPs that offer more comprehensive services such as crisis intervention and brief treatment are attractive to employers because of the easy access to services and absence of additional expense for employees. Employees can "continue with their initial counselor, avoiding a disruptive referral to a new therapist. ... [These EAP] counselors will work toward returning the employee to his or her normal level of functioning as soon as possible, having no incentive to 'overtreat' or to overutilize costly inpatient resources" (Winegar, 1992, p. 75).

Finally, both HMOs and EAPs are putting more and more emphasis on prevention and wellness programs because these programs can bring considerable cost savings and benefits to the total population (subscribers or employees). Thus, communication skills training, assertiveness training, parenting, support for dealing with loss and death issues, victim assistance, and information on changing workplace expectations are now being offered through the modalities of individual counseling, therapy groups, or seminars (Dickman & Challenger, 1997).

A countervailing force to both the prevention of illness and reduction of job-related stress in EAP work is the restriction placed on the counselor's advocacy or mediating functions in many EAP contracts with employers. Thus, when a client's psychiatric disturbance or stress reaction is related to workplace conditions, the counselor may be enjoined from contacting the work site to advocate on behalf of the client. This presents an ethical dilemma for counselors. In these situations, the counselor should work to empower the client to advocate on his or her own behalf, as in the following case illustration.

> Mrs. H, a 39-year-old divorced mother of three children, applied for help with depressive symptoms that were jeopardizing her employment as a data entry clerk. Her severe depression appeared to be related to problems with an abusive boyfriend, conflicts with her adolescent daughter, and job stresses. After the depression had been ameliorated and she had ended her relationship with her boyfriend, the focus shifted to her job, where she was under fire for not meeting new production levels, which required higher rates of keystrokes. Mrs. H was showing signs of repetitive-motion injury, which prevented her from meeting the new production demands. When appeals to management did not result in a change in work conditions, she was encouraged and coached in how to work with her union representative. The union supported her and helped her to take legal action to receive compensation for her injury.

Individual Counseling

EAPs and HMOs frequently get referrals for assessment or treatment for persons who are having difficulty functioning on the job. Individuals also request help because of their concern that their personal or family problems are interfering with their ability to perform their jobs. Depression, anxiety, substance abuse, and interpersonal relationship problems are among the more common reasons for disabling levels of distress and declining functioning. For example, depression is significantly correlated with diminished productivity, and in fact it is more debilitating than most medical conditions in terms of both role functioning and other domains of functioning. The dramatic loss of competency found in individuals experiencing a major depressive episode and the diminished productivity seen in dysthymic individuals are a function of the negative impact of depression on concentration, memory, energy level, motivation, self-esteem, optimism, creativity, autonomy, problem solving, and coping capacity in general. Often the individual will attempt to compensate for lost productivity by working longer and harder but fall further behind, leading to an increasing sense of inadequacy and hopelessness and loss of satisfaction in working. Difficulty in getting along with and communicating with coworkers further diminishes the depressed individual's functioning at work. Sometimes depressed individuals present themselves as suffering from burnout on the job. The clinician must then sort out to what extent the depression is reactive to actual job stresses and to what extent the patient's experience of stress is related to having a mood disorder, and what the complex interactions are between the two (Shuchter, Downs, & Zisook, 1996). In any case, clients experiencing vocational or academic failure often present in crisis and require a crisis intervention assessment and treatment plan (Klein & Wender, 1993).

Productivity lost due to employee stress or distress or incapacity to work is of great concern to employers because of the significant direct and indirect costs. In 1990, the estimated indirect cost in the United States for reduced productivity due to depression was $24 billion, while direct treatment costs were $12 billion (Wells, Sturm, Sherbourne, & Meredith, 1996). Employers would like to see distressed employees have easy access to treatment and a rapid return to functioning (McCall-Perez, 1994). HMO and EAP mental health services strive to meet employer needs through crisis intervention services and the use of brief treatment methods.

In the following case vignette, the EAP and HMO goals of rapid access to service, amelioration of symptoms, and return to functioning are demonstrated.

Interpersonal Conflict and Depression

Tony, a 32-year-old single Italian American man employed as a teacher, requested help for escalating feelings of anxiety and depression that were interfering with his ability to manage his classroom. He described himself as becoming increasingly irritable and indecisive, and perceived that this state was affecting his interactions with his students and fellow teachers. He was also having difficulty concentrating on and completing classroom duties. He was worried about whether he would be able to continue teaching or whether he should take a leave of absence. He also complained of frequent migraine headaches. Tony sounded both angry and very anxious on the telephone. He denied feeling suicidal, but he wanted an appointment as soon as possible because of the degree of distress he was feeling.

Tony reported that he had experienced two previous episodes of depression 10 and 5 years earlier, for which he had received treatment. The first occurred after college, when he failed to find a good job, and the second was when he was not accepted to law school. Tony met the DSM criteria for Dysthymia and Generalized Anxiety Disorder, but not for major depression. It appeared that he experienced his depression more intensely than the number and severity of symptoms of depression would indicate. Intense anxiety appeared to be making the stronger contribution to his problems in functioning. In addition, a long history of low self-confidence and inability to assert himself was making it difficult for him to make key relationship and vocational decisions. He was at a point where he had to decide whether he would marry someone his family disapproved of and whether he would attend a law school prep course that both his mother and his girlfriend opposed his attending. Tony lived with his widowed mother, with whom he had a chronically conflicted relationship. They fought daily about all aspects of his life, but particularly about his non-Catholic, non-Italian girlfriend. At the same time, his girlfriend and his sister, who was considered the success in his family, derided his plan to attend the prelaw course as a waste of time and money.

Tony's strengths were his intelligence, perseverance, and capacity for setting and achieving goals. He had performed well in both jobs he had held since graduating from college. He was a valued teacher because of his commitment to his students and willingness to help out with after-school activities. Tony played basketball regularly, which had been his main social outlet before his chronic depression and anxiety had become more disabling

The first phase of treatment, the crisis intervention phase, focused on diminishing Tony's distress, reducing his symptoms of depression and anxiety, and supporting his efforts to continue working. Early interventions included the use of reframing and normalizing techniques, stress management, and interpersonal conflict management techniques. Tony appeared to respond well to the immediate reframing of his self-denigrating statements about himself into positive goals. For example, he frequently castigated himself for not "being a man" because he didn't have a high-status career and because the women in his life told him what to do. This was reframed for him as his desire to achieve goals that most people his age were striving for—that is, wanting to establish himself in a career and in a satisfying, intimate relationship. Tony's usual method of stress reduction was supported and built upon. Thus, the first homework tasks were to return to daily playing of basketball and to practice the breathing and relaxation exercises given in the first session. The third intervention was to remove him from the interpersonal conflicts that were causing him such distress. Through the use of role plays, he was able to change two significant interactions. Instead of responding to his mother's criticisms with angry denunciations of her meddling, he would thank her for her suggestions and offer to take them into consideration in his decisions. With his girlfriend, Tony was able to request a time-out from their arguments so that he would be able to make a good decision for both of them.

Once Tony's anxiety and depressive symptoms diminished and he felt he was coping adequately with his job, the focus shifted from skills development to exploratory work around his unsatisfying interactions with women and his personal goals and needs. In particular, a core belief that people would desert him if he were to assert his thoughts and feelings was examined in terms of the consequences for his mood states and his ability to achieve his goals. Recognizing the origin of this belief in the early death of his father and the impact of that death on his relationship with his mother allowed Tony to contemplate alternative interactions with his mother, sister, and girlfriend. Success in being able to remove himself from arguments with them also motivated him to learn assertiveness skills and to use them in his interactions with them. In addition, exercises in which he ranked values, goals, and commitment to goals enabled him to make decisions about what he wanted to do about his career goals and his relationship with his girlfriend. He decided to attend the prelaw program because it offered him the best chance of becoming a lawyer, and to leave his relationship with his girlfriend because it replicated what was problematic in his interactions with his mother and sister. One follow-up visit was scheduled for a time after he completed the prelaw program. At this session, he reported that he had successfully completed the program and had been accepted into law school. This final session focused on reviewing his experiences of depression and anxiety, his skills in managing these mood disorders, and planning for how he would address these problems if they should reoccur in the future.

Substance Abuse Treatment and Managed Care

Both employers and managed care organizations have been dissatisfied with the high cost and the lack of proven efficacy of inpatient substance abuse reha-bilitation programs. In fact, follow-up studies have shown a high rate of recidi-vism: following an inpatient stay, 70–90% relapse by the end of the first year (Brownell, Marlatt, Lichtenstein, & Wilson, 1986). One of the concerns about traditional treatment approaches was their failure to understand and prevent relapses. In particular, it was thought that not enough attention had been paid to the roles of family, friends, and community environments in the recovery process. A person is at high risk for relapsing on returning to the same social environment, especially if the social network is made up of other substance abusers. On the other hand, if the client has a job, a stable living arrangement, and family and friends supportive of recovery, the client is more motivated to maintain sobriety, and the chances of success are greater (Berg, 1994).

Other emerging developments in substance abuse treatment under man-aged care are an increase in the number of treatment options available and a rejection of the one-size-fits-all approach of the traditional 12-step disease model of substance abuse treatment. Spurred on by the high cost of addiction treatment and by research evidence that individualized treatment programs show better outcomes and that outpatient brief treatment programs are as effective as longer term inpatient programs, substance abuse treatment under managed care has become flexible, brief, and provided on an outpatient basis. The goal now is to match the appropriate level of treatment to the severity of the client's substance abuse problem and to select the treatment approach that best meets the client's needs and preferences (Johnson, 1995).

Among the newer treatment models that clinicians can use are (1) brief intervention therapy or motivational interviewing, (2) solution-focused therapy, (3) holistic, lifestyle change, and (4) the Community Reinforcement Approach.

Motivational interviewing is a brief treatment approach that seeks to help the individual to become aware of the nature of his or her problems with alcohol and then help the person to find a way to change by offering treatment options. It is a consciousness raising rather than confrontational approach and a persuasive rather than coercive or argumentative approach. The goals of treatment are to motivate clients who are ready to take action to make the necessary changes in their drinking behaviors, and to motivate clients who have been denying a drinking problem and resisting change to enter treatment (Miller & Rollnick, 1991).

Solution-focused substance abuse therapy is an approach that challenges chemically dependent clients' beliefs about their inability to stop abusing alcohol or drugs. It does this by shifting their attention to times when they were abstinent and focusing on the strengths or existing coping skills that made control possible, however briefly (Johnson, 1995). The holistic or life-process substance abuse treatment program is a lifestyle change approach in which all aspects of the client's well-being are addressed: (1) *physical* through diet, exercise, and stress management; (2) *mental* through the cognitive restructuring of substance-using beliefs and enhancement of motivation to abstain; (3) *emotional* through individual, family, and group therapy; and (4) *spiritual* through encouraging participation in religion, a 12-step program, or meditation (Meyers & Smith, 1995).

The Community Reinforcement Approach (CRA) specifically addresses the environmental forces that encourage or discourage drinking. CRA seeks to shape social, recreational, familial, and vocational forces so that sober behavior becomes more rewarding than drinking behavior (Meyers & Smith, 1995).

Substance Abuse Assessment Issues

The emphasis in substance abuse treatment planning under managed care is on the individual assessment and on the tailoring of a treatment program to that individual based on the assessment. Assessment from this perspective follows the traditional elements of assessing the physiological, psychological, and psychosocial consequences of the substance abuse, but in addition evaluates the potential for relapse. Thus, what is needed is a functional analysis of the personal and environmental factors that place the client at risk for abusing substances and the factors that protect against abuse. In the EAP setting, the assessment usually entails working with an involuntary client. Therefore, the clinician needs to combine the skills of engagement and assessment in order to establish rapport and arrive at an accurate assessment of the client's substance abuse problem. The techniques described in Chapter 3 for engaging involuntary or resistant clients can be helpful. Strategies that may lower treatment resistance include exploring the client's concerns about the referral, particularly concern about losing his or her job, eliciting negative feelings about the referral and loss of freedom of choice about treatment, and restoring a sense of control over the process wherever possible.

The strategies and techniques of motivational interviewing are particularly useful in the initial assessment session with involuntary clients because they are designed to reduce resistance. The first strategy is to move in the interview from less threatening subjects to more threatening ones, and to employ the techniques of open-ended questioning, reflective listening, and summarizing to facilitate the process of establishing rapport and trust. A good topic to open up discussion about substance use is that of stress on the job or at home. Once the details about stressful situations have been obtained, particularly the details of what they are like for the client emotionally and physically, it is easy to extend the discussion to how the client copes with stress and inquire whether he or she uses alcohol or drugs to cope. Rollnick and Bell (1991) suggest that, in addition to the topic of stress management, other topics such as health problems, child care, recreational outlets, or just the details of a typical day could be used to open up the discussion on substance use. The following is an example.

> Jennifer, a 32-year-old woman, presented with an initial complaint about having difficulty concentrating on the job because of her unhappiness about her marriage. An inquiry about health concerns led her to reveal that she was experiencing pain in the kidney area. As we explored this topic, it became evident that she was avoiding seeking medical care because she was afraid that her drinking might be creating the problem. She did not believe she had a drinking problem, but our focus on her health concerns gave her the motivation to begin attending AA.

After use of alcohol and drugs has been established, details of the usage need to be discussed. In motivational interviewing, this inquiry begins with the less threatening issue of the impact of the drinking or drug use on the individual. This is followed by a discussion from the client's perspective of the good things gotten from substance use and then by an inquiry into the negative consequences. A careful history of substance use is also taken so that the client can begin to see the pattern of increasing tolerance and the negative impact of the substance abuse on health, relationships, and job performance (Rollnick & Bell, 1991).

The Community Reinforcement Approach also avoids a confrontational and authoritarian approach and instead seeks to understand the function of substance abuse in the client's life—for example, as a way of managing stress or avoiding a difficult marital situation. In CRA, where the focus is on the role of environmental contingencies in the recovery process, the assessment examines the antecedents and consequences of substance use in order to understand what is creating and maintaining the push toward substance use. CRA assessment also begins with gathering information about the nature of the substance abuse, that is, the quantity and frequency of use and its impact on the health and the psychological, marital, familial, occupational, and legal functioning of the individual. This information can be gathered through direct interviewing or through the use of the numerous diagnostic instruments available (e.g., the Addiction Severity Index, the Brief Drinker Profile, the Drinker Inventory of Consequences, the CAGE questionnaire, and the Stages of Change Readiness and Treatment Eagerness Scale) (Meyers & Smith, 1995; Maxmen & Ward, 1995).

To determine the function of substance abuse in the client's life, information is collected about factors promoting substance abuse and abstinence. The evaluator looks for information about the triggers to substance use (what clients are thinking and feeling, and who they are with and where, before use begins), the pattern of substance abuse behaviors, the short-term positive and negative consequences, and the long-term positive and negative consequences. The positive triggers for the nonuse of substances and the negative and positive consequences of nonuse are also examined. Out of this assessment should come a picture of the risks for relapse and the resources for countering substance abuse for each client (Meyers & Smith, 1995).

Evaluation and Referral

Clinical social workers, particularly in EAP and HMO settings, frequently provide assessment and referral services for individuals with substance abuse problems. Often this is a one-session contact. Although it is not thought of as single-session therapy, when viewed from within a motivational interviewing framework, it can be seen as sharing the aims and techniques of single-session therapy. In order to be effective, the single session for evaluation and referral of substance-abusing clients must enable clients to "uncover something significant about themselves," that is, "to become more aware of some aspect of their cognitive and affective lives," so that making a change in their drinking or drug use behaviors seems possible (Bloom, 1992, p. 101). Evaluation and referral within this framework are something more than providing information and advice about the substance abuse problem and referring the client for treatment.

It is an approach in which clients come to see their drinking or drug use from a different perspective. By creating dissonance between stated concerns they have about their drinking or drug use or personal goals and the reality of the substance abuse, clients become aware of what drinking or using drugs means in their lives. The skill for the clinician then is to convey a sense of hope that clients have the resources to make changes in their problem behaviors and thereby motivate them to take action (Miller & Rollnick, 1991).

The strategies and techniques that the worker can employ to help clients to make this move from the precontemplation stage to the contemplation stage include using the results of the assessment in a motivating fashion. That is, the client is informed in an empathic, concerned manner about the risks and problems that the drinking or drug use is presenting, with an emphasis on the discrepancies between goals and concerns and the assessment findings. The client's reactions to the evaluation are encouraged and attended to, particularly fears and worries about the results and any problem recognition statements or expressed wishes to see his or her situation change. The emerging awareness and motivation can then be reinforced by exploring in a nonjudgmental way the client's ambivalence toward making changes while offering support for the client's positive goals. A balance sheet of pros and cons for making changes can be written up for the client as well as a statement of the client's ideas about how the problem could be solved and what steps he or she would like to take next. A final summarizing statement can then be used to highlight the gains the client has made in recognition of the problem(s) as well as the steps he or she has indicated a willingness to pursue. At the end of this session, the treatment options are explored, including potential obstacles to following through with a referral (Rollnick & Bell, 1991). Some clients may need more direct assistance in making a connection to an agency, self-help group, or addiction specialist. Clients should be encouraged to contact the worker if they run into difficulty with the referral.

Many clients will need more than one session before they are able to commit themselves to taking action about their substance abuse, particularly when there are coexisting disorders or when there are impinging stresses such as unemployment or homelessness. Such clients will need additional sessions of motivational interviewing along with supportive therapy, crisis intervention, direct assistance with concrete needs, or some combination of help. If, after the denial has diminished, the client is still resisting taking action, then techniques for handling resistance will need to be employed. When clients present arguments for not doing anything about their substance abuse problem, the most effective approach is to move with the resistance rather than offering counterarguments, which tends to only heighten the resistance (Shea, 1998). If resistance is understood as a reflection of underlying fears or anxieties or as a reaction to the clinician moving faster than the client, then feelings of countertransference are better managed and the clinician will be able to employ reflecting and reframing techniques to help clients work through their concerns. Reflective listening and amplified reflection, in which the client's concerns are highlighted in the clinician's reflecting-back statement, are ways of communicating to clients that their concerns are heard and validated. Reflective statements can also be used to highlight client ambivalence, while reframing brings into awareness the functions served by the client refusing to take action (Miller & Rollnick, 1991).

> Sandra, an employed 24-year-old mother of two who lived with her parents, sought help for depression and constant conflict with her mother. Sandra had been seen in long-term treatment twice before as an adolescent and young adult for the same problems. She was described in therapy notes as locked in a hostile dependent relationship with her mother. Sandra saw herself as a disappointment to her well-educated parents, who were administrators in the public school system. Sandra had a learning disability and had had difficulty completing high school. She held a low-level data-processing job, which did not pay enough for her to live in her own apartment.
>
> Sandra began the interview with a litany of complaints about her mother's mistreatment of her. When asked to describe the most recent argument in detail, which was over her mother's anger that Sandra did not have the money to make her monthly auto loan payment, it became clear that this had been a recurrent problem for over a year. Further exploration about why this problem was constantly recurring revealed a worsening substance abuse problem. Sandra had been abusing substances since adolescence, but in the last year had begun using cocaine. Sandra was able to accept the results of the assessment that she was addicted to cocaine when she could see how the cocaine use repeatedly undercut her plans to move to her own apartment and live independently. However, she could not accept the need to enter the chemical dependency program at the HMO, because it would be one more thing her mother could hold against her. Over the next three sessions, Sandra's desire to raise her children without her mother's interference (as she saw it) was supported while the role of her cocaine use in the constant conflicts with her mother was carefully examined. When Sandra could see that her drug use was a real threat to her retaining custody of her children, she accepted a referral to the chemical dependency program.

Parallel Treatment

There are situations in which a clinician may continue to be involved in brief treatment with a substance-abusing client after the client has accepted specialized addiction help. For example, if a client elects to attend AA or another self-help group, or if the substance abuse treatment program does not have comprehensive services, the client may still need help with psychological or family and marital problems that either hamper recovery or make the client vulnerable to relapse. For these clients, because the primary disorder is still the substance abuse, the appropriate strategies would be Level I interventions aimed at supporting and stabilizing the recovery. Thus, symptom reduction, concrete assistance with vocational and recreational needs, cognitive-behavioral interventions (cognitive restructuring of dysfunctional substance-abusing beliefs, stress management, and problem-solving skill development), behavioral family or marital therapy, and psychoeducation would be used to reduce vulnerability to relapse (Berg, 1994; Meyers & Smith, 1995).

For a client with a coexisting Axis I disorder, symptom reduction and psychoeducation, as outlined in Chapter 7 for dual-diagnosis patients, are the techniques of choice. For clients with personality disorders, cognitive restructuring and the management of impulsive behaviors would be the interventions most useful for support of recovery. Clients with a history of substance abuse beginning in adolescence will often need assistance with life skills and relationships, because such abuse tends to arrest the development of other coping skills and of social and recreational skills. The parallel treatment process can be used to reduce these risk factors for relapse, as the individual therapist can help work through the grief about what was lost to substance abuse and at the same time work with the client to develop life skills.

Finally, because substance abuse causes distress in marital and family relationships, and because such conflicted relationships in turn can lead to increased use of alcohol or drugs, marital and family work is an important part of the treatment. The focus in this type of marital and family work is on increasing satisfying relationships and reducing the behaviors that reinforce substance abuse, such as nagging and attempts at controlling, and inadequate styles of communication, conflict resolution, and problem solving (Meyers & Smith, 1995). Reciprocity marriage counseling, for example, involves the establishment of contracts for conflict resolution and for positive interactions that make alcohol abuse incompatible with the marital relationship (Barber, 1995). Typical points of tension such as money management, disciplining of children, or social life are discussed and contracts made for each partner to agree to do something pleasing for the other in these areas, but only when the abusing partner or family member is sober (Barber, 1995).

The Community Reinforcement Approach uses a similar approach by having couples complete a Marriage Happiness Scale, in which each couple ranks their degree of satisfaction with the partner in such areas as household responsibilities, sex and affection, child-rearing, and so on, and then completes a goals-of-counseling form in which they state in specific ways what they would like the partner to do in areas where there is dissatisfaction. Therapy is then directed toward helping the couple to communicate, negotiate, and reinforce each other's efforts (Meyers & Smith, 1995). Each of these approaches is specifically geared to reducing substance use and preventing relapse and therefore would meet the managed care requirement that the family and marital treatment be in the service of remediating the problem for which there is a medical necessity for treatment.

Motivational Interviewing with an Alcoholic Client

The following case study illustrates the use of motivational interviewing to help a client with a long history of resisting treatment for his alcoholism to become motivated to work toward sobriety. It also illustrates the use of an environmental contingency assessment to help him achieve sobriety and the use of relapse prevention strategies to help him maintain his sobriety. This case study also demonstrates how a parallel treatment process can support the treatment of the addiction through enhancing the client's motivation to pursue sobriety.

Dave, a 34-year-old single man, entered treatment only after receiving an ultimatum from his boss that he would be unable to continue working for his firm unless he stopped drinking. After a physical examination in which his liver function tests indicated elevated enzyme levels (liver damage), Dave was informed that he would not be eligible to receive medical insurance, which was a necessity for his work. When Dave came in for his intake appointment, he indicated that he didn't think he had a drinking problem, but he wanted to pass his physical and therefore needed to cut back some on his drinking. He also didn't think he needed to be in therapy, because he thought he could cut back on his drinking on his own. On the other hand, he knew that his employer was expecting him to be in treatment for his alcohol use and, therefore, he planned to continue treatment.

A review of Dave's daily alcohol intake revealed that he routinely drank eight to ten double vodka highballs per day and more on the weekends. He denied blackouts, but he did acknowledge that his previous attempts at cutting back had not succeeded. He had also been under pressure from his family for over 5 years to get treatment. This resulted in one detoxification stay 5 years previously, but he signed out after the counselors had confronted him about his lack of commitment to his treatment, and he did not seek treatment again. Over the 18 years since he began drinking, Dave had been arrested several times for driving while intoxicated, twice resulting in suspension of his driving license. He exhibited no awareness of the negative consequences of his alcohol abuse for him. He reported that his father had died of cirrhosis of the liver when Dave was 15 years old. He did not see his drinking as being as severe as his father's because his father had been a binge drinker who was abusive when he was drunk, which Dave was not.

At the end of the assessment interview Dave was given feedback about the degree of harm that his drinking was creating for him now and the potential danger to him in the future in terms of his health, job, legal liability, and problems with his family, based on the information he had provided. He did not agree with the assessment, but he indicated that he would try to cut back on his drinking. He rejected the suggestion that he join AA to reduce his drinking, because from his previous treatment experience he believed he was not an alcoholic like the other people in AA. While seeking to find a goal that would motivate him to do something in therapy about his alcohol abuse,

Dave expressed a concern that appeared to be an opening. At 34 he was still living in an apartment, although he seemed to be earning enough money to own a condominium. He contrasted his situation with that of his brother, who had recently moved to a new house. The initial contract therefore was to work toward removing the obstacles to his purchasing a condominium. The first homework assignment was for him to monitor his expenditures during the week to determine why he could not save money.

The following excerpt from the second session illustrates the use of the motivational interviewing technique of creating dissonance between stated goals and actual behavior.

WORKER: *Well, how did the week go?*

DAVE: *(sighs) I spent the weekend fishing. It was our annual bluefish fishing trip that a bunch of us guys have gone on since high school. We usually have a good time, but this year, I don't know why, I found the whole thing annoying.*

WORKER: *Can you remember one thing that you found annoying?*

DAVE: *It wasn't one thing. It was more that everyone spent the time talking about their kids, their wives, their houses. I felt out of it, because I don't have a wife, a house, or kids.*

WORKER: *We talked last week about your wanting to save money for a condo. Are you also thinking about wanting to get married and have children?*

DAVE: *I don't know about getting married, but I would like to have a steady girlfriend. I really haven't had one since I was 20 years old. I have a son, you know, but I've never seen him. She wouldn't let me see him.*

WORKER: *Are you talking about the girlfriend you had back then? (Dave: Yes.) I can see from your face that you have feelings about this. Can you talk about this?*

DAVE: *I hadn't thought about this for a long time. At the time, I thought she was right. I was pretty wild then and I just didn't care. I was too busy partying, but lately I've started to wonder what he's like. He'd be 14 years old now.*

WORKER: *It sounds like you feel you are at a crossroads in your life. You are questioning whether the way you've lived your life for the past 15 years is the way you want to continue living. This is really an important question to be asking. It's one that a lot of people your age ask.*

DAVE: *Really. That's good to hear. I just thought I was a loser, because I don't have what everyone else I know has. I look at my brother. He's just 3 years older than me and he's already moved up to a bigger house. He's got a great wife and kids. I spend a lot of time with Cindy and the kids, because I don't have anyone in my life.*

WORKER: *We can certainly take a look at what that's about, why it's been hard for you to have someone in your life. We can take a close look at the situation in the same way we are looking at what makes it hard for you to reach your goal of buying a condo. I see you have some numbers written down on that sheet. Let's take a look at them.*

DAVE: *This wasn't a good week. I not only didn't save any money, but I had to borrow money to pay the rent. I started the week with 500 dollars left from my paycheck and at the end of the week I had 20 dollars left.*

WORKER: *Let's take a look at where the money went. You have written 60 dollars down for food and 60–80 dollars a day spent at the Merry-Go-Round. Is that a bar?*

DAVE: *Yeah. It looks like I'm buying way too many drinks for people.*

WORKER: *Well, at least it's clear where the bulk of your money is being spent and where you would have to cut back if you want to save money.*

DAVE: *That's what I want to do; cut back on my spending at the bar.*

WORKER: *Does that mean you are going to try again to cut back on your drinking?*

DAVE: *Yes. I can do that.*

By the fifth week, it was clear that Dave was not able to cut back on his drinking or save money. Focusing on the discrepancy between his goals and his behavior provided enough motivation for him to reconsider attending AA to cut back on his drinking. Attending AA was reframed as a step in his plan to take charge of his life rather than giving in to what his family wanted him to do. The early sessions revealed how important it was for Dave to see himself and to have others see him as someone who could take charge and get things done. He needed to begin each session with a recitation of his accomplishments for that week and to receive positive feedback before he would move back to talking about the difficult issues, usually issues of loss associated with his drinking that he had talked about at the end of the previous session. For the next five sessions Dave slowly became involved in and committed to attending AA and achieving sobriety, although he had many doubts and frequently thought about quitting, particularly when he could not stay sober for any length of time. It became clear to Dave that he had few supports for remaining abstinent, and in fact his whole social life centered around drinking at bars. He did not feel comfortable socializing with women outside of a bar, and drinking was his only way of dealing with stresses and tension. However, by continually refocusing on his goals of owning a home and finding the type of enduring relationship that he had missed out on due to his drinking, he was able to remain in the action stage of change. Consequently, he was able to accept the need for an inpatient stay for the purposes of detoxification and time away from the multiple triggers in his environment for drinking.

The inpatient stay led to Dave becoming involved in a comprehensive outpatient substance abuse treatment program. Dave returned for two termination sessions to help reinforce his commitment to his recovery program and to solidify the gains made in being able to talk about loss and problems in interpersonal relationships, so that he could begin dealing with these issues in his group therapy. On follow-up 6 months later, Dave continued to be involved with AA and his therapy group and had maintained his sobriety.

Brief Group Therapy: Rationale and Description

Time-limited group therapy has been growing in use as a treatment modality since the establishment of community mental health centers in the 1960s, when responsibility for meeting the mental health needs of a population in a specified catchment area necessitated the development of innovative ways of serving larger numbers of patients. HMOs and EAPs faced with the same need to serve large numbers of clients have, since the 1970s, turned increasingly to group therapy as a means of serving client populations efficiently and effectively (Spitz, 1996). They have been in the vanguard in developing brief group treatment principles and techniques and in expanding the use of groups for treating a greater range of problems and life cycle challenges. Over the past decade, due to the emergence of managed mental health care, brief group treatment has become a preferred treatment approach in many mental health settings besides community mental health centers and HMOs.

The following section provides an introduction to the utility of brief therapy groups, the principles and techniques of brief treatment in groups, the types of and uses for groups, and the structure and process of effective brief group therapy. The focus of this section is on the points of distinction between long-term and time-limited group therapy. A full discussion of brief group therapy is beyond the scope of this book, but there are several books that address brief group treatment in depth. Among these are MacKenzie, K. R. (1990), *Introduction to Time-Limited Group Psychotherapy;* and Spitz, H. I. (1996), *Group Psychotherapy and Managed Mental Health Care: A Clinical Guide for Providers.*

Research over several decades on the effectiveness of group therapy has consistently shown that group therapy is as effective as individual therapy, and with certain problems such as anxiety disorders it can be more effective. The same result has been reported from outcome studies on brief group therapy and brief individual therapy (Zuercher-White, 1997). In addition, medical cost offset studies have demonstrated the benefit of brief group therapy for clients with chronic medical illness or disability. For example, Kelly et al. (1993) found that depressed individuals with HIV infection who participated in brief group therapy (cognitive-behavioral and supportive therapy) showed a greater reduction in emotional distress than a comparison group of individuals who did not participate in group therapy. Similar outcomes were found with cancer patients undergoing radiotherapy who participated in brief, coping-oriented group therapy. In one study, even though the group therapy patients exhibited higher levels of psychological distress at baseline in comparison with other cancer patients, "at the end of the 6-week structured group intervention, the experimental subjects (n = 38) exhibited significantly lower levels of distress than did the control subjects (n = 28)" (Fawzy, Fawzy, Hyun, & Wheeler, 1997, p. 153).

In brief group treatment, basic brief treatment principles and techniques are linked with the inherent power of groups to advance interpersonal and behavioral skills, promote mutual aid, and reduce feelings of isolation or stigmatization (Hoyt & Austad, 1992). There are several different models of brief group treatment, but they share a common set of principles and techniques that allow group therapy to be brief whatever the theoretical orientation of the group. Among these factors are (1) a high degree of group structure and therapist involvement in structuring the group; (2) targeted, limited goals; (3) use of time limits to motivate members to make changes; (4) transfer of knowledge and skills gained in group to outside life; (5) use of tasks to extend and transfer learning; (6) use of educational methods to impart knowledge and skills; and (7) a commitment to utilize and mobilize family and community resources (Spitz, 1996). Contracting about group purpose and objectives, rapidly establishing group cohesion, maintaining a focus on objectives and themes, and an emphasis on homogeneous elements in group composition are also considered characteristic of brief therapy groups (MacKenzie, 1994).

Types of Brief Therapy Groups

Brief therapy groups are now being used with a wide range of problems and needs—for example, specific clinical disorders such as panic or depression, stresses associated with life stage developmental challenges, medical crises and losses, or the need to develop interpersonal or behavioral skills. They can be broadly classified according to the degree of structure maintained in the group therapy process, the degree of homogeneity sought in the selection of group members, and whether the groups are closed or open in enrollment. The more highly structured groups are used for imparting knowledge and skills about specific disorders or problems. The less structured groups are more experiential and insight-oriented in nature and tend to focus on issues of selfhood and self-in-relationship (MacKenzie, 1994).

Folkers and Steefel (1991) split the two broad categories of highly structured and less structured groups into four subtypes of therapy groups—the psychoeducational, crisis intervention, developmental, and experiential models, with the first two subtypes being more structured than the latter. The psychoeducational model uses the group to impart coping skills related to specific problem areas or needs, such as those needed for adaptation to chronic medical or psychiatric illnesses or for improving parent-child conflicts. In this model, cognitive-behavioral and resource enhancement interventions are emphasized. The crisis intervention model is designed to provide immediate help to individuals suffering from acute distress and disruption in their lives through the use of a variety of supportive, educational, and experiential interventions. The developmental stage model addresses the needs of individuals who are facing similar difficulties in adjusting to life stage demands, particularly interpersonal relationship shifts. The inherent potential of groups for interpersonal learning experiences is emphasized in this model.

Group Structure and Process

Brief therapy groups tend to be more homogeneous in composition than long-term therapy groups, although the common factors that unite the group will differ depending on the type of group. Thus, factors such as a shared life situation or lifestyle, developmental stage of life, problems in living, or a prior history of psychiatric or group therapy experience may be the basis of the group composition. Group members can quickly establish points of common ground on the basis of shared backgrounds. Homogeneity in composition is preferred because of the need for rapidly establishing a group culture and cohesion in order for clients to achieve their goals in a limited period of time (Hoyt, 1995). Therefore, there is a greater emphasis in brief treatment on screening, orienting, and preparing potential members for group therapy before the first session. An evaluation of suitability for group therapy should also be a part of the initial, diagnostic session for all clients in order to determine what level of preparation the client will need to satisfactorily participate in a group or whether group therapy is contraindicated. Thus the evaluation of suitability for group therapy will need to include a history of the client's object relations, interpersonal style, and roles he or she played in naturally occurring groups in life (Spitz, 1996).

Over the years, selection criteria for whether an individual would be placed in a more structured, skills-oriented group or a more unstructured, exploratory, or experiential group have become more flexible as the distinction between these two categories has become less sharply defined (see Folkers and Steefel's expanded typology of 1991 cited previously). However, a consensus has begun to emerge that certain clients do not do well in exploratory, experiential groups. These include clients in crisis; clients who exhibit poor impulse control, highly manipulative behavior, or severely diminished interpersonal relatedness or have rigid defensive styles with high use of projection, denial, or projective identification; and clients with cognitive impairment due to psychosis or brain injury (MacKenzie, 1990).

Once a client is determined to be a suitable candidate for group therapy, clinicians operating within a managed care situation will need to complete the precertification process. The process is essentially the same as a request for authorization of individual therapy; that is, the clinician must provide evidence for the medical necessity for treatment, and there must be a clear linkage between the defined problem and functional impairments, the specific, concise goals and associated behavioral objectives, and the selected treatment intervention. In this instance, it must be demonstrated that the problems to be worked on would be appropriately or best addressed by group therapy (Spitz, 1996). Paleg and Jongsma's *The Group Therapy Treatment Planner* (1998) can be used to help develop treatment plans for each group member.

The population-oriented practice management approach of HMOs, with the subsequent emergence of brief group therapy as a preferred practice approach, has fostered the development of strategies for increasing the efficiency and efficacy of group therapy (Sabin, 1991). Thus, orientation to and preparation of the client for group therapy is widely used in HMOs as a means of rapidly fostering group cohesion. Group cohesion is defined as the capacity of group members to become interested and invested in each other, trust one another, cooperate toward group goals, remain focused on the work at hand, and express support for each other. Preparation for group treatment and the presence of group cohesion have been found to reduce the dropout rate (Budman & Gurman, 1988).

A range of methods of group preparation has evolved out of the HMO experience. "The continuum extends from informal discussions with individual members to structured pre-training programs, . . . the distribution of written orientation manuals, group orientations involving many or all members at the same time, and others" (Spitz, 1996, p. 69). In general, the preparation time is used to impart information about the particular group experience in which the client will be participating; provide the prospective member time to deal with fears and confusions about the group process and to clarify personal treatment goals; and review the rules for the group, including expectations for attendance, participation, and interaction with other group members. The group therapy contract may be a written one such as the one provided in the *Therapist's Guide to Clinical Intervention* (Johnson, 1997), in which the group goals are specified and the rules for attendance, confidentiality, and prohibitions on substance use and family members' presence are spelled out in a contract that the client signs.

Brief therapy groups are generally closed—that is, not open to new members for the contracted length of the group. This is because of the need in short-term groups to maintain group cohesion and not lose focus. A shifting membership requires the leader and group to divert attention to helping the new members catch up, which can reduce the amount of time available for reaching the group goals. In addition, when significant attention has been paid to pregroup preparation, there is less likelihood of dropouts, thereby obviating the need to maintain an open membership approach. On the other hand, Zuercher-White (1997) has successfully conducted open groups where the format was highly structured around a specific psychiatric disorder. In an effort to reduce the long periods of waiting for another group to form for clients with panic and phobia disorders, she ran an ongoing group with shifting membership as clients progressed through the group treatment modules (14 two-hour sessions with four sessions each for the first three modules and two for the final module). Reading and assignments for each module were given before the session so that everyone was working on the same tasks. New members were incorporated into the group in the first session of any module, and then they worked along with the group until they completed all four modules.

The Brief Group Therapist's Roles and Functions

From the pregroup orientation and preparation phase to termination, the brief group therapist is more active and assumes more roles than the therapist in a long-term group. This is true whether the group is a structured, psychoeducational one or an experiential, exploratory one. From the beginning the brief group therapist must both structure and cultivate the group experience while facilitating interpersonal interactions and learning experiences. In the pregroup preparation stage and in the initial session, the group leader is responsible for defining the purpose of the group, screening and selecting appropriate candidates, explaining and maintaining the ground rules, assisting the group in defining treatment goals, guiding the group in selecting a focus and in staying goal focused, and helping group members to identify areas of common ground. Even in psychosocial or experiential groups, the brief therapist initially has a more active educational and guidance role. The therapist's functions in a less structured, interpersonal group format might proceed as follows: In the pregroup preparation phase, the therapist gives potential members a written introduction to the group and several questionnaires addressing interpersonal issues, such as their current views of significant relationships and past relationship experiences. Then the therapist might ask each member of the group to talk about what they learned from the assessment process. This enables group members to share information about significant relationship experiences and begin the "task of building cohesion through a universalization process" (MacKenzie, 1994, p. 421).

In the experiential or psychodynamic brief group format, the therapist's role may shift from a more active one initially to a less active one in the middle sessions and then back to a more active role in the termination phase. The therapist's role shifts with the tasks and challenges at each stage of the group development. Close attention is paid in brief, experiential group therapy to the group's stage of development because of the need to select and time interventions according to the group's ability to handle difficult or threatening issues (Spitz, 1996). Thus, the different developmental stages in a group reflect the vicissitudes of group cohesion. The first two stages, "starting the group" and "early therapy," have as their central tasks engagement, affiliation, creation of group boundaries, and the establishment of trust among members and for the leader. In these early stages, the group leader fosters cohesion by stressing similarities among group members with regard to problem issues, unsuccessful attempts at solutions, and the resulting states of demoralization; and by encouraging cohesion-building skills such as listening to one another and empathically responding. The third or middle stage is marked by a resurgence of individual needs and wishes, followed by an awareness of the time limits and members' concern that their needs will not be met before the group ends. The leader in this stage must acknowledge and work through the disappointments and disenchantment with the group to rebuild group cohesion. In the next stage, the fourth or late stage, cohesion is strong and there is a group culture centered on working on focal tasks. The fifth stage, that of termination, requires the group leader to become more active again, but now the tasks are to help members disengage from the group and work through the loss of the group and group leader. The final stage is the planned follow-up 6 months to a year later, in which the members have the opportunity to reflect on their group experience and consolidate gains made (Budman & Gurman, 1988).

In the more structured skills-building group format, the role of the clinician tends to remain fairly constant. In Zuercher-White's panic and phobia group, for example, the therapist maintains an educational, skills-facilitating role through each of the four modules. The modules move the group progressively through learning about anxiety and progressive relaxation skills to gaining an understanding and correction of the linkage between thoughts or beliefs and anxiety reactions. The final modules then focus on overcoming the fear of physical reactions, developing assertiveness skills, and preventing relapse. Each session begins with a discussion of the workbook readings and assignments, with the therapist serving in the role of a technical expert. At the same time, the group leader promotes group interaction so that the curative factors of mutual aid, corrective feedback, socialization, and interpersonal growth can aid in skill development and commitment to change (Zuercher-White, 1997). Follow-up or booster sessions are usually included as a part of the structured group therapy approach.

As the Folkers-Steefel typology suggests, there is considerable overlap between structured and unstructured brief therapy groups in terms of technique and group process, but positive outcomes will still depend on an accurate assessment of clients' central concerns and needs as well as their suitability for a particular group approach. A systematic method of strategically matching clients to the appropriate group format is still evolving, but given the cost and time effectiveness of group therapy, refinement of evaluation criteria as well as the development of additional group formats will continue.

EAP Assessment–Intervention Exercise: Carolyn

Use the following vignette to answer the questions in this exercise.

Carolyn, a 40-year-old office manager, was referred by her EAP for the treatment of panic attacks that had been increasing in severity and frequency to the point that she had exhausted all of her sick leave and vacation time. She was contemplating leaving her job because she was growing fearful about having panic attacks while driving to work. Carolyn had been prescribed an antianxiety medication, which was helpful in reducing her chronic anxiety but had not affected the frequency of the attacks. Her first panic attack had occurred 1 year before, shortly after the death of her father. Carolyn reported feeling anxious that her mother, whom she described as a clinging, dependent woman, would transfer that dependence to her after her father's death.

Carolyn described her relationships with her husband and her 10- and 13-year-old daughters as generally good up until she began having panic attacks. Her husband was growing increasingly impatient and angry with the decline in her functioning and her inability to go to certain public places. Further exploration of family functioning revealed suppressed anger and resentment on Carolyn's part toward her husband for his refusal to let her participate in financial planning and decisions. Her job involved considerable responsibility for budget preparation and management of company finances. Carolyn was a highly valued employee, having received several promotions. Her close relationships with colleagues and job satisfaction made her very reluctant to leave her job. In addition to supportive colleagues, she had a close, mutually supportive relationship with her brother, which made caring for their mother easier for both of them.

1. Following the EAP/HMO model of treatment, what problems should the initial treatment plan address and in what order?
2. Following best-practices guidelines, what would be the most appropriate methods for addressing Carolyn's panic attacks?
3. Identify Carolyn's strengths and resources and indicate how they could be used to help Carolyn to continue working.
4. When the most pressing problems are brought under control and there is sufficient time remaining, what other problem areas could be addressed as part of the relapse prevention work?

Answers to this exercise appear in the Appendix.

Summary

HMOs and EAPs have been at the forefront in developing brief-treatment models. Their approach to service delivery based on population rather than individual clients has resulted in a number of innovations in conceptualizing and delivering services for individuals beset by mood disorders, substance abuse problems, and interpersonal conflicts that are interfering with their capacity to function effectively, particularly in the workplace. This chapter has outlined some of the paradigm shifts that have taken place with regard to the treatment of mood disorder and substance abuse and has summarized the salient aspects of a central modality of treatment—brief group treatment.

Recommended Reading

Dickman, F., & Challenger, B. R. (1997). Employee assistance programs: A historical sketch. In W. Hutchinson & W. G. Emener (Eds.), *Employee assistance programs: A basic text* (2d ed.) (pp. 50–58). Springfield, IL: Charles C. Thomas.

Meyers, R. J., & Smith, J. E. (1995). *Clinical guide to alcohol treatment: The community reinforcement approach.* New York: Guilford Press.

Spitz, H. I. (1996). *Group psychotherapy and managed mental health care: A clinical guide for providers.* New York: Brunner/Mazel.

AFTERWORD: PRINCIPLED PRACTICE

The book began with a discussion of the economic and technological forces that have been reshaping the behavioral health care environment and fueling the movement toward time-limited therapy. As was indicated in the first chapter, managed care ideas and management techniques will continue to determine how social service and mental health services will be delivered, even as managed care organizations undergo significant changes in structure or change their methods of monitoring the health care system. Pressures to deliver efficient and effective therapy are likely to continue whether financial problems force HMOs to go out of business or reorganize, state or federal governments come to regulate managed care organizations, or mental health insurance benefits approach parity with the cost of coverage for medical illnesses. It is hoped that you have gained from using this book a way of thinking about time-limited practice and of developing new practice strategies that will hold you in good stead, whatever the future transformations in the delivery of social, mental health, or health care services.

The approach to brief treatment advocated in this book centered on three main tenets. The first is that becoming competent in brief treatment involves a process of letting go of certain assumptions about what constitutes effective practice—for example, that longer term treatment is more beneficial than short-term, that therapy necessarily involves the uncovering of the historical origins of problems or the expression of feelings, or that symptom relief and rapid return to functioning are not enduring changes. The second tenet is that acceptance of a set of basic principles and techniques will naturally shorten the treatment process and lead to effective brief treatment. The final tenet is that within these treatment guidelines there is enough latitude for clinicians to adapt their personal therapy style and favored theoretical orientation so that they will be able to practice the art and not just the mechanics of treatment.

Friedman (1997) has characterized these basic principles and techniques as "The Five Cs." In the conceptual framework developed in this book, it would be more appropriate to characterize the central principles as "The Ten Cs." These are (1) competency, (2) client-determined therapy, (3) collaboration, (4) context, (5) circumscribed goals, (6) current-problems focus, (7) coping, (8) calculated change, (9) community resources, and (10) catalytic function of therapist. These are the concepts or themes that are present in the case illustrations of practice. In each of these interventions, the therapist is always searching for the client's areas of competency that can be used for improving motivation and fostering change. Always the client's definition of the problem is used initially in the treatment plan, and his or her continued collaboration is sought on the methods and pace of the treatment process. Evaluation of the client's context, particularly family and community resources, is essential in facilitating the change process and preventing relapses. To achieve gains in treatment in short periods of time, the prevailing goals are narrow or circumscribed and meaningful to the client (e.g., getting a good night's sleep, reducing the morning chaos getting off to school, etc.). A focus is maintained on resolution of the current, most pressing problems, again to achieve positive outcomes in a short period of time. The clinician's role is primarily an enabling or catalytic one in which the client is empowered by the knowledge and skills provided by the clinician to make changes in his or her life. Finally, connection to community resources is a frequent and highly valued intervention, because the gains in treatment or changes set into motion in therapy are more likely to endure if community supports are in place.

These central concepts will be incorporated into practice within the context of a managed mental health care system. This means that the managed care requirements (that the need for treatment should be documented, that an appropriate level of care should be provided, and that treatment should result in symptom reduction and rapid return to functioning) must also be taken into account when devising treatment plans. The book contended that the pragmatic, triage approach of a Levels of Intervention model is in fact an ethical, good-practices approach, because it guarantees that the most distressing, disabling, and potentially harmful problems will be addressed first. Once clients are experiencing less distress and are functioning better, they are more likely to have the ego strengths needed to make use of more exploratory, expressive treatments.

Finally, it is hoped that you, the reader, will have observed the benefits of turning to the empirical literature for guidance as to best-practice methods and insights that can lead to practice innovations. As could be seen from the discussion of the literature on stress and resiliency, the findings from the research in this area are proving useful in devising better ways of serving children and families. Similarly, findings from research on life histories of those with borderline personality disorder have yielded new insights into the role of trauma and chaos in the development of the disorder and have consequently led to a restructuring of treatment strategies. Additionally, the literature on the life course of the borderline illness has provided clues as to how to structure the delivery of services to match the natural history of the illness and shifting clinical needs. Armed with a receptiveness to brief treatment ideas, guidelines for practicing, and means for developing new practice strategies, students and clinicians will be able to respond to whatever changes occur in the mental health care delivery system.

Appendix
Answers to Case Exercises

The following are suggested answers to the case exercises that appear at the end of Chapters 3–9. The answers are derived from actual treatment approaches that were successful in abbreviation of treatment and had positive outcomes, but alternative problem definitions and intervention plans could also have led to similar results. Therefore, the answers provided here should be seen primarily as a starting point for discussion.

Chapter 3
Assessment Exercise: Donna

1. Donna was at the contemplation level in the Prochaska-DiClemente Stages of Change model. While she was concerned about her job performance and fearful about losing her job, she would not yet have sought help on her own without the recommendation of the EAP counselor. Even though she was suffering, she did not want to be a burden to others. Therefore, she was prepared to put forth more effort to keep on functioning as she had before she became depressed rather than seek help for her depression.
2. Donna's history of being the caregiver in her family presented potential problems for the establishment of a helping alliance. She was not comfortable in focusing on her own needs and feelings and strongly valued her commitment to her family. This commitment needed to be respected while helping her to find a better balance between taking care of herself and taking care of her family.
3. Beck Depression Inventory and ecomap.
4. The developmental dyssynchrony focus in the I-D-E model, although an interpersonal conflict or loss focus could also have been selected. The developmental dyssynchrony focus was selected because it resonated deeply with Donna, as she was at a normative transition point in which she was questioning herself and her relationships and because her role as caregiver was central to the onset of her depression.
5. Depression was manifesting itself in a relatively healthy personality. Donna had positive self-esteem and a sense of pleasure and accomplishment in a number of arenas, including her work and volunteer activities. She had a number of interpersonal skills that made her a valued and liked colleague and family member in a large, supportive extended family. Until becoming depressed, she had social outlets for tension and anxiety and a range of coping skills (defenses such as sublimation and altruism).
6. **Problem definition**: A moderate level of depression as manifested by work problems (i.e., decreased productivity, increased level of errors, and social withdrawal) and vegetative signs (i.e., depressed affect, sleeplessness, lack of energy, poor concentration, indecisiveness, and diminished interest and enjoyment).

Goals: (1) Alleviate depressed mood and return to previous level of functioning at work and home. (2) Develop capacity to recognize personal stressors and thoughts that lead to depression and anxiety. (3) Resolve developmental challenges. **Objectives**: (1) Learn to recognize sources of depression, particularly interpersonal stresses. (2) Learn signs and symptoms of stress overload at work and home. (3) Learn alternative ways of coping with stress. (4) Recognize dysfunctional cognitions about self and relationships. (5) Clarify personal needs, wants, and goals. (6) Reestablish social supports and satisfactions. **Interventions**: (1) Refer for medication evaluation. (2) Provide education about causes and care of depression. (3) Teach stress management skills. (4) Support the developmental task of reevaluating self and life goals. (5) Provide Donna with alternative perspectives on her self-worth beyond caregiving roles. (6) Assign homework tasks that will reestablish social relationships and support network.

Chapter 4
Treatment Plan Exercise: Janet

1. **Problems and priority**: (1) anorexia, (2) depression, and (3) family stressors.
2. **Behavioral definitions**: (1) dieting resulting in significant weight loss, (2) loss of appetite, (3) diminished interest and enjoyment of social activities, (4) diminished self-esteem, (5) social withdrawal, (6) mother self-preoccupied and unavailable to provide support and guidance around adolescent concerns for Janet, (7) father creating anxiety and insecurity because of his reckless behavior when drinking.
3. **Long-term goals**: (1) Maintain current normal eating patterns. (2) Solidify commitment to gaining weight and maintaining weight gain. (2) Gain an understanding of the nature of depression and of the long-term management of depressed mood and symptoms. (3) Alleviate signs and symptoms of depression. (4) Reestablish social network and increase sources of social support.

   Short-term objectives: (1) Continue cooperation with physician and mental health staff concerning monitoring of weight and diet. (2) Verbalize and demonstrate an acceptance of the need to maintain a healthy weight. (3) Recognize and attend to depressed mood. (4) Identify irrational beliefs about self-worth and self-image. (5) Find alternative ways of dealing with distress about parents, including using extrafamilial supports. (6) Increase social activities. (7) Explore ways of managing transmandibular joint (TMJ) pain.
4. **Interventions**: (1) Refer for medical evaluation of TMJ. (2) Refer for medication evaluation for depression. (3) Establish conditions of safety and trust in therapeutic relationship through joining and building on strengths. (4) Restructure distorted cognitions about body and self-image. (5) Educate Janet about the nature and course of depression and the impact of depression on the whole family. (6) Support areas of competency such as school and work performance. (7) Expand and enhance social supports in school and in extended family. (8) Support a return to social activities through the use of homework tasks. (9) Connect Janet with support group for sufferers of TMJ.

Chapter 5
Assessment–Intervention Exercise: Mark

1. In the initial interview, the C family demonstrated several potential areas of strength, including abilities to identify potential problems, prepare for a major transition, and seek out resources for making the transition, as well as an affection and support for

each other. Mrs. C displayed a thoughtful, purposeful approach to dealing with the challenge of Mark's return, and she was able to express worries and fears as well as positive feelings toward her son. She also was sensitive to the needs and potential points of conflict between her children. Mr. C appeared to be concerned and involved with his stepson, as shown by his visit to Mark's future school. Mark appeared to be a bright child who now has the skills to express his thoughts and feelings.

2. Identifying and building on the family strengths at this uncertain point would help to build a positive alliance. For example, supporting the relationship between Mark and his stepfather through homework centering on activities they both enjoy could strengthen family bonds and lessen the competition for the mother's attention. Providing guidance about managing problems that Mrs. C anticipates will occur with Mark's return also should strengthen the family alliance, because treatment is more likely to be seen as meeting her needs rather than just a requirement for discharge from the hospital.

3. The parents may be worried that Mark will see his hospitalization as rejection or punishment and will not trust them anymore. They may also fear that Mark will become suicidal again and are afraid of saying or doing the wrong things. Mark seems concerned that there isn't a place for him and that they don't really want him back home. Everyone seems to fear that they don't know how to live with each other anymore and that they can't be a family again. Becoming comfortable and secure as a family again is everyone's goal, and interventions that help them resolve problems of transition should be very motivating to them.

4. A combination of Level I and Level II interventions is indicated. The initial focus will be on stabilizing the family with case management, problem-solving, and psycho-educational interventions. With the family's apparent capacity for meeting the basic physical and emotional needs of its members, Level II interventions can be introduced after the family has stabilized. The central problems identified by this family concern the adjustment and bereavement issues related to family reunification. Also, there are concerns about Mark's adjustment to home and school and the potential reemergence of depression and suicidal feelings. Goals for this family might include (1) managing the predictable and unpredictable reunification adjustment difficulties; (2) working through their grief about the year of separation; (3) strengthening family bonds; and (4) facilitating transition to a new school. Objectives for reaching these goals might include (1) helping the family tell their story through supportive family sessions and individual play sessions for Mark and for Mark and his sister conjointly; (2) decreasing guilt and fear through family psychoeducational sessions about the typical reactions of children and families to placement out of the home; (3) increasing the family's ability to plan for points of tension through family and parental guidance sessions in which the problem-solving method is introduced and homework is assigned to aid in the development of conflict resolution and communication skills; (4) increasing the number of positive family activities and decreasing negative interactions by encouraging pleasant family activities such as father-son fishing trips; (5) aiding Mark's adjustment to school through parental guidance and regular telephone contacts with his teacher and guidance counselor.

5. Family work, individual play therapy, parental guidance, and collateral work with the school can be used as needed to assist in the reunification process. When Mark returns home, sessions will be more frequent and then will be gradually phased out when the family and Mark appear to be adequately coping with the demands of the transition.

Chapter 6
Assessment–Intervention Exercise with a Child: Jessica

1. **Multisystem, multimodal intervention plan**:
   Goals: (1) Process trauma. (2) Grieve the loss of her father. (3) Increase family and community supports. (4) Decrease anxiety. (5) Alleviate tic symptom.
   Modalities: (1) individual play therapy, (2) joint play therapy, (3) caregiver guidance, (4) school guidance, (5) family sessions. Therapy sessions to be held twice a week at the beginning and then spaced further apart.
   Interventions: (1) Provide opportunity for Jessica to recollect and express thoughts and feelings about her father's death. (2) Enable Jessica to remember and talk about her father. (3) Educate mother and grandmother about how children grieve and Jessica's particular mourning needs. (4) Connect Jessica with school social worker and children's loss group. (5) Strengthen family's capacity to grieve as a family. (6) Strengthen ties with church and playmates.
2. Jessica's mother and grandmother and her school can be informed about the nature of trauma responses and grief reactions in children. They can also be educated about the need for the adults in her life to support the grieving process and to reassure Jessica that she is not to blame for her father's death. The minister in the church can assist the family by providing them with healing rituals, and the school can increase support and decrease Jessica's sense of isolation by including her in a bereavement group.
3. Play therapy can help with the trauma process by providing the media (play cars and dolls) by which Jessica can replay the traumatic event as often as she needs. Encouraging her to bring in photographs of her father and gifts from him gives her permission to recollect her positive feelings for her father. Books about losing a parent can also be helpful by putting into words the thoughts and feelings that her family has not been comfortable expressing. Joint play therapy sessions with her sister will give them both an opportunity to discuss their memories and for misunderstandings about their responsibility for their father's death to be corrected.
4. Jessica's skill and interest in reading could be used both within sessions and in assigning homework tasks for her and her caregivers to help her to process the trauma and loss. Keeping a journal about her thoughts and feelings could also be helpful for this shy, introspective child.

Chapter 7
Exercise in Selecting a Focus When Working with Severe Mental Illness: John

1. John was at a number of critical turning points in his life that were creating stresses for him and leading to an upsurge in self-destructive behavior, but they were also strong motivating forces to resolve long-standing self-esteem and interpersonal difficulties. As a late adolescent, he was struggling with issues of identity formation, vocation selection and preparation, separation and individuation, and formation of intimate relationships. The crisis in his relationship with his girlfriend could also serve as a vehicle for dealing with problems with self-esteem and mood regulation.
2. Behind the self-destructive actions appeared to be a healthy striving for connection and intimacy. John's strengths included his pleasure in and competence as a disk jockey and his part-time employment. He was doing reasonably well in high school, had plans to attend college, and had a number of friends. Although it had been tempestuous, he had sustained a 2-year relationship with his girlfriend. John's parents

were concerned about him and committed to his well-being. They were steadily employed and the family life was structured, predictable, and free of major conflict.

3. The developmental focus was selected initially because it was less threatening and disorganizing for John than his interpersonal problems and because John had a strong interest in sorting out vocational interests and in developing a positive identity. These interests and goals also provided a means for dealing with the substance abuse and parasuicidal behaviors, because of the dissonance between stated goals and behaviors.

4. A Level I crisis intervention approach is indicated because of the high risk for self-destructive behaviors and substance abuse.

> **Treatment plan**:
>
> **Problems**: (1) suicidal behavior as evidenced by reckless driving and accidents, (2) parasuicidal behaviors including cutting, drinking to excess, and driving while intoxicated, (3) binge drinking, (4) intense, unstable relationship with girlfriend, (5) high level of dependence on girlfriend and fear of losing her.
>
> **Goals**: (1) Reduce frequency of impulsive, destructive acts. (2) Accept problem of binge drinking and engage in a recovery program. (3) Develop ability to handle conflicts in relationships in less self-destructive manner. (4) Develop tolerance for separation from girlfriend and for being alone. (5) Begin development of an independent self with capacity for regulating own self-esteem and mood states.
>
> **Objectives**: (1) Develop awareness of precipitants to and consequences of impulsive behavior. (2) Increase ability to self-monitor moods and tension levels. (3) Learn alternative ways of managing tensions and fears, including using mental health and social support systems at times of distress. (4) Join recovery group. (5) Develop understanding of connection between relationship conflicts and alcohol abuse. (6) Identify own needs, values, goals, and interests. (7) Recognize accomplishments and strengths. (8) Develop additional sources of emotional and social support.
>
> **Interventions**: (1) Refer for psychiatric evaluation of ADHD and medication review. (2) Refer to chemical dependency group and support recovery process. (3) Teach stress management and anger and impulse control skills. (4) Support positive identity formation through focusing on the identification of personal goals, vocational interests, and areas of strength. (5) Help client identify distorted beliefs about self in relationship. (6) Increase sense of efficacy within relationships. (7) Increase dissonance between valued goals and reckless, self-destructive behavior. (8) Provide parents with guidance about coping with John's impulsivity and alcohol abuse. (9) Educate parents about the developmental challenges John is facing and provide guidance about how to support him at this time. (10) Encourage extracurricular activities and recreational interests as means of developing more positive social interactions.

Chapter 8
Case Management Exercise: Duane

1. A Level I intervention strategy was necessary because the risk of violence, the severity of Duane's symptoms, and the pending out-of-school placement made this a family crisis situation.

2. The community mental health and social service agencies that served as resources for this family were (1) male batterers program, (2) child protection service and public school system to provide funding for a special education, community-based program for children with severe emotional disabilities, (3) child welfare agency to provide

homemaking and respite care services, (4) child and family services agency (crisis intervention team) to provide treatment of the mother's depression, counseling for the father, and individual therapy for Duane, and (5) YMCA to provide recreational and socialization opportunities. An interagency team led by the crisis intervention worker took responsibility for monitoring and coordinating services to this family.

3. Duane was a friendly, trusting, verbal child with positive relationships with his parents and sibling. His parents were caring and loving and were committed to helping Duane regain bowel control and move forward with his development. Mr. O also responded readily to the request that he get help to gain control of his violent behavior. The father's efforts at gaining control over his aggression should enable Duane to feel comfortable in asserting himself and in expressing his fears and feelings of anger. The positive family bonds can also be used to cushion the discomfort of changes in individual behavioral patterns and in family interactions.

4. Individual play therapy sessions, parental guidance, and family therapy used in different combinations in each session and from session to session would be the preferred way to address the number and severity of problems in this family. Intensive case management, including the coordination of services among school, child welfare, and community agencies, and the crisis intervention approach of seeing the family several times per week in the first few weeks could also be used to quickly reduce the family violence and the disruptive symptoms of encopresis. The combination of treatment approaches and modalities might include (1) individual work with the father to secure his commitment to nonviolence and to following through with a referral to a domestic violence treatment program; (2) individual work with the mother to empower her to ensure her own safety and to alleviate her depression; (3) individual play therapy to reduce Duane's high level of anxiety and his fears about expressing anger; (4) instituting a behavior modification program based on rewards for expression of feelings; (5) work with parents in using behavior chart and responses to soiling; (6) referral for special education placement; (7) family work to address impact of violence on family functioning and individual emotional distress.

Chapter 9
EAP Assessment–Intervention Exercise: Carolyn

1. Following the EAP approach of rapid reduction in symptoms and return to functioning, problems were selected in the following order: (1) panic disorder as evidenced by palpitations, nausea, shortness of breath, trembling, dizziness, and fear of losing control; (2) increasing inability to get to work; and (3) intimate relationship conflicts as evidenced by daily unsatisfying interactions with her husband and constant undermining of her self-confidence.

2. Best practices for the treatment of panic disorder are cognitive-behavioral interventions and antianxiety medication. Clients with panic disorder benefit from education about the nature of panic attacks and gaining coping skills for managing their anxiety, learning, for example, to self-monitor, use relaxation and breathing techniques, use anticipatory guidance for problem situations, restructure dysfunctional beliefs about physiological responses and ability to cope with these sensations, and learn assertiveness skills. To address interpersonal stresses, an examination of the nature of her relationship with her husband and why this relationship is distressing to her are indicated, along with the development of assertiveness skills.

3. Carolyn's competencies on the job and in managing her household while helping both her mother and her husband with his business could be identified for her and used to disconfirm her belief that she cannot cope with panic attacks and to counter the

message from her husband that she is incompetent. Her intelligence and capacity for self-reflection should enable her to make good use of workbooks on coping with panic disorder. Carolyn's positive relationship with her brother can also be used to help her develop a perspective on herself that is different from the one that she has carried since childhood, that she is helpless and ineffectual in managing her life.

4. Once the panic attacks have diminished and are under sufficient control in Carolyn's view and she is able to go to work without experiencing acute anxiety, there is an opportunity to work on core beliefs about herself that have led her to suppress her own thoughts and feelings and fail to assert herself in her marriage. Couple therapy might be useful at this point if there is enough time and if this is what the client wants. She may prefer to use the remaining sessions to reinforce assertiveness skills and explore the origins of her beliefs about herself in relationships.

References

Abramson, J. S. (1992). Health-related problems. In W. J. Reid, *Task strategies: An empirical approach to clinical social work* (pp. 225–249). New York: Columbia University Press.

Achenbach, T. M. (1991). *Manual for the child behavior checklist and 1991 profile.* Burlington, VT: University of Vermont, Department of Psychiatry.

Ackermann-Engel, R. (1992). Brief cognitive therapy. In L. Bellak, *Handbook of intensive brief and emergency psychotherapy* (2d ed., pp. 165–229). Larchmont, NY: C.P.S. Inc.

Adams, P., & Nelson, K. (Eds.). (1995). *Reinventing human services: Community- and family-centered practice.* Hawthorne, NY: Aldine De Gruyter.

Akiskal, H. S., & Cassano, G. B. (1997). *Dysthymia and the spectrum of chronic depression.* New York: Guilford Press.

Aldwin, C. M. (1994). *Stress, coping and development.* New York: Guilford Press.

American Psychiatric Association. (1994). *Diagnostic and statistical manual of mental disorders* (4th ed.). Washington, DC: Author.

Anderson, H., & Goolishian, H. (1992). The client is the expert: A not-knowing approach to therapy. In S. McNamee & K. J. Gergen (Eds.), *Constructing therapy: Social construction and the therapeutic process* (pp. 22–39). London: Sage.

Austin, C. D. (1990). Case management: Myths and realities. *Families in Society, 71*(7), 398–405.

Ballew, J. R., & Mink, G. (1996). *Case management in social work: Developing the professional* (2d ed.). Springfield, IL: Charles T. Thomas.

Barber, J. D. (1995). Working with resistant drug abusers. *Social Work, 40*(1), 17–23.

Beck, D. F., & Jones, M. A. (1973). *Progress on family problems.* New York: Family Service Association of America.

Beck, A. T., Rush, A. J., Shaw, B. F., & Emery, G. (1979). *Cognitive therapy of depression.* New York: Guilford Press.

Beckham, E. E., & Leber, W. R. (Eds.). (1995). *Handbook of depression* (2d ed.). New York: Guilford Press.

Bellak, L. (1992). *Handbook of intensive brief and emergency psychotherapy.* Larchmont, NY: C.P.S. Inc.

Bennett, M. (1989). The catalytic function in psychotherapy. *Psychiatry, 52,* 351–364.

Berg, I. K. (1994). *Family based services: A solution-focused approach.* New York: W. W. Norton.

249

Berkman, B. (1996). The emerging health care world: Implications for social work practice and education. *Social Work, 41*(5), 541–552.

Berlin, S. (1983). Cognitive-behavioral approaches. In A. Rosenblatt & D. Waldfogel (Eds.), *Handbook of clinical social work* (pp. 1095–1119). San Francisco: Jossey-Bass.

Bernier, D. (1992). The Indochinese refugees: A perspective from various stress theories. In A. S. Ryan (Ed.), *Social work with immigrants and refugees* (pp. 15–30). Binghamton, NY: Haworth Press.

Beutler, L. E., & Clarkin, J. F. (1990). *Systematic treatment selection: Toward targeted therapeutic intervention.* New York: Brunner/Mazel.

Birelson, P., Hudson, I., Buchannon, D., & Wolff, S. (1987). Clinical evaluation of a self-rating scale for depressive disorder in childhood (Depression Self-Rating Scale). *Journal of Child Psychology and Psychiatry, 28,* 43–60.

Bloom, B. L. (1992). *Planned short-term psychotherapy: A clinical handbook.* Needham Heights, MA: Allyn & Bacon.

Bowlby, J. (1979). *The making and breaking of affectional bonds.* London: Tavistock Publications.

Bray, R. (1998). *Unafraid of the dark: A memoir.* New York: Random House.

Breakey, W. R. (1996). Developmental milestones for community psychiatry. In W. R. Breakey (Ed.), *Integrated mental health services: Modern community psychiatry* (pp. 29–42). New York: Oxford University Press.

Brownell, K. D., Marlatt, G. A., Lichtenstein, E. & Wilson, G. T. (1986). Understanding and preventing relapse. *American Psychologist, 41,* 765–782.

Browning, C. H., & Browning, B. J. (1994). *How to partner with managed care: A do-it-yourself kit for building working relationships and getting steady referrals.* Los Alamitos, CA: Duncliff's International.

Budman, S. H., & Gurman, A. S. (1988). *Theory and practice of brief therapy.* New York: Guilford Press.

Budman, S. H., Hoyt, M. F., & Friedman, S. (1992). First words on first sessions. In S. H. Budman, M. F. Hoyt, & S. Friedman (Eds.), *The first session in brief therapy* (pp. 3–8). New York: Guilford Press.

Burns, G. L., & Patterson, D. R. (1990). Conduct problem behaviors in a stratified random sample of children and adolescents: New standardization data on the Eyberg Child Behavior Inventory. *Psychological Assessment, 2,* 391–397.

Butler, S. F., Strupp, H. H., & Binder, J. L. (1992). Time-limited dynamic psychotherapy. In S. H. Budman, M. F. Hoyt, & S. Friedman (Eds.), *The first session in psychotherapy* (pp. 87–110). New York: Guilford Press.

Cabaj, R. P. (1998). Substance abuse and HIV diseases: Entwined and intimate entities. In E. F. McCance-Katz & T. R. Kosten (Eds.), *New treatments for chemical addictions* (pp. 113–150). Washington, DC: American Psychiatric Press.

Calhoun, K. S., & Resick, P. A. (1993). Post-traumatic stress disorder. In D. H. Barlow (Ed.), *Clinical handbook of psychological disorders* (2d ed., pp. 48–98). New York: Guilford Press.

Clark, D. C. (1995). Epidemiology, assessment, and management of suicide in depressed patients. In E. E. Beckham & W. R. Leber (Eds.), *Handbook of depression* (2d ed., pp. 526–538). New York: Guilford Press.

Clarkin, J. F., & Haas, G. L. (1988). Assessment of affective disorders and their interpersonal contexts. In J. F. Clarkin, G. L. Haas, & I. D. Glick (Eds.), *Affective disorders and the family: Assessment and treatment* (pp. 29–50). New York: Guilford.

Clinton, J. J., McCormick, K. & Besteman, J. (1994). Enhancing clinical practice: The role of practice guidelines. *American Psychologist, 49*(1), 30–34.

Collins, A., & Collins, T. (1990). Parent-professional relationship in the treatment of severely emotionally disturbed children and adolescents. *Social Work, 35*, 522–537.

Combs, G., & Freedman, J. (1994). Narrative intentions. In M. F. Hoyt (Ed.), *Constructive therapies* (pp. 67–91). New York: Guilford Press.

Congress, E. P. (1994). The use of culturagrams to assess and empower culturally diverse families. *Families in Society, 75*(9), 531–540.

Cooper, J. F. (1995). *A primer of brief psychotherapy.* New York: W. W. Norton.

Corcoran, K., & Vandiver, V. (1996). *Maneuvering the maze of managed care: Skills for mental health practitioners.* New York: Free Press.

Corwin, M. D. (1996). Early intervention strategies with borderline clients. *Families in Society, 77*(1), 40–49.

Cournoyer, B. R. (1996). Converging themes in crisis intervention, task-centered, and brief treatment approaches. A. R. Roberts (Ed.), *Crisis management & brief treatment: Theory, technique, and applications* (pp. 3–15). Chicago: Nelson Hall.

Cowger, C. D. (1992). Assessment of client strengths. In D. Saleeby (Ed.), *The strengths perspective in social work practice* (pp. 139–147). White Plains, NY: Longman.

Cowger, C. D. (1994). Assessing client strengths: Clinical assessment for client empowerment. *Social Work, 39*(3), 262–269.

Craske, K. S., & Barlow, D. H. (1993). Panic disorder and agoraphobia. In *Clinical handbook of psychological disorders* (2d ed., pp. 1–47). New York: Guilford Press.

Cummings, N., & Sayama, M. (1995). *Focused psychotherapy: A casebook of brief, intermittent psychotherapy throughout the life cycle.* New York: Brunner/Mazel.

Cutler, D. L. (1992). A historical overview of community mental health centers in the United States. In S. Cooper & T. H. Lentner (Eds.), *Innovations in community mental health* (pp. 1–22). Sarasota, FL: Professional Resources Press.

Dejong, P., & Miller, S. D. (1995). How to interview for client strengths. *Social Work, 40*(6), 729–736.

Delgado, M. (1998). *Social services in Latino communities.* Binghamton, NY: Haworth.

de Shazer, S. (1985). *Keys to solution in brief therapy.* New York: W. W. Norton.

Dhooper, S. S. (1997). *Social work in health care in the 21st century.* Thousand Oaks, CA: Sage Publications.

Dickman, F., & Challenger, B. R. (1997). Employee assistance programs: A historical sketch. In W. Hutchinson & W. G. Emener (Eds.), *Employee assistance programs: A basic text* (2d ed., pp. 50–58). Springfield, IL: Charles C. Thomas.

Dorfman, R. (Ed.) (1988). *Paradigms of clinical social work.* New York: Brunner/Mazel.

Drake, R. E., Osher, F. C., & Bartels, S. J. (1996). The "dually diagnosed." In W. R. Breakey (Ed.), *Integrated mental health services: Modern community psychiatry* (pp. 339–352). New York: Oxford Press.

Drake, R. E., & Sederer, L. I. (1986). The adverse effects of intensive treatment of chronic schizophrenia. *Comprehensive Psychiatry, 27*, 313–326.

Druss, R. G. (1995). *The psychology of illness: In sickness and in health.* Washington, DC: American Psychiatric Press.

Duncan, B. L., Solovey, A. D., & Rusk, G. S. (1992). *Changing the rules: A client-directed approach to therapy.* New York: Guilford Press.

Dziegielewski, S. F., & Resnick, C. (1996). Crisis assessment and intervention: Abused women in the shelter setting. In A. R. Roberts (Ed.), *Crisis management & brief treatment: Theory, technique, and applications* (pp. 123–141). Chicago: Nelson-Hall Publishers.

Eaton, M. C. (1996). The psychotherapy of schizophrenia. In W. R. Breakey (Ed.), *Integrated mental health services: Modern community psychiatry* (pp. 206–221). New York: Oxford University Press.

Eysenck, H. J. (1988). Psychotherapy to behavior therapy: A paradigm shift. In D. B. Fishman, F. Rotgers, & C. M. Franks (Eds.), *Paradigms in behavior therapy: Present and promise* (pp. 45–76). New York: Springer.

Falloon, I. R. H., & Fadden, G. (1993). *Integrated mental health care: A comprehensive community-based approach.* Cambridge, UK: Cambridge University Press.

Farley, J. E. (1994). Transitions in psychiatric inpatient clinical social work. *Social Work, 39*(2), 207–212.

Fawzy, F. I., Fawzy, N. W., Hyun, C. S., & Wheeler, J. G., (1997). Brief coping-oriented therapy for patients with malignant melanoma. In J. L. Spira (Ed.), *Group therapy for medically ill patients* (pp. 133–164). New York: Guilford Press.

Fisch, R. (1994). Basic elements in the brief therapies. In M. F. Hoyt (Ed.), *Constructive therapies* (pp. 126–139). New York: Guilford Press.

Fischer, J., & Corcoran, K. (1994). *Measures for clinical practice: A sourcebook* (2d ed.). New York: Free Press.

Fleischer, D., & Kaplan, B. H. (1988). Employee assistance/counseling typologies. In G. M. Gould & M. L. Smith (Eds.), *Social work in the workplace* (pp. 31–44). New York: Springer.

Folkers, C., & Steefel, N. M. (1991). Group psychotherapy in HMO settings. In C. S. Austad & W. H. Berman (Eds.), *Psychotherapy in managed mental health care: The optimal use of time and resources.* Washington, DC: American Psychological Association.

Ford, D. H., & Urban, H. B. (1998). *Contemporary models of psychotherapy: A comparative analysis* (2d ed.). New York: J. Wiley & Sons.

Forman, S. G. (1993). *Coping skills interventions for children and adolescents.* San Francisco: Jossey-Bass.

Fortune, A. (1985). *Task-centered practice with families and groups.* New York: Springer.

Frank, J. D. (1982). Therapeutic components shared by all psychotherapies. In J. H. Harvey & M. M. Parks (Eds.), *Psychotherapy research and behavior change* (pp. 5–38). Washington, DC: American Psychological Association.

Fraser, M. W., & Galinsky, M. J. (1997). Toward a resilience-based model of practice. In M. W. Fraser (Ed.), *Risk and resiliency in childhood: An ecological perspective* (pp. 265–276). Washington, DC: NASW Press.

Freeman, A., Pretzer, J., Fleming, B., & Simon, K. (1990). *Clinical applications of cognitive therapy.* New York: Plenum.

Friedman, S. (1997). *Time-effective psychotherapy: Maximizing outcomes in an era of minimized resources.* Needham Heights, MA: Allyn & Bacon.

Garfield, S. L. (1994). Research on client variables in psychotherapy. In A. E. Bergin & S. L. Garfield (Eds.), *Handbook of psychotherapy and behavior change* (4th ed., pp. 190–228). New York: J. Wiley & Sons.

Garmezy, N. (1985). Stress-resistant children: The search for protective factors. In J. E. Stevenson (Ed.), *Recent research in developmental psychology* (pp. 213–233). Tarrytown, NY: Pergamon Press.

Garnick, D. W., Hendricks, A. M., Dulski, J. D., Thorpe, K. E., & Horgan, C. (1994). Characteristics of private-sector managed care for mental health and substance abuse treatment. *Hospital and Community Psychiatry, 45*(12), 1201–1205.

Germain, C. B. (1991). *Human behavior in the social environment.* New York: Columbia University Press.

Globerman, J., & Bogo, M. (1995). Social work and the new integrative hospital. *Social Work in Health Care, 21*(3), 1–22.

Goering, P. N., & Wasylenki, D. (1996). Case management. In W. R. Breakey (Ed.), *Integrated mental health services: Modern community psychiatry* (pp. 310–322). New York: Oxford University Press.

Golan, N. (1981). *Passing through transitions: A guide for the practitioner.* New York: Free Press.

Goodman, M., Brown, J., & Dietz, P. (1992). *Managing managed care: A mental health practitioner's survival guide.* Washington, DC: American Psychiatric Press.

Granvold, D. K. (1996). Constructivist psychotherapy. *Families in Society, 77*(6), 345–359.

Granvold, D. K., & Wodarski, J. S. (1994). Cognitive and behavioral treatment: Clinical issues, transfer of training, and relapse prevention. In D. K. Granvold (Ed.), *Cognitive and behavioral treatment: Methods and applications* (pp. 353–375). Belmont, CA: Brooks/Cole.

Green, B. L., Wilson, J. P., & Lindy, J. D. (1985). Conceptualizing post-traumatic stress disorder: A psychosocial framework. In C. R. Figley (Ed.), *Trauma and its wake: The study and treatment of post-traumatic stress disorder* (pp. 53–72). New York: Brunner/Mazel.

Grigsby, R. K. (1995). Interventions to meet basic needs in high-risk families with children. In A. C. Kilpatrick & T. P. Holland, *Working with families: An integrative model by level of functioning* (pp. 69–84). Needham Heights, MA: Allyn & Bacon.

Gunderson, J. G. (1997). Effects of childhood abuse on treatment of borderline clients. In M. C. Zanarini (Ed.), *Role of sexual abuse in the etiology of borderline personality disorder* (pp. 225–236). Washington, DC: American Psychiatric Press.

Gunderson, J. G., & Links, P. (1996). Borderline personality disorder. In G. O. Gabbard and S. D. Atkinson (Eds.), *Synopsis of treatments of psychiatric disorders* (2d ed.) (pp. 969–978). Washington, DC: American Psychiatric Press.

Gunderson, J. G., & Sabo, A. N. (1993). The phenomenological and conceptual interface between borderline personality disorder and PTSD. *American Journal of Psychiatry, 150,* 19–27.

Hall, M. J., Arnold, W. N., & Crosby, R. M. (1990). Back to basics: The importance of focus selection. *Psychotherapy, 27*(4), 578–226.

Hamberger, L. K., & Hotzworth-Munroe, A. (1994). Partner violence. In F. M. Dattilio & A. Freeman (Eds.), *Cognitive-behavioral strategies in crisis intervention* (pp. 302–324). New York: Guilford Press.

Hardley, G., & Guerney, B. G. (1989). A psychoeducational approach. In C. R. Figley (Ed.), *Treating stress in families* (pp. 158–184). New York: Brunner/Mazel.

Hargrove, D. S. (1992). Community mental health center staff development for service to special populations. In S. Cooper & T. H. Lerner (Eds.), *Innovations in community mental health* (pp. 141–170). Sarasota, FL: Professional Resource Press.

Harrison, A. O., Wilson, M. N., Pine, C. J., Chan, S. Q., & Buriel, R. (1990). Family ecologies of ethnic minority children. *Child Development, 61,* 347–362.

Hartman, A. (1978). Diagrammatic assessment of family relationships. *Social Casework, 59*(8), 465–476.

Hecker, L. L., Deaker, S. A., & Associates (1998). *The therapist's notebook: Homework, handouts, and activities for use in psychotherapy.* Binghamton, NY: Haworth Press.

Heinssen, R. K., Levendusky, P. G., & Hunter, R. H. (1995). Client as colleague: Therapeutic contracting with the seriously mentally ill. *American Psychologist, 50*(7), 522–532.

Hepworth, D. H., Rooney, R. H., & Larsen, J. (1997). *Direct social practice: Theory and skills* (5th ed.). Pacific Grove, CA: Brooks/Cole.

Hoff, L. A. (1995). *People in crisis: Understanding and helping* (4th ed.). San Francisco: Jossey-Bass.

Horowitz, M., Field, N. P., & Classen, C. C. (1993). Stress response syndromes and their treatment. In L. Goldberger & S. Breznitz (Eds.), *Handbook of stress: Theoretical and clinical aspects* (2d ed., pp. 757–774). New York: Free Press.

Howard, K. L., Kopta, S. M., Krause, S. M., & Orlinsky, D. E. (1986). The dose-effect relationship in psychotherapy. *American Psychologist, 41,* 159–164.

Hoyt, M. (1994). Introduction: Competency-based, future-oriented therapy. In M. Hoyt (Ed.), *Constructive therapies* (pp. 1–10). New York: Guilford Press.

Hoyt, M. (1995). *Brief therapy and managed care: Readings for contemporary practice.* San Francisco: Jossey-Bass.

Hoyt, M. F. & Austad, C. S. (1992). Psychotherapy in a staff model health maintenance organization: Providing and assuring quality care in the future. *Psychotherapy, 29*(1), 119–129.

Hoyt, M. F., Rosenbaum, R., & Talmon, M. (1992). Planned single-session therapy. In S. H. Budman, M. F. Hoyt, & S. Friedman (Eds.), *The first session in brief therapy* (pp. 59–86). New York: Guilford Press.

Hudson, W. W. (1992). *The WALMYR Assessment Scales Scoring Manual.* Tempe, AZ: WALMYR Publishing Co.

Hunter, R. H. (1995). Benefits of competency-based treatment programs. *American Psychologist, 50*(7), 509–513.

Jenkins, J. H. (1995). Culture, emotion, and psychopathology. In S. Kitayama & H. R. Markus (Eds.), *Emotion and culture: Empirical studies of mutual influence* (pp. 307–338). Washington, DC: American Psychological Association.

Jobes, D. A., & Berman, A. L. (1996). Crisis assessment and time-limited intervention with high risk suicidal youth. In A. R. Roberts (Ed.), *Crisis management and brief treatment: Theory, technique, and applications* (pp. 60–82). Chicago: Nelson-Hall.

Johnson, L. D. (1995). *Psychotherapy in the age of accountability.* New York: W. W. Norton.

Johnson, S. L. (1997). *Therapist's guide to clinical intervention: The 1-2-3's of treatment planning*. Fresno, CA: Academic.

Johnson, H. C., Cournoyer, D. E., & Bond, B. M. (1995). Professional ethics and parents as consumers: How well are we doing? *Families in Society, 76,* 408–421.

Johnson, H. C., Cournoyer, D. E., & Fisher, G. A. (1994). Measuring worker cognitions about parents of children with mental and emotional disabilities. *Journal of Emotional and Behavioral Disorders, 2*(2), 99–108.

Jongsma, A. E., & Peterson, L. M. (1995). *The complete psychotherapy treatment planner*. New York: J. Wiley & Sons.

Jongsma, A. E., Peterson, L. M., & McInnis, W. P. (1996). *The child and adolescent psychotherapy treatment planner*. New York: J. Wiley & Sons.

Julia, M. C. (1996). *Multicultural awareness in the health care professions*. Needham Heights, MA: Allyn & Bacon.

Katz, M. (1997). *On playing a poor hand well*. New York: W. W. Norton.

Kazdin, A. E. (1998). Psychosocial treatments for conduct disorder in children. In P. E. Nathan & J. M. Gorman (Eds.), *A guide to treatments that work* (pp. 65–89). New York: Oxford Press.

Kelly, J. A., Murphy, D. A., Bahr, R., Kalichman, S. C., Morgan, M. G., Stevenson, Y., Koob, J. J., Brasfield, T. L., & Bernstein, B. M. (1993). Outcome of cognitive-behavioral and support group brief therapies for depressed, HIV-infected persons. *American Journal of Psychiatry, 150*(11), 1679–1686.

Kilpatrick, A. C., & Holland, T. P. (1995). *Working with families: An integrative model by level of functioning*. Needham Heights, MA: Allyn & Bacon.

Klein, A. R., & Cnaan, R. A. (1995). Practice with high-risk clients. *Families in Society, 76,* 203–212.

Klein, D. F., & Wender, P. H. (1993). *Understanding depression: A complete guide to its diagnosis and treatment*. New York: Oxford Press.

Koerner, K., & Linehan, M. M. (1992). Integrative therapy for borderline personality disorder: Dialectical behavior therapy. In J. C. Norcross & M. R. Goldfried (Eds.), *Handbook of psychotherapy integration*. New York: Basic Books.

Koss, M. P., & Butcher, J. N. (1986). Research on brief therapy. In A. E. Bergin & S. L. Garfield (Eds.), *Handbook of psychotherapy and behavior change* (3d ed., pp. 627–670). New York: J. Wiley & Sons.

Koss, M. P., & Shiang, J. (1994). Research on brief psychotherapy. In A. E. Bergin & S. L. Garfield (Eds.), *Handbook of psychotherapy and behavior change* (4th ed., pp. 664–700). New York: J. Wiley & Sons.

Kreilkamp, T. (1988). *Time-limited intermittent therapy with children and families*. New York: Brunner/Mazel.

Lambert, M. J., & Bergin, A. E. (1994). The effectiveness of psychotherapy. In A. E. Bergin & S. L. Garfield (Eds.), *Handbook of psychotherapy and behavior change* (4th ed., pp. 143–189). New York: J. Wiley & Sons.

Lambert, M. J., Chiles, J. A., Kesler, S. R., & Vermeersch, D. A. (1998). Compendium of current psychotherapy treatment manuals. In G. P. Koocher, J. C. Norcross, & S. S. Hill (Eds.), *Psychologists' desk reference* (pp. 202–207). New York: Oxford University Press.

Land, H., Nishimoto, R., & Chau, K. (1988). Interventive and preventive services for Vietnamese Chinese refugees. *Social Service Review, 62*(3), 468–484.

Lebow, J. (1995). Open-ended therapy: Termination in marital and family therapy. In R. H. Mikesell, D. Lusterman, & S. H. McDaniel (Eds.), *Integrating family therapy: Handbook of family psychology and systems* (pp. 73–88). Washington, DC: American Psychological Association.

Legault, G. (1996). Social work practice in situations of intercultural misunderstandings. In Y. Asamoah (Ed.), *Innovations in delivering culturally sensitive social work services.* (pp. 49–66). Binghamton, NY: Haworth Press.

Links, P. S., Boiagoa, I., Huxley, G., Steiner, M., & Mitton, J. E. (1990). Sexual abuse and biparental failure as etiologic models in borderline personality disorder. In P. S. Links (Ed.), *Family environment and borderline personality disorder* (pp. 105–120). Washington, DC; American Psychiatric Press.

Lock, J. (1997). Depression. In H. Steiner (Ed.), *Treating school-age children* (pp. 65–92). San Francisco: Jossey-Bass.

Ludgate, J. W. (1995). *Maximizing psychotherapeutic gains and preventing relapse in emotionally distressed clients.* Sarasota, FL: Professional Resource Press.

Lukton, R. (1982). Myths and realities of crisis intervention. *Social Casework, 63,* 275–285.

Lum, D. (1996). *Social work practice & people of color: A process-stage approach* (3d ed.). Pacific Grove, CA: Brooks/Cole.

Lyons, J. S., Howard, K. I., O'Mahoney, M. T., & Lish, J. D. (1997). *The measurement & management of clinical outcomes in mental health.* New York: Wiley & Sons.

McCall-Perez, F. (1994). What employers want in managed care programs. *Hospital and Community Psychiatry, 44*(7), 682–683.

McCubbin, H. I., & Thompson, A. I. (Eds.). (1991). *Family assessment inventories for research and practice.* Madison, WI: University of Wisconsin.

McGovern, M. P., Lyons, J. S., & Pomp, H. C. (1990). Capitation payment systems and public mental health care: Implications for psychotherapy with the seriously mentally ill. *American Journal of Orthopsychiatry, 60*(2), 288–303.

MacKenzie, K. R. (1990). *Introduction to time-limited group psychotherapy.* Washington, DC: American Psychiatric Press.

MacKenzie, K. R. (1994). Where is here and when is now? The adaptational challenge of mental health reform for group psychotherapy. *International Journal of Group Psychotherapy, 44*(4), 407–428.

Markowitz, J. C., & Weissman, M. M. (1995). Interpersonal psychotherapy. In E. E. Beckham & W. R. Leber (Eds.), *Handbook of depression* (2d ed., pp. 376–390). New York: Guilford Press.

Marley, J. (1992). Content and context: working with mentally ill people in family therapy. *Social Work, 37*(5), 412–417.

Maxmen, J. S., & Ward, N. G. (1995). *Essential psychopathology and its treatment* (2d ed.). New York: W. W. Norton.

Mays, M., & Croake, J. W. (1997). *Treatment of depression in managed care.* New York: Brunner/Mazel.

Medical Source (1999): http:\\www.medicalinternet.net.

Meichenbaum, D. (1996). *Mixed anxiety and depression: A cognitive-behavioral approach*. New York: Newbridge Professional Programs.

Meyers, R. J., & Smith, J. E. (1995). *Clinical guide to alcohol treatment: The community reinforcement approach*. New York: Guilford Press.

Miller, W. R. (1983). Motivational interviewing with problem drinkers. *Behavioral Psychotherapy, 11*, 147–172.

Miller, W. R., & Rollnick, S. (1991). *Motivational interviewing: Preparing people to change addictive behavior*. New York: Guilford Press.

Moffat, P., & Kay, N. (1996). Brief coping-oriented therapy for patients with malignant melanoma. In J. L. Spira (Ed.), *Group therapy for medically ill patients* (pp. 133–164). New York: Guilford Press.

Myer, R. A., & Hanna, F. J. (1996). Working in hospital emergency departments: Guidelines for crisis intervention workers. In A. R. Roberts (Ed.), *Crisis management & brief treatment: Theory, technique, and applications* (pp. 37–59). Chicago: Nelson-Hall Publishers.

Nathan, P. E., & Gorman, J. M. (1998). *A guide to treatments that work*. New York: Oxford Press.

O'Connor, K. J., & Ammen, S. (1997). *Play therapy: The ecosystemic model and workbook*. San Diego, CA: Academic Press.

Orlinsky, D. E., Grawe, K., & Parks, B. K. (1994). Process and outcome in psychotherapy—noch einmal. In A. E. Bergin & S. L. Garfield (Eds.), *Handbook of psychotherapy and behavior change* (4th ed., pp. 270–378). New York: J. Wiley & Sons.

Paleg, K., & Jongsma, A. E. (1998). *The group psychotherapy treatment planner*. New York: J. Wiley & Sons.

Parad, H. J. (1965). *Crisis intervention: Selected readings*. New York: Family Service Association of America.

Paulson, R. I. (1996). Swimming with the sharks or walking in the garden of Eden: Two visions of managed care and mental health practice. In P. R. Raffoul & C. A. McNeece (Eds.), *Future issues for social work practice* (pp. 85–96). Boston, MA: Allyn & Bacon.

Pekarik, G. (1996). *Psychotherapy abbreviation: A practical guide*. Binghamton, NY: Haworth Press.

Perkinson, R. R., & Jongsma, A. E. (1998). *The chemical dependence treatment planner*. New York: J. Wiley & Sons.

Perris, C., & Skagerlind, L. (1994). Schizophrenia. In F. M. Dattilio & A. Freeman (Eds.), *Cognitive-behavioral strategies in crisis intervention* (pp. 104–118). New York: Guilford.

Poertner, J., & Ronnau, J. (1993). A strengths approach to children with emotional disabilities. In D. Saleeby (Ed.), *The strengths perspective in social work practice* (pp. 111–121). White Plains, NY: Longman.

Pollack, D. A., & Cutler, D. L. (1992). Changing roles: Psychiatry in community mental health centers. In S. Cooper & T. H. Lentner (Eds.), *Innovations in community mental health* (pp. 125–140). Sarasota, FL: Professional Resources Press.

Pollin, I., & Kanaan, S. B. (1995). *Medical crisis counseling*. New York: W. W. Norton.

Primm, A. B. (1996). Assertive community treatment. In W. R. Breakey (Ed.), *Integrated mental health services: Modern community psychiatry* (pp. 222–237). New York: Oxford Press.

Primm, A. B., Lima, B. R., & Rowe, C. L. (1996). Culture and ethnic sensitivity. In W. R. Breakey (Ed.), *Integrated mental health services: Modern community psychiatry* (pp. 146–159). New York: Oxford Press.

Prochaska, J. O., & DiClemente, C. C. (1986). The transtheoretical approach. In J. C. Norcross (Ed.), *Handbook of eclectic psychotherapy* (pp. 163–200). New York: Brunner/Mazel.

Prochaska, J. O., DiClemente, C. C., & Norcross, J. C. (1992). In search of how people change: Applications to addictive behaviors. *American Psychologist, 47*(9), 1102–1114.

Ramirez, M. (1991). *Psychotherapy and counseling with minorities: A cognitive approach to individual and cultural differences.* New York: Pergamon Press.

Reid, W. J. (1978). *The task-centered system.* New York: Columbia University Press.

Reid, W. J. (1992). *Task strategies: An empirical approach to clinical social work.* New York: Columbia University Press.

Reid, W. J., & Epstein, L. (1972). *Task-centered casework.* New York: Columbia University Press.

Reid, W. J., & Shyne, A. W. (1969). *Brief and extended casework.* New York: Columbia University Press.

Reinecke, M. (1994). Suicide and depression. In F. M. Dattilio & A. Freeman (Eds.), *Cognitive-behavioral strategies in crisis intervention* (pp. 67–103). New York: Guilford Press.

Richman, J. M., & Bowen, G. L. (1997). School failure: An ecological-interactional-developmental perspective. In M. W. Fraser (Ed.), *Risk and resilience in childhood: An ecological perspective* (pp. 95–116). Washington, DC: NASW Press.

Roberts, A. R. (1984). *Battered women and their families: Intervention strategies and treatment programs.* New York: Springer.

Roberts, A. R. (1996). Overview. In A. R. Roberts (Ed.), *Crisis management & brief treatment* (pp. 3–15). Chicago, IL: Nelson-Hall Publishers.

Rogler, L. H., & Cortes, D. E. (1993). Help-seeking pathways: A unifying concept in mental health care. *American Journal of Psychiatry, 150,* 554–561.

Rolland, J. S. (1994). *Families, illness, and disability.* New York: Basic Books.

Rollnick, S., & Bell, A. (1991). Brief motivational interviewing for use by the nonspecialist. In W. R. Miller & S. Rollnick, *Motivational interviewing: Preparing people to change addictive behavior* (pp. 203–213). New York: Guilford Press.

Rooney, R. H. (1988). Socialization strategies for involuntary clients. *Social Casework, 69,* 131–140.

Rothman, J. (1994). *Practice with highly vulnerable clients: Case management and community-based service.* Englewood Cliffs, NJ: Prentice Hall.

Rubenstein, E. (1991). An overview of adolescent development, behavior, and clinical intervention. *Families in Society, 72,* 220–226.

Rutter, M. (1987). Psychosocial resilience and protective mechanisms. In *American Journal of Orthopsychiatry, 57*(3), 316–331.

Rutter, M. (1989). Pathways from childhood to adult life. *Journal of Child Psychology and Psychiatry, 30*(1), 23–51.

Ryglewicz, H., & Pepper, B. (1992). The dual-disorder client: mental disorder and substance use. In S. Cooper & T. H. Lentner (Eds.), *Innovations in community mental health*. Sarasota, FL: Professional Resource Press.

Sabin, J. (1991). Clinical skills for the 1990's: Six lessons from HMO practice. *Hospital and Community Psychiatry, 42*(6), 605–608.

Safran, J. D., & Segal, Z. V. (1990). *Interpersonal process in cognitive therapy*. New York: Basic Books.

Saleeby, D. (Ed.) (1992). *The strengths perspective in social work practice*. White Plains, NY: Longman.

Saleeby, D. (1996). The strengths perspective in social work practice: Extension and cautions. *Social Work, 41*, 296–305.

Santos, A. B., Henggler, S. W., Burns, B. J., Arana, G. W., & Meisler, N. (1995). Research on field-based services: Models for reform in the delivery of mental health care to populations with complex clinical problems. *American Journal of Psychiatry, 152*(8), 1111–1123.

Saunders, E. A., & Arnold, F. (1993). A critique of conceptual and treatment approaches to borderline psychopathology in light of findings about childhood abuse. *Psychiatry, 56*, 187–203.

School Health Policy Initiative (1996). *A partnership for quality and access: School-based health centers and health plans*. New York: Montefiore Medical Center.

Schultheis, G. M. (1998). *Brief therapy homework planner*. New York: J. Wiley & Sons.

Schwarz, R. A., & Prout, M. F. (1991). Integrative approaches in the treatment of posttraumatic stress disorder. *Psychotherapy, 28*(2), 364–373.

Sciacca, K. (1997). Removing barriers: Dual diagnosis and motivational interviewing. *Professional Counselor*, February 1997, 41–46.

Seaburn, D. B., Lorenz, A. D., Gunn, W. B., Gawinski, B. A., & Mauksch, L. B. (1996). *Models of collaboration: A guide for mental health professionals working with health care practitioners*. New York: Basic Books.

Selekman, M. D. (1993). *Pathways to change: Brief therapy solutions with difficult adolescents*. New York: Guilford Press.

Seligman, M. E. (1995). *The optimistic child*. New York: Harper Perennial.

Selzer, M. L. (1971). The Michigan Alcoholism Screening Test: The quest for a new diagnostic instrument. *American Journal of Psychiatry, 127*, 89–94.

Shea, C. S. (1998). *Psychiatric interviewing: The art of understanding* (2d ed.). Philadelphia: W. B. Saunders.

Shuchter, S. R., Downs, N., & Zisook, S. (1996). *Biologically informed psychotherapy for depression*. New York: Guilford Press.

Simon, C. E., McNeil, J. S., Franklin, C., & Cooperman, A. (1991). The family and schizophrenia: Toward a psychoeducational approach. *Families in Society, 72*, 323–333.

Sledge, W. H., Moras, K., Hartley, D., & Levine, M. (1990). Effect of time-limited psychotherapy on patient dropout rates. *American Journal of Psychiatry, 147*(10), 1341–1347.

Smyrnios, K. X., & Kirkby, R. J. (1993). Long-term comparison of brief versus unlimited psychodynamic treatments with children and their parents. *Journal of Consulting and Clinical Psychology, 61*(6), 1020–1027.

Spitz, H. I. (1996). *Group psychotherapy and managed mental health care: A clinical guide for providers*. New York: Brunner/Mazel.

Stiffman, A. R., Orme, J. G., Evans, D. A., Feldman, R. A., & Keeney, P. A. (1984). A brief measure of children's behavior problems: The behavior rating index for children. *Measurement and Evaluation in Counseling and Development, 16,* 83–90.

Stone, M. (1990). *The fate of borderline patients*. New York: Guilford Press.

Straus, M. A., & Gelles, R. J. (1990). *Physical violence in American families: Risk factors and adaptations to violence in 8,145 families*. New Brunswick, NJ: Transaction Books.

Strayhorn, J. M. (1988). *The competent child: An approach to psychotherapy and preventive mental health*. New York: Guilford Press.

Strom-Gottfried, K. (1997). The implications of managed care for social work education. *Journal of Social Work Education, 33*(1), 7–18.

Sue, D. W., & Sue, S. (1990). *Counseling the culturally different: Theory and practice* (2d ed.). New York: J. Wiley & Sons.

Sue, S., & Zane, N. (1987). The role of culture and cultural techniques in psychotherapy: A critique and reformulation. *American Psychologist, 42*(1), 37–45.

Sue, S., Zane, N., & Young, K. (1994). Research on psychotherapy with culturally diverse populations. In A. E. Bergin & S. L. Garfield (Eds.), *Handbook of psychotherapy and behavior change* (pp. 783–820). New York: J. Wiley & Sons.

Taylor, S. E., & Aspinall, L. G. (1993). Coping with chronic illness. In L. Goldberger & S. Breznitz (Eds.), *Handbook of stress* (2d ed., pp. 511–531). New York: Free Press.

Tseng, W., & Hsu, J. (1991). *Culture and family: Problems and therapy*. Binghamton, NY: Haworth Press.

Turner, R. M., Becker, L., & DeLoach, C. (1994). Borderline personality disorder. In F. M. Dattilio & A. Freeman (Eds.), *Cognitive-behavioral strategies in crisis intervention* (pp. 25–45). New York: Guilford Press.

Wakefield, J. C., & Kirk, S. A. (1996). Unscientific thinking about scientific practice: evaluating the scientist-practitioner model. *Social Work Research, 20*(2), 83–96.

Walker, L. E. (1995). *Abused women and survivor therapy*. Washington, DC: American Psychological Association.

Wallace, C. J., & Liberman, R. P. (1996). Psychiatric rehabilitation. In G. O. Gabbard & S. D. Atkinson (Eds.), *Synopsis of treatments of psychiatric disorders* (2d ed., pp. 439–446). Washington, DC: American Psychiatric Press.

Waters, D. B., & Lawrence, E. C. (1993). *Competence, courage, & change: An approach to family therapy*. New York: W. W. Norton.

Webb, N. (1996). *Social work practice with children*. New York: Guilford Press.

Webster-Stratton, C., & Herbert, M. (1994). *Troubled families, problem children*. New York: J. Wiley & Sons.

Weick, A. (1997). Family therapy and social constructionism: A good marriage. *Families in Society, 78*(4), 366.

Weisz, J. R., & Weiss, B. (1989). Assessing the effects of clinic-based psychotherapy with children and adolescents. *Journal of Consulting and Clinical Psychology, 57,* 741–746.

Wells, K. B, Sturm, R., Sherbourne, C. D., & Meredith, L. S. (1996). *Caring for depression*. Cambridge, MA: Harvard University Press.

Wells, R. A. (1994). *Planned short-term treatment* (2d ed.). New York: Free Press.

Werner, E. E., & Smith, R. S. (1992). *Overcoming the odds*. Ithaca, NY: Cornell University Press.

Westermeyer, J. J. (1993). Cross-cultural psychiatric assessment. In A. C. Gaw (Ed.), *Culture, ethnicity, and mental illness* (pp. 125–146). Washington, DC: American Psychiatric Press.

White, M. S., & Epston, D. (1990). *Narrative means to therapeutic ends*. New York: W. W. Norton.

White, R. W. (1963). *Ego and reality in psychoanalytic theory*. New York: International Universities Press.

Whittaker, J. K. (1986). Formal and informal helping in child welfare services: Implications for management and practice. *Child Welfare, 65*(1), 17–25.

Winegar, N. (1992). *The clinician's guide to managed mental health care*. Binghamton, NY: Haworth Press.

Winegar, N. (1993). Managed mental health care: Implications for administrators and managers of community-based agencies. *Families in Society, 74,* 171–177.

Yanamoto, J., Silva, J. A., Justice, C. Y., Chang, & Leong, G. B. (1993). Cross-cultural psychotherapy. In A. C. Gaw (Ed.). *Culture, ethnicity, and mental illness*. Washington, DC: American Psychiatric Press.

Zayas, L. H., & Dyche, L. A. (1992). Social workers training primary care physicians: Essential psychosocial principles. *Social Work, 37*(3), 247–252.

Zuercher-White, E. (1997). *Treating panic disorder and agoraphobia: A step by step clinical guide*. Oakland, CA: New Harbinger Publications.

Index
